From Object to Experience

From Object to Experience

The New Culture of Architectural Design

HARRY FRANCIS MALLGRAVE

BLOOMSBURY VISUAL ARTS
LONDON • NEW YORK • OXFORD • NEW DELHI • SYDNEY

BLOOMSBURY VISUAL ARTS
Bloomsbury Publishing Plc
50 Bedford Square, London, WC1B 3DP, UK

BLOOMSBURY, BLOOMSBURY VISUAL ARTS and the Diana logo are trademarks of
Bloomsbury Publishing Plc

First published in Great Britain 2018

Copyright © Harry Francis Mallgrave, 2018

Harry Francis Mallgrave has asserted his right under the Copyright,
Designs and Patents Act, 1988, to be identified as Author of this work.

Cover design by Eleanor Rose
Cover photograph: Interior of Fünf Höfe shopping centre, Germany
© Francis Wu Architectural Photography / Flickr

All rights reserved. No part of this publication may be reproduced or
transmitted in any form or by any means, electronic or mechanical, including
photocopying, recording, or any information storage or retrieval system,
without prior permission in writing from the publishers.

Bloomsbury Publishing Plc does not have any control over, or responsibility for,
any third-party websites referred to or in this book. All internet addresses given
in this book were correct at the time of going to press. The author and publisher
regret any inconvenience caused if addresses have changed or sites have ceased
to exist, but can accept no responsibility for any such changes.

A catalogue record for this book is available from the British Library.

A catalog for this book is available from the Library of Congress.

ISBN:	HB:	978-1-3500-5952-8
	PB:	978-1-3500-5953-5
	ePDF:	978-1-3500-5956-6
	ePub:	978-1-3500-5954-2

Typeset by Integra Software Services Pvt. Ltd.

To find out more about our authors and books visit www.bloomsbury.com
and sign up for our newsletters.

Contents

List of Figures   vi

Foreword by Sarah Robinson, "Architects Make Culture"   viii

Introduction   1

1   Architecture Is the Practice of Culture   7
2   The Culture Wars   27
3   A Cultural Model for Design   43
4   New Models of Perception   57
5   Aesthetic Perception   85
6   Feeling-for-Form … Feeling-for-Space   99
7   The Atmosphere of Place   117
8   The Hearth and the Storyteller   135
9   Ritualization and the Ethos of Design   155

Notes   176

Select Bibliography   211

Index   230

List of Figures

1.1 Louis Sullivan, detail from the National Farmers' Bank of Owatonna, Minnesota (1906–08). Photo courtesy of Carptrash at English Wikipedia, Creative Commons 12

1.2 Ignazio Gardella, House on the Zattere, Venice (1953–58). Photo by author 21

1.3 Aldo Rossi, Cemetery of San Cataldo, Moderna (1961–84). Photo courtesy of Bob Condia 22

4.1 The Neocortex. Image courtesy of Dan Costa Baciu 58

4.2 Pathway of the mirror-neuron system in visual action-perception. Visual input processed in the visual cortex (VC) activates mirror areas in the inferior parietal lobe (IPL) and premotor cortex (PMC), and ignites Motor Evoked Potentials (MEPs) in the motor cortex (MC), preparing the body for action in response to what it is seeing 68

4.3 "Where" and "What" streams. Image courtesy of Dan Costa Baciu 77

5.1 Herzog & de Meuron, Dominus Winery, Napa (1995–98). Photograph by author 96

6.1 Bapistry of Pisa (1152–1363). Photograph courtesy of Jan Drewes. Creative commons 103

6.2 Donato Bramante, Temple in the Courtyard of San Pietro in Montorio, Rome (1502). Courtesy of Angelo Hornak, Getty Images 104

LIST OF FIGURES

6.3 Francisco Borromini, San Carlo alle Quattro Fontane, Rome (1638–41). Photograph by author 109

7.1 Petroglyph from Dinosaur National Monument, near McKee Springs, Utah (c. 1100 AD). Photo courtesy of Bob Condia 119

7.2 An African savannah. Photo courtesy of Tim Graham, Getty images 124

7.3 Oculus of the Pantheon, Rome (27 BC–14 AD). Photograph by author 126

7.4 Carlo Scarpa, Bridge to the Fondazione Querini Stampalia, Venice (1961–63). Photograph by author 128

7.5 Doge's Palace, Venice (begun 1340). Photograph by author 132

8.1 Reconstruction of a shelter from Terra Amata, France. Courtesy of Karen Carr Studio and the Smithsonian National Museum of Natural History 136

8.2 Cultural timeline 142

8.3 Blombos cave, ochre, and artifacts. Photo by Chris Henshilwood. Permission: CC-BY-2.5; Release under GNU free documentation license 145

9.1 Portio of the west porch of San Marco Basilica, Venice. Photograph by author 161

9.2 Laocoön, Copy after Hellenistic original. Museo Pio-Clementino, Vatican. Photograph by Marie-Land Nguyen. Creative Commons 166

9.3 Balthasar Neumann, Basilica of Vierzehnheiligen, Staffelstein, Germany (1743–72). Photograph by Bbb. Creative Commons 171

Architects Make Culture

Sarah Robinson

Why do we continue to pretend that derelict living environments play no role in the pathologies of human health and behavior? Why is it that we never question the hardened premises of our glass-and-concrete cities?

HARRY FRANCIS MALLGRAVE

No one could deny that architects are essentially makers. We create the plans that, in the complex collaboration that making involves, become buildings, artifacts, and cities. We draw boundaries, lay down lines, define paths along which our daily lives unfold. The grooves of habit are deepened along the routes suggested by the material world, and it is we who arrange, organize, and transform that physical domain. Yet how exactly do we arrive at the declaration that architects make culture? Is culture something higher, set apart from the matter of walls, roofs, paths, and streets? Or, is culture the amalgam of myriad forces—the climate of place, the economic and social affordances offered by light and topography, a compound of collective human habits—those very habits that we have a hand in directing?

These questions lie at the very heart of Mallgrave's inquiry. Why do we persist in thinking that environmental forces are opaque to psychological and cultural ones? Why do we dismiss derelict living environments as the consequence of social and psychological devastation, rather than its mutually arising cause? His message is that we can no longer afford to think in terms of such easy oppositions. The fundamental truth of our anthropocene era is that humans have altered the very topography and atmosphere of earth. Nature is no longer conceived to be a fixed, immutable opposite to human culture, which has long been considered to operate in its own separate sphere. Human action cannot be disentangled from nature, but rather produces the very scientific phenomena it once set out to observe. It is impossible to draw lines between culture and nature, sociology and ecology, and the consequences of human actions and biological processes. We are embedded, enmeshed, intertwined in a complex weave that we ourselves have spun. The human capacity and drive to make, construct, shape, and transform our surroundings have unleashed forces the magnitude of which we have only scarcely reckoned. Indeed, confronting the consequences of our actions, understanding the implications of our cherished habits, and coming to terms with the deeply relational and interactive nature of our entanglement in these complex global processes are the most urgent challenges of our time.

Decades of work from diverse disciplines ranging from philosophy, cultural anthropology, neuroscience, evolutionary psychology, and aesthetics—to name only a few—have broken down the dichotomies that have held us captive in the delusion that we can exist apart from our environment without any real consequence. Thanks to their work, we can consign the long-cherished divisions between mind and body, nature and culture, self and world to the trash heap of obsolete theory. This profound shift in thinking is causing the academy, which for centuries has been faithfully built on such dualities, to crumble, realign, and metamorphose. Emerging from the rubble of the tired dichotomies that have ruled Western thinking are new collaborations, hybrid fields, and unimagined possibilities. Interdisciplinary discourse is no longer the exception; it is today the rule.

Yet strangely, this revolution in thinking has gone practically unnoticed by architects. Perhaps we have just simply had our heads down, struggling in the trenches to confront the urgent set of problems with which the vacuity of recent architectural theory has left us ill-equipped to face. Working between the traditional boundaries separating culture from biology and the built from the natural, we are strategically placed to harvest the bounty of insights that have quickly accumulated over the last forty years. Yet our discipline has been torn between abstract cultural theory on one side, and reductionistic technology and hard evidence on the other, with scant recognition of the merits or necessity of both sides. Rather than remaining locked in such a standoff, Mallgrave has shown us a plausible way forward.

From the beginning, he reminds us that the word "culture" originally referred to agriculture, to the life of plants. The culture of the plant still today refers to the many variables that make it possible for lives to flourish. Deriving from the Latin *cultura*, culture meant to "to tend, guard, to till and cultivate." Culture shares the same root as the word "to care." And it is this caring of, this tilling of the soil, which makes civilization possible. Mallgrave reminds us further that our fundamental task as architects is to create culture in this most primal sense: to tend, to create, and to arrange the countless variables that make human life and its flourishing possible.

John Dewey, a thinker whose voice resonates throughout these pages, shared a similar understanding of culture. Among the very few philosophers who critically considered architecture, he was not interested so much in its form, as he was in its potential to form. He was interested in architecture's formative role in directing human evolution. Dewey did not think that human nature was forever fixed, but rather considered human nature to be a developmental and evolutionary open-ended process shaped by myriad bio-cultural factors. According to Dewey, the human organism is patterned physiologically, emotionally, psycho-sociologically, and intellectually by habits. And since architecture sediments habit, he recognized its potential to uplift and heal. Implicit in his writings is the truth that as we shape our environments, our environments also shape us. Our habitat is the locus of our habits, the context that allows and reinforces our daily routines. As the makers of habitat, architects are not mere arbiters of taste; we are sculptors of habits who "shape the nervous make-up of generations,"[1] as Richard Neutra so rightly noted more than fifty years ago.

Dewey's pivotal insight was that we are living beings inseparable from and shaped by our environments, a reality that seems ridiculously obvious if it were not for 300 years of intellectual discourses that have convinced us otherwise. We are just beginning to recognize just how subtly and deeply our environment influences our being. Consider the daily experience of light touching your skin: the light that makes its way through a window not only warms your skin, it also expands the space around you, making both it and you feel a little larger. The light shifts your mood as it regulates your hormone levels and tunes your body to seasonal and cosmic cycles. The light filtering through a room captures your imagination in multiple directions, unveiling the hidden, and inviting the imagination to trace its path. Without awareness, your mind begins to fill in the shadows the light has brought newly into relief. At the same time, light tugs your mind outward, towards the opening, inviting you to seek the source of this sure and quiet power. Here, in a single experiential incident, countless subtle shifts and nuances have transpired; the light has touched not only your skin, it has also touched your mind and reminded you of your place on the ground, your position in the larger scheme of things. This ordinary experience has biological, psychological, and spiritual dimensions to be sure, but it cannot be reduced to any one of these many factors. Experiencing architecture involves our whole being in a dense immersive weave in which the line between the inside and the outside cannot be clearly drawn. Where you stop and the world begins is an open question.

We have barely reckoned with these facts of our embodiment. Beneath the long-held, if mistaken, notion that we exist in isolation from our environment, lurks the idea that the body is separate from the mind. It is difficult to fully comprehend the real nature of the interdependence between body, mind, and world when language reinforces their division rather than their connection. Dewey complained that we lack a term to describe or think about the body-mind as an integrated whole, and even the term "embodiment" does not sufficiently address the problem. The philosopher-biologist-dancer Maxine Sheets-Johnstone laments that the term "embodiment" is "little more than a lexical band-aid" covering a 300-year-old semiotic wound. According to her, using the term perpetuates "a divide that has not healed and will never heal so long as the terms of the division remain part of our thinking. They remain part of our thinking because we have not fathomed what it is to be the bodies we are." We use the term "embodiment" in order to make the abstract concrete, but in doing so, we inadvertently do just the opposite. We make the concrete abstract, in our effort, as she puts it, "to make the thing we prize the most at home *in* this thing we call the body."[2]

The crucial step, the one that has not yet been fully taken, is to recognize, in the words of Tim Ingold,

> that the body *is* the human organism and that the process of embodiment is one and the same as the development of that organism in its environment. Once this step is taken, then one or the other of the two terms, body and organism, becomes effectively redundant. Given the choice of which term to retain, I would opt for the latter, since it better conveys the sense of organized process, of movement, connectivity, and relationality, that I take to be fundamental to life. Substituting life for mind and organism for body, the notion of a mindful body may be replaced by that of living organism, a substitution that has the effect both of restoring human beings to their proper place within the continuum of organic life, and laying the Cartesian dualism finally to rest.[3]

The implications of this shift in thinking are radical indeed, and those committed to phenomenological and hermeneutic approaches have been reluctant to go this far. Their resistance to taking this step is understandable in light of former deterministic approaches, but those theories have long since been refuted, and, as Mallgrave insists, it is a debate that belongs to the nineteenth century and should remain there. As Dewey once observed— knowing our physiology: knowing our physiology does not by itself help us understand our psychology, any more than knowing the geography of a country, helps us understand the history and culture that developed in that place. However crucial the quality and attributes of the land are in forming the nation's character, geography by itself cannot explain the history of the nation, any more than one's physiology can explain one's psychological life and history—one cannot completely and wholly understand one dimension without integrating knowledge about the other. A holistic understanding of cultural history and experience must include biological facts. In order to deal with the urgent issues with which the architect is confronted, we need to correct the conceptual errors that have led to these damaging dualities in the first place.

This book imagines the possibility of thinking and making architecture that overcomes and heals this wound. Mallgrave traces the implications of what it means to be a full-bodied organism immersed with its surroundings in architectural terms. Our most immediate surroundings are the buildings and dwellings in which we live and work; this is the context in which 95 percent of our life unfolds. He imagines the possibility of an architecture that is an integrated whole, an architecture that responds to our bodies as well as to our capacity for empathy and imagination, one that understands the human and the natural as a shared continuum.

We now know that we experience architecture at a visceral level; our organism responds immediately and unconsciously to the overall texture and mood of the place. We do not experience places intellectually, though the intellect comes into play to be sure. The intellectual surfaces later, not so much in the experience, but through reflecting on and unraveling the meaning of experience over the course of time. The intellectual is an outer layer of a multidimensional whole-organism encounter, and it is time to integrate this basic fact into the training of an architect.

"The role of the architect, it needs to be highlighted, is not to theorize the 'making' but to construct or give life to the places in which we dwell," Mallgrave insists. The student has precious little time in our care, so we must ask ourselves what values best serve an architect's sustained and generative practice, and what knowledge prepares one to make things of lasting social and human value. According to Juhani Pallasmaa, the capacity for empathy is fundamental to the creation of profound architecture, and essential to the practice of an architect. "In my way of thinking, a sincere architect cannot authentically design a house facing the client as an external other," he writes, "the architect has to internalize the client, to turn himself into the client, and eventually design the building for him/herself. At the end of the design process, the architect offers the house to the real dweller as a gift … The process is similar to the gift a woman makes when she offers her womb to give birth to a child on behalf of the woman who is physiologically unable to bear one. Architecture is born of imaginative empathy, and the talent of compassion is as important to the architect as formal fantasy."[4]

Empathy is a talent that can be developed and refined, and it is more important to the practice of the architect than technical skill—indeed empathy should be honed as one of the most valuable assets in our repertoire of skills. Mallgrave has introduced us to the rich history of empathy theory, *Einfühlungstheorie*, whose advocates anticipated many of the findings of modern neuroscience. Voluminous literature has developed around the importance and cultivation of empathy, and the human capacity to empathize illustrates a way that theory and practice can be joined in experience. We understand the evolutionary and, I would add, the revolutionary importance of empathy when we experience it ourselves, and that knowledge becomes a skill that allows us to anticipate our clients' needs, to viscerally apprehend the materials of the situation, and to establish a scale of values unique to the task at hand, allowing us to create something better than anyone ever imagined. In this way, architectural form is not the consequence of an authoritarian imposition; it is a melody written from a posture of humility.

Our role as architects is to make the song. And in order to do that, we must, as Mallgrave has stressed, be able philosophers, cosmologists, and interpreters of these truths of our embodiment. We need to understand the whole of the facts so that we might apply them in a way that transforms their discordant notes into music. Good design emerges from a host of variables to become something completely unique, something that could not have been foreseen by the composition of any one of its component parts, and one whose experiential depth cannot be predicted by the most elaborate algorithm. Living processes, like the processes of design and making, defy simple strategies—they are inexplicable processes of transformation that give birth to new worlds. Such an undertaking does not call for anything utopian, and the possibility of making a lasting song does not involve a flight from matter—the secret lies in a fuller embrace of who we are as living organisms.

Introduction

Theory is insufficient for life and does not respond to all its requirements.
EILEEN GRAY AND JOHN BADOVICI[1]

For 2,000 years or so, architecture has been viewed through the two lenses of history and theory. The former provided the discipline with a taxonomic or stylistic framework in which to house knowledge and traditions. On some occasions, it even provided a platform from which to depart from accepted practices. Theory, as it came to be construed in both Greek and Roman times, became architecture's ideological framework. Yet when Claude Perrault, in 1673, questioned the superiority of the "Ancients" over the "Moderns," he problematized the relationship between history and theory.[2] The latter could not only confront history in a critical fashion, but it, as it gained ascendency over the following two centuries, increasingly came to oppose the very notion of history. The victory was more or less complete by the 1820s when Karl Friedrich Schinkel, in service to the new state of Prussia, embarked on his project of constructing an "architectural theory" (*Baulehre*) in line with the new industrial realities—one, incidentally, he never completed.[3] Modernists in the decades surrounding the start of the twentieth century again struggled with the problem of defining a theoretical position adequate to the revolution taking place in practice. Implicit in these endeavors was the belief that architecture was a language that should represent the new cultural realities. The symbolism of ornament and the historicity of styles, as many modernists argued, should be replaced by a more functional language expressing itself simply through form.

By the 1960s we began to see the endgame to this strategy—the clear priority of *theōria* over *praxis*.[4] The premise that architecture is a visual language exemplified by its representational meanings remained intact. In fact, both semiotic and poststructural ideologies revolved around the importance of meaning: the belief that meanings should either reinstitute or deconstruct the conventional symbolisms of practice. Meaning, through an elaborate ideological paradigm, was thereby reduced to an ocular-centric and highly conceptualized reading of form, and architecture became, in many design circles, a formalistic exercise in service to its speculative ambitions. There were, of course, oppositional camps to this ideological hegemony, but few forces had the resources or weight to gain traction.

The central tenet of this book is that the sovereignty of speculative theory over the past six decades has run its course and today has become antiquated by the momentous leaps that have been made in the humanities and natural sciences. The literature currently emanating from circles in anthropology, philosophy, aesthetics, biology, and neuroscience is pointing to a new way of thinking about ourselves and, by extension, how we might design our habitats. Perhaps the most consequential lesson of these insights is that we should *center our design efforts less on the formalist "objects" of linguistic expression and more on the deeply rooted dimensions of human "experience"*—that is, how we might align practice with the primal needs and great complexities of the human organism. This change of viewpoint has come about because we are beginning to understand how profoundly our built habitats influence and condition the very core of our being.

This shift of perspective is more than just another theoretical tack; it is a recognition of the limitations and deflation of conventional architectural theory—at least that body of theory that, in its preening manner, strutted across the last decades of the twentieth century. It is as well the understanding that we can no longer view the built environment through the Cartesian lens of a mind interpreting meanings found in objects or buildings. The humanities and sciences today have simply discarded such dualities, and designers should do the same. We need to acknowledge the fact that minds, bodies, environments, and cultures collectively enact or interact with each other in a developmental process on multiple levels of organismic expression, one that plays out differently with each new generation. This is the context or reality for today's designers to take into account.

Such a perspective has a number of implications for designers. One is that the Heideggerian "openness" of our "being there" (our "forward and backward" relatedness to things as a mode of being) has found support in the newer models of emotion.[5] If emotion in past years has been defined as the response of a biological organism to a stimulus, a different dynamic is now beginning to be revealed. Not only are emotional systems now viewed as motivational processes in themselves giving life to or shaping conceptualization, but affectivity also and already posits a "postural attitude" or a readiness to act within the environment in which we dwell.[6] Saying this another way—emotion, a "whole-organism event," is a sense-making cognitive system of worldly engagement from the beginning, one that pervades our consciousness through and through.[7] Upon entering a room, for instance, we, in a multisensory way, take in the gist of the evolving perception, its positive or negative valences, long before we stand back and reflect on what we have experienced. Every perception is in this way an evolving "experience," whose embodied intricacies can now be viewed in real time by ever more sophisticated technologies.

Supporting the newer models of perception are the recent insights into the sensorimotor or motoric underpinnings of it workings. The discovery of mirror mechanisms over the last three decades was the pivotal event in this regard and it carries with it a score of architectural implications. We have learned much, for instance, about the cellular activities of our cortical and subcortical realms, the neurological interworking of our sensory modalities, and the multiple motoric processes involved with our simulations of actions and movements—and yes, even about the experience of form and space—within our surroundings. Sigfried Giedion, not so long ago, advanced the intellectual construct of "space-time" as an architectural concept that was enormously attractive and influential.[8] However ingenious it was as a paradigm—it was an intellectual construct entirely speculative in its premises and little more than an abstraction in its application to practice. Today we are learning the actual dynamics of our motor cognition, or how our bodies actually engage with forms and continually interact with the boundaries of space. The dynamics of how people perceive or experience the built environment would seem to be a delightfully rich field for designers to explore.

Our expanding knowledge of human evolution has similarly led to a host of additional insights into the social roots of human nature. Human sociality is no longer explained as a learned behavior, because it, like emotion, is more deeply situated in our ancestral past. The human brain did not enlarge itself in relation to our primate cousins simply by making better hand axes; its growth and development emerged from the need to manage our increasingly complex social relationships and expanded social circles. The human brain, however, at some point took a unique turn with respect to other primates in the way it began to restructure its neural pathways. The underpinnings to rituals, gestures, and play, for this reason, can no longer be taken as a sociological abstraction of an anonymous "user." They are deeply implicated in our humanity and the creative designer, above all others, should be attracted to these motivational forces, because they take us to the heart of what it means to be a designer.

The fact that we are beginning to understand the depth of our sociality has a number of other ramifications. If, as some psychologists now insist, behaviors such as ethics or morality have a discernible neurobiological basis, but one only expressed ontogenetically or through the environment in which one is raised—then the designer might want to take notice. Newer models of enculturation again provide us with a platform to speak of such things that have in the recent past fallen out of favor, such as the importance of qualitative standards of design and the larger cultural ethos by which a social structure is shaped. Who is not moved, for instance, by what is intriguing and attractive? Why is it that our building "solutions" today differ so little from those of a half-century ago? Why do we continue to pretend that derelict living environments play no role in the pathologies of human health and behavior? Why is it that we never question the hardened premises of our glass-and-concrete cities?

If the idea of "culture" today sounds foreign to practice, it is because the word has scarcely been voiced in architectural circles for the past half-century. And it is not so much that the conceptual frameworks of the postmodern era specifically sought to expunge the word from its preferred newspeak; it is rather that cultural theory, as it was conceived and practiced in the second half of the century, *was* in fact quite removed from any relevance to practice—giving some cause for the increasingly erratic line of inquiry to manifest itself in architectural practice. If one believes, for instance, that the metanarrative of "progress" can be consigned to the void of Alice's rabbit hole, then culture (perhaps best imagined in the biological sense of growing something in a prepared medium, the human organism in its built and cultural environments) has little to say to designers. Yet allowing the ethic of building a world in sympathy with the human organism to dissipate into the rarified air of philosophical abstractions, or to reduce design to a formalist exercise of crafting novel "objects" also in the end proved to be unsuccessful, we must now admit. We may, if we truly want to be critical, entertain the idea that perhaps we have looked at the problem from the wrong end of the glass. Cultural factors do to some extent condition the habits of designers, but, more importantly, architecture is also a powerful means for *creating* the very culture that sets this process in motion.

Supporting the premise that architecture is the making of culture is the assertion, which this study will attempt to show, that cultural models today are quite different from those of just a few decades ago. The proverbial divide between the human and natural sciences has been repairing itself and coevolutionary and interdisciplinary models are today vastly extending the boundaries of cultural thought. The newer collaborative models are less speculative in their foundations, even as our greater understanding of human complexity becomes manifest.

Let us take the example of "niche construction," a field of population biology that appeared in the 1990s. Its basic idea is that when organisms alter their physical and cultural environments, these altered environments change the biological and cognitive structures, as well as the evolutionary track, of the organisms housed within them. The human species, of course, is the most prolific organism of change in this respect, and buildings, as we are now learning, also alter perceptions and influence how we think. They make us feel and do things in different ways. Because architects are professionally charged

INTRODUCTION

with the task of designing environments, is it not time for designers—as Richard Neutra long ago suggested—to take a measure of responsibility for our survival?

We gain something else by broadening our perspective beyond the limits of twentieth-century theory and directing our attention to the human experience of the built environment. For one thing, we can reclaim a measure of dignity and forbearance by returning the focus of design to what Dalibor Vesely once referred to as "the practical nature of situations," or our everyday activities.[9] In doing so, we might begin to see that architects are not charged with designing structures or spaces for specific functions but places for human life to flourish. And only by viewing design within the full temporal spectrum of our affective, perceptual, social, and cultural dimensions will we begin to see the range of our responsibilities as designers.

It need not be emphasized here that architecture is standing on the threshold of stirring change. Not only will pedagogical and accreditation programs in the coming years have to undergo a radical rethinking of their most basic premises, but the products of the designer's office—our built and natural habitats—themselves will be judged by different standards. If we look back on twentieth-century theory today, we must admit that much of it was remarkably selective and reductive in the parameters with which design was concerned. If design is not to fall into another trap of theory, it will have to become not only more multifaceted in its reach but also more radically interpretive in its approach—the traditional and historical purview of the architect. Yet hermeneutics also requires a text and the palimpsest we have before us is not the speculative model or conceptual affectation of the past but a living and breathing organism with specific environmental needs. And it is here that the insights gathered by the biological sciences must be joined with the new perspectives of philosophy, cultural studies, and human evolution to provide the designer with a better understanding of who we are and how we actually engage the world. My interest in what follows is neither human behavior nor the mechanics of our nervous system, but the existential foundation on which we come to terms with the world. In this regard, the interdisciplinary models from which we learn will not in themselves determine any course of action; they can only inform the designer about the embodied "nature" of the human organism for whom we design. The taking of this knowledge and dealing with it creatively and aesthetically remain the humble task of the thoughtful designer.

***

The material presented here has been gathered from many sources and I have prospered from the informed comments of many people who have read parts of the manuscript, among them Sarah Robinson, Bob Condia, Jonathan

Hale, Michael Arbib, Isabella Pasqualini, David Leatherbarrow, Michelangelo Sabatino, and Alberto Pérez-Gómez. On aspects of this study, I have benefited over the years by my conversations with Juhani Pallasmaa, Vittorio Gallese, Alessandro Gattara, Olaf Blanke, and Davide Ruzzon. I dedicate the work to my beautiful wife Susan.

1

Architecture Is the Practice of Culture

When the artist amasses these sensual and emotional talents, then a true culture will take shape:
BECAUSE THESE THINGS ARE OF THE SPIRIT AND SUBSTANCE OF CULTURE!

LOUIS SULLIVAN[1]

To say architecture is the practice of culture would scarcely seem to be a contentious assertion. After all, the Roman architect Vitruvius became so stricken with the beauty of Hellenic culture that he devoted a good part of his life attempting to explain the elusive principles behind the elegance and grace of its architectural forms. Isidore of Miletus assembled his vision of Byzantine culture out of Egyptian porphyry, Thessalian marble, and columns from the Temple of Artemis at Ephesus. Gothic builders attempted to recreate the culture of afterlife in stone by extending the vault to ethereal heights and painting the atmosphere with opalescent glass. The artistic dream of Filippo Brunelleschi took shape amid the mounds of a Roman culture that had for centuries been viewed as perplexing. And who can deny that Leon Battista Alberti anchored his scholarly vision of Humanist culture in the Platonic and Ciceronian cultures with which he was most familiar.

Yet where are our cultural idealists today? The path of design education has for decades been narrowing and adapting itself to the technological and software demands of the workplace. Traditional areas of cultural thinking—philosophy, anthropology, sociology, and psychology—have been pushed aside in architectural curricula, where they have not disappeared altogether. Design studios attempt to teach design, yet with a very attenuated view of what constitutes the art—often reducing the complexity of life simply to form making sheathed with the ubiquitous glass facade. Does today's "culture" have any relevance for designers? And what does it really mean to say that design is the practice of culture?

Many tend to think of culture in vague terms, such as the multiculturalism of academic pretension or the lack of culture for someone exhibiting rude behavior. Seldom does the word today carry any weight, although this was not always the case. The English word "culture" comes from the Latin word *cultura*, which means the growing, tending, or cultivation of the land. In the sixteenth century the word came to acquire the additional meanings of cultivating the mind or one's manners, but its contemporary usage of signifying the customs, beliefs, or ways of life of a society only came about in the late eighteenth century. One of the first writers to employ culture in this sense was Johann Gottfried Herder, who made the argument that because the collective achievements of a people are rooted in the local landscape, climate, language, traditions, and spirit of the people, cultures are both varied and relative in their trajectories.[2] Yet observe that for him culture was still rooted in tangible things, like landscape, climate, and the traditions of a people—similar to how a biologist might today speak of growing something in a prepared medium. Culture for Herder implied an inextricable connection with the soil and traditions, rather than with virtue signaling or the fanning of airs.

My definition of the word "culture" draws upon these earlier meanings. The medium of culture—to put it in biological terms—is the built and social environments in which the human organism either flourishes or withers. In this sense, architects and designers quite literally create cultures for the human organism.

The word "practice" is similarly problematic. In design, we have come to think of practice as the application of theory, but the Greek root word *praxis* carried with it the notion of "acting" or "doing." It was a *practicality* or experience grounded in the ethos of everyday life, one demanding a tacit understanding of our existential needs. The concept implied some kind of human activity, in design terms, "the table on which we take our daily meal, or the walls that protect the intimacy of our conversation within a room."[3] To say that design is the practice of culture is therefore to imbue design with the cultural values or practices that fill out our existence. Yet how do we today reclaim this practical grounding, one that has for decades been occluded by theory?

I believe the answer to this question lies in a critical understanding of the interdisciplinary models now coming to the fore. Over the last few decades the human and biological sciences have seen an explosion of knowledge about ourselves and—by extension—the cultures in which we are embedded. As a result, the artificial divide between biology and culture has today dissolved. The fields of philosophy, history, psychology, anthropology, and sociology have undergone a massive transformation, one that has shaken their traditional foundations. It is foolish to think that architecture can stand its ground or that it can be practiced with its own sheltered set of premises. History teaches us otherwise, and from the sources cited in the following chapters we hope to draw out at least two implications. First, architecture is intertwined with human culture in a very profound sense. This is true even though the field of design is weighed down, as one likes to say, with its hallow traditions. The second implication is that design is not only the practice of culture but also the *making of culture*. Again, I do not mean culture in the superficial or academic sense of the word. When we design the world around us, we are at the same time designing who we are—biologically, intellectually, morally, and aesthetically. Architecture, when viewed from this perspective, is the shaping of the environmental medium in which the human organism dwells.

II.

Louis Sullivan, more than a century ago, well understood these two points. Early modern historians portrayed him as a functionalist, but beginning in the 1960s writers began to highlight the cultural context of his ideas, in particular the American transcendentalist tradition of Ralph Waldo Emerson and Walt Whitman. The latter's imperative that the United States must fulfill its social destiny to lead the world into a new era of human culture—"or else prove the most tremendous failure of time"—seems also to define Sullivan's mission.[4] Yet the determination to create a new approach to design in line with the new ideal of democracy would have supplied Sullivan only with a motivation and not with any specific strategy for design. This vision also does not explain how or why his designs, particularly from the late 1880s forward, would achieve what Richard Etlin has aptly described as Sullivan's "life-enhancing symbiosis of music, language, architecture, and ornament."[5]

Etlin also provides us with an important clue as to what aspects of his culture informed Sullivan's practice, when he speaks of the accord of the architect's ideas with the body of psychological theory dominant around the turn of the twentieth century in Germany—that of *Einfühlung* or "empathy" theory. Its focus was largely with aesthetic perception, and the discussion concerning the idea often employed such terms as *Formgefühl* (feeling-for-form) and *Raumgefühl* (feeling-for-space).[6]

The historian Sherman Paul had earlier noted this connection. In his monograph on Sullivan of 1962 he informs us that Sullivan's vast and multifaceted library (auctioned off during his later bankruptcy) contained a large number of books devoted to the relatively new field of psychology and physiology—books by Wilhelm Wundt, Johan Wilhelm Lavater, A. E. Willis, William James, G. Stanley Hall, Lester Ward, and Alexander Chamberlain.[7] Paul also reports that in 1893 the newly created American Psychological Association set up a booth in Sullivan's Transportation Building at the Columbian Exposition, as well as the fact that John Dewey arrived in the city one year later to assume a professorship of psychology at the University of Chicago.

Paul even gives us the gist of Dewey's psychological approach from a paper published in 1884, "The New Psychology," in which the psychologist argued that it was impossible to consider the "psychical life" of any organism outside of the environment in which it resides.[8]

Let us consider Dewey's paper in greater detail. The revolution in psychology taking place, Dewey argues, was born of two factors. One is the introduction of empirical studies of our psycho-physiological nature mainly originating in Germany. These studies follow upon the premise, in Dewey's words, that "the most complex landscape" is not a simple impression seen from without, "but is built up from color and muscular sensations, with, perhaps, unlocalized feelings of extension, by means of the psychical laws of interest, attention, and interpretation. It is, in short, a complex judgment involving within itself emotional, volitional, and intellectual elements."[9] Note in this passage the reference to sensorimotor "muscular sensations" and "feelings of extension," of emotion and volition, which Dewey posits as the basis of the new psychology—ideas now confirmed by today's neuroscience.

The second point emphasized in Dewey's paper, as Paul noted, is the force of culture in shaping how one thinks, the idea that the human individual can no longer be considered in isolation but only within the encultured context of an environment, which for him also entails the "organic relation of the individual to that organized social life into which he is born."[10]

What insights would these points hold for Sullivan as a designer? One might be that design is the material and emotional expression of the living human spirit, whose essence might well reside in the psycho-physiological animation of the rhythmic forms found in nature. The perception of our designed environments possesses a physiological dimension, and their forms, if successful, become animated through the "muscular sensations" they invoke within us. Second, if democracy is to produce a living culture, it must become, in Sullivan's words, "a *moral* principle, a *spiritual* law, a perennial subjective reality in the realm of man's spirit," one allowing the ascendance of the artist's true creative powers within its "organized social form."[11]

It is instructive to follow the changes in Sullivan's language and designs from the late 1880s through the first decade of the twentieth century. In 1886, the year he received the commission for the Auditorium Building, he penned his "Essay on Inspiration," a full-blown Emersonian rhapsody on nature—its growth and "noble decay," its "entrancing song of the Great Spirit," and how a new art can only be formed "by amplifying the rhythms of nature as these are interpreted by the sympathetic soul."[12] In "The Artistic Use of the Imagination," written in 1889 as Sullivan was putting the finishing touches on the auditorium's interiors, he begins to characterize artistic activity in both physiological and emotional terms: "The sensations of a true artist are always complex, for to susceptibility of the senses, he adds susceptibility of the heart. Every object, therefore, that he regards, will give him a double sensation, specifically the sensual and the emotional."[13]

In his often-cited essay of 1892, "Ornament in Architecture," Sullivan further develops this theme of animation. Here he underscores the need for the designers to express their individual artistic "rhythms" in order to animate architectural form, because the essence of a building resides in its "emotional expression." If a building is to express such life, he goes on to say, "an ornamented structure should be characterized by this quality, namely, that the same emotional impulse shall flow throughout harmoniously into its varied forms of expression—of which, while the mass-composition is the more profound, the decorative ornamentation is the more intense."[14]

His cultural and psychological polemic shifts into high gear with the publication of *Kindergarten Chats* in 1901, where the philosophical mentor—the "gardener" and "horticulturalist"—attempts, through a series of conversations, to cultivate the mind of the student. Early on, Sullivan notes that "the critical study of architecture" is not the study of art but of "the social conditions producing it." In this way, "architecture becomes naturally and logically a branch of social science; and we must bend our facilities to this bow if we would reach the mark."[15] And if the designer is to plant the seed of a true democratic culture, he or she must do so not with words but "in terms of *images*, of pictures, of states of feeling, of rhythm," and above all by nurturing the ability to "think organically."[16] When the artist amasses these sensual and emotional talents, a true culture will take shape: "BECAUSE THESE THINGS ARE OF THE SPIRIT AND SUBSTANCE OF CULTURE!"[17]

Nowhere is Sullivan's implementation of these sensual and emotional values better displayed than in his National Farmers' Bank in Owatonna, designed and built in 1906–08. Completed a few years after Hendrik Berlage's Amsterdam Exchange and while Otto Wagner's Postal Office Savings Bank was still under construction, Sullivan's bank has never received the historical recognition that it merits—perhaps first because of its remote location, but also because few historians have understood its cultural grounding in the "new psychology."

The thinking behind the work is actually well documented. In a letter to the bank's vice president early in the design process, he noted that "I want a color symphony and I am pretty sure I am going to get it. I want something with many shades of the strings and the wood winds and the brass"[18] (Figure 1.1). The textural effects of the exterior are indeed striking: the felicitous contrast of the exterior brickwork banded within a small but luxurious framework of colorful tiles and lush-green terra-cotta. In working with the suppliers, Sullivan also went to great lengths to achieve the plastic finish that he wanted. The shale with which the brick was formed was ground coarser and cutting wires in the formwork impressed on the face "a texture with a nap-like effect, suggesting

FIGURE 1.1 *Louis Sullivan, detail from the National Farmers' Bank of Owatonna, Minnesota (1906–08). Photo courtesy of Carptrash at English Wikipedia, Creative Commons.*

somewhat an Anatolian rug; a texture giving innumerable highlights and shadows, and a moss-like softness of appearance."[19] Raking the 3/8" joints 3/8" deep, Sullivan also sought textural effects with his hues, varying them "from the softest pinks through delicate reds, yellows, (varying the intensity) through the light browns, dark browns, purples and steel blacks—each of these colors with its own graduations and blendings—the possibilities of chromatic treatment are at once evident."[20]

Sullivan also radically rethought the interior of the people's (democratic) bank with an open floor plan, an abundance of natural light, and a large measure of human dignity afforded by its imposing spatial and atmospheric effects. The dominant hues are green, yellow, red, and red-orange. The flooring is green tile, wainscoting is formed of a reddish brick capped with a green terra-cotta frieze, counters are veined marble, grillwork is copper plate, and the wall murals are lit by the leaded glass with orchestrated shades of green, yellow, blue, and orange. The bank fulfills all of his earlier criteria for creating a new culture of democracy: the victory of feeling over intellect, emotion over reason, the dreamy vision of a gardener or colorist seeking to transcend the limits of the drab and colorless "feudal" world that preceded the new democratic era. What comes through particularly strong in Sullivan's majestic polychromy are the *plastic* effects of the materials. With the bank's design, Sullivan clearly intimated, as Dewey did with his "muscular sensations," that visual processing always induces activity in sensorimotor areas of the brain. Architecture, for Sullivan, was first and foremost a haptic experience, one veritably intended to touch the human soul.

III.

Gustav Klemm's *General Cultural History of Mankind* appeared in ten large volumes between 1843 and 1852. The Dresden native was an avid collector of ethnographic artifacts, and he proposed that the new "science" of cultural history should deal with defining the "stages" of human development, from its rudest beginnings to culture's organization "into organic social bodies," resulting in customs, knowledge, skills, domestic and public life, religion, art, and science.[21] He tied the origin of culture to the fixed abode, fire, weaponry, and property ownership—first evident for him in the cultures of Malaysia, China, Mexico, Egypt, and the Middle East. He methodically cataloged every known culture through its physical and mental characteristics, family and social life, eating and burial habits, dwellings, dress, personal decorations, tools, weapons, utensils, religion, and language.

Klemm's efforts stood at a forefront of a long string of related cultural studies, among the most prominent of which were James Prichard's *The Natural History of Man* (1843), Charles Darwin's *The Origin of Species* (1859), Adolf Bastian's *Mankind in History: Toward a Foundation for a Psychological Worldview* (1860), John Lubbock's *Pre-Historic Times* (1865), and Edward Tylor's *Primitive Culture* (1871). A number of archaeological findings played into these interests, among them Jacques Boucher de Perthes's discovery of stone flints in the Somme Valley of France in 1838 and Édouard Lartet evidence for the coexistence of humans with extinct animals in 1852. Both suggested that human existence might go as far back as the Ice Age. Another finding of great importance, the Neanderthal skeleton unearthed by Johann Fuhlrott in 1856, would also have had a major impact had not Rudolf Virchow, Germany's leading natural scientist, dismissed it as the remains of a rachitic idiot.

This ethnological interest also figured prominently into the decision to hold London's Great Exhibition of the Works of Industry of All Nations in 1851, where for the first time the cultural artifacts of many nations across the globe were assembled on one grand stage. We need not dwell upon Joseph Paxton's monumental greenhouse (ironwork colorfully painted by Owen Jones), for it was the sheer pageantry of the event that made it a "must see" for millions of visitors from home and abroad. The grand opening alone attracted a half-million visitors to Hyde Park simply to observe the 30,000 invited guests assembled inside the building, many of whom were anxious that the royal salute to be fired from a model frigate on nearby Serpentine Pond might shatter the glass roof. Artifacts from around the globe—African skirts, native North American headdresses, models and implements of Maori villages, West Asian carpets—were placed alongside Western art and the latest industrial machinery. One astonished visitor, William Whewell, referred to the Crystal Palace as the "magical glass" cabinet that brought together in time and space goods from different nations in different stages of artistic progress, revealing that mankind "is, by nature and universally, an artificer, and artisan, an artist."[22] When, in 1854, the exhibition hall was reerected and expanded in Sydenham (since destroyed by a fire), the ethnographic collections were considerably enlarged. Life-size models of humans were displayed in their native clothing and habitats: Zulu tribesmen, Ethiopian "Danakils," West Africans, "Hindoos," Chinese Tartars, Papuans, aboriginal Australians, "Sumartrans," North American and Brazilian tribesmen, and Arctic "Esquimaux" or Eskimos.[23]

Gottfried Semper's *Style in the Technical and Tectonic Arts or Practical Aesthetics* (1860–63) was much inspired by this event. If in an earlier book the architect had traced the origin of architectural culture to the four primordial motives of the social hearth, mounding, roofing, and walling—*Style* can be read as a cultural history, as many ethnologists did in the day. It discussed everything from Scandinavian stave churches to Chinese incense holders, Venetian glass, and the pleasing ornamental systems used by Canadian Native Americans on their canoes. The depth of his cultural thinking can be found in the way he opens his important section on the "Masking of Reality in the Arts" not with a discussion of architecture, but with a commentary on the colorful undergarments of Ephesian women in classical times. His point was that if these Hellenic robes had attained such exquisite refinement in their lines, materials, and coloration, the lines and polychrome dressings of the culture's architectural monuments must have been similarly inspired.[24] Few architects would make such a cultural bridge today.

Semper's influence on German cultural theory was large, but others soon took up the challenge. In 1866, Bastian, together with Virchow, founded the first museum devoted exclusively to ethnographic collections. One of their first students was Franz Boas, who would later bring the newly minted field of anthropology to the United States. Still another new field coming into view at this time was sociology and in Germany its first major voice was that of Max Weber, who would also play a significant role in the formation of German modernism.

Germany became a unified country only in 1871 and it was immediately confronted with the task not only of building a national government but also of coming to terms with the social upheavals associated with industrialization. Weber's first book, *The Protestant Ethic and the Spirit of Capitalism*, published in 1904–05, accepted the challenge of appraising the new industrial reality from a purely sociological perspective. In some ways, it was a critique of the materialist underpinning to Karl Marx's political notion of capital, as Weber sought to place capitalism's genesis not within the teleological forces of history but rather with the rise of modernity itself—that is, the coming together of such disparate cultural forces as the secularization of society and the erosion of earlier social values.

The importance of Weber's research resides in the nuances of his argument. Capitalism in his view—and in employing his famous architectural metaphor of the "iron cage"—has fundamentally altered the cultural conditions of Europe by enslaving the individual within a social structure predicated on rationality, centralization, and ever-expanding bureaucracy. In a way recalling Sullivan's contemporary polemics, Weber concludes that industrial conglomerates and the mechanization of all aspects of life were producing a citizenry of "specialists without spirit, sensualists without heart."[25] This overwhelming force of "reason" in every facet of life was at the same time creating an emotionally debilitating "disenchantment of the world"—a sense of the individual's spiritual disorientation and disempowerment, resulting from the loss of the irrational, the sensuous, and the mysterious aspects of life. Capitalism had also undermined the moral foundation of the agrarian society by substituting for it a set of impersonal values lacking any ethical conviction. This condition was being felt across Germany as a shared feeling of pathos. While conceding that one cannot reverse the trend toward an industrial economy, Weber goes on to argue that we should at least address this imbalance in our social relations, and thus the question posed to the new field of cultural theory was how to repair modernity's damage to the human spirit.

What is particularly interesting about Weber's commentary was that many German-speaking architects were at the same time engaging in similar discussions. At one end stood those who openly embraced the rationalism of modernity, as we see in Otto Wagner's *Modern Architecture* (1896). At the other end were those who espoused the "painterly" principles of the garden-city movement, which rejected the harshness of the metropolis and offered a vision of the city scaled to the pedestrian and accommodative of the natural landscape. Somewhere in between lay the creation of the German Werkbund, upon which the ideas of Weber would have considerable influence.

The title of Fritz Schumacher's inaugural address to the Werkbund Congress in 1907, "The Reconquest of Harmonious Culture," was scarcely accidental.[26] The theme owes much to Weber's writings, but also to the contemporary efforts of many German architects, as Francesco Dal Co has noted, to define a new *Wohnkultur* or "culture of living" suited to the new economic realities.[27] At the center of these discussions were the social ideas of the politician Friedrich Naumann. He was a close friend of Weber, and through his friendship with Herman Muthesius he became the political force behind the Werkbund. In 1907 Naumann was elected to the German Reichstag and his political future would remain on an upward trajectory until his death in 1920. An opponent of Marxism and a supporter of Christian socialism, he lobbied for constructing an ethical society in line with the capitalist economy, which meant elevating the living standards of workers and focusing on affordable and high-quality goods for Germans at home and exportation abroad.

Naumann also had a strong interest in the arts and architecture. It was through his invitation to speak at the Dresden Arts and Crafts Exhibition of 1906 that he met Schumacher and the furniture manufacturer Karl Schmidt, both of whom were political supporters. At the first Werkbund conference in 1907, Naumann tapped another of his political friends, Wolf Dohrn, to be the executive director of the Werkbund, and in the ensuing months Naumann assisted in writing the guild's constitution and the first pamphlet outlining the organization's multiple aims.[28] It should also be noted that Dohrn has just taken his doctorate under the psychologist Theodor Lipps, who was the preeminent theorist of *Einfühlungstheorie*, or "empathy theory," in the first decade of the new century.

It is significant in this regard that the first undertaking of the Werkbund was the creation of Hellerau, a garden city outside of Dresden—the new "German Olympus"—in which Dohrn, Schmidt, Muthesius, Richard Riemerschmid, and

Heinrich Tessenow were involved.[29] It was more than a city for Schmidt's industrial workers; it was a grandiose attempt to realize the *Wohnkultur* ideal—that is, to build a culturally vibrant middle-class community heavily invested in the arts. Not only were high housing standards mandated by ordinance but also were a number of social and recreational amenities put into place, chief of which was Émile Jaques-Dalcroze's institute of dance and "eurhythmics," which opened in 1910. The institute was a program of dance and musical education (in keeping with the latest psycho-physiological theories to which Dewey and Sullivan were attracted) to train one to become better attuned with one's natural rhythms and thereby boost the efficiency of the nervous system and artistic creativity.

Dalcroze's music and dance festivals, held annually from the years 1912 to 1914, created a sensation across Germany and lured crowds in the tens of thousands to view the performances, among them a stream of intellectuals from both Europe and North America. Many architects, especially those within the Werkbund, were fascinated with the experiment. Le Corbusier's brother Albert Jeanneret was an instructor under Dalcroze, and Le Corbusier made a trip to the new town on no fewer than four occasions. Alma Mahler, the future wife of Walter Gropius, was a visitor, and Ada Bruhn, the fiancée of Mies van der Rohe, was a student at the institute in 1912–13. The experiment in reinjecting "enchantment" back into the social fabric unfortunately would end with the outbreak of the First World War in 1914.

Max Weber remained in the background to these events, but he was observing the experiment closely. In a letter to her husband in 1908, Marianne Weber recorded the pleasant conversations of a day she had spent with Schmidt and Dohrn in Hellerau as they were directing the construction of the city, how Dohrn, in particular, "reads your methodological writings with ardour."[30] Weber's interest in architecture was also rooted in his family. His younger brother Carl was an architect who had studied under Carl Schäfer at Karlsruhe's polytechnic school, and Schäfer's son Hermann, also an architect, was married to Weber's younger sister Lili. Max's older brother Alfred, a sociologist, joined the German Werkbund after the war and he addressed the Congress of 1928 on the issue of German modernism.

Lawrence Scaff, one of Weber's more able interpreters, has suggested that his metaphor of the "iron cage" was more than a poetic turn of phrase and—as later interpreted by Jürgen Habermas at least—was a foreboding of the steel-and-glass phenomenon of modern architecture, a challenge to Germany's traditional cultural forms and scale of building.[31] Scaff points to comments in a speech made by Weber in 1918, in which he cautioned Germany—in an age "characterized by rationalization and intellectualization and, above all, by the 'disenchantment of the world'"—against any forced attempt to create a new monumental style of art, which he felt would only replicate the "miserable monstrosities" that have been produced in the last two decades.[32] Weber's comment, penned two years before his death, can be read as antimodern, but in its context it is better seen as a response to the horrors of the war, to the pace of life upended by industrial change, the loss of personal intimacy, and to the fruitless search for some compensating factor amid the destruction widely attributed to industrialization. In any case, the devastation of the war and the resulting political instability would haunt cultural theory for much of the twentieth century.

One manifestation of this anxiety was the Frankfurt Institute for Social Research, founded in 1923, and made famous by the writings of Max Horkheimer, Theodor Adorno, Herbert Marcuse, and Walter Benjamin. Politically, most of its members were communists, and the institute seized upon the failure of the German Communist Revolution of 1918 to revisit the question of how (in view of the economic failings of Russia's proletarian revolution) to construct a socialist society that would retain basic human values.

Germany's political instability, beginning in 1930, would soon disrupt the discussions, but from their relocated venue in southern California, Horkheimer and Adorno would respond with their polemic *Dialectic of Enlightenment*. The book can be read as a commentary on Weber's metaphor of the "iron cage" of instrumental reasoning and the illusive myth of progress. If the European Enlightenment had promised freedom, the secularization of values had only wrought war, genocide, the destruction of nature, and the intellectual debasement of people. Capitalization had not collapsed, as Marx had naively predicted. Western liberal economies, with their bureaucratic expansion and concentrations of wealth, had simply evolved into mass-consumer cultures in which individuals were now the iron-cage tenants of their own "culture industry," seduced into political conformity by the sale of commodities that are repackaged each new shopping season under the guise of novelty.[33] Art, which in preindustrial times had offered a place of refuge from mass culture, had similarly indentured itself to the allure of the marketplace. In their defense of modernity, Horkheimer and Adorno encouraged artists not to pander to the culture industry but to regard their work as an act of "resistance" against bourgeois culture, and it was this somewhat evolved Weberian theme that, as we will see, helped to touch off the cultural upheaval of the 1960s—with less than positive consequences.

IV.

Much has been written about the 1960s from a cultural perspective and no one has denied it was an acutely transformative period. It was a time of great political and social agitation engendered by the unresolved tensions stemming from the First and Second World Wars—a Korean peninsula split in two, the Cold War, the communist revolution in Cuba, the Indo-Pakistani War, the Arab-Israeli Six Day War, the Nigerian Civil War, the "Cultural Revolution" in China, and the American escalation of France's colonial conflict in Vietnam into a full-scale war. The thirteen-day Cuban Missile Crisis of 1962 even raised the very real specter of an apocalyptic nuclear war. The cultural values of earlier generations were under attack from all sides. The Civil Rights movement, the birth-control pill and the feminist movement, environmental awareness, campus radicalism, psychedelics, and rock music—all came of age in the 1960s. The cultural, or one might say the countercultural, divide between generations had never before been so large, nor defined with such unconcealed anger and frustration.

Architecture was, of course, not exempt from this clash of values and two books published in 1966 give testimony to the underlying disquiet. Both can be seen as sallies upon the hegemony of orthodox modern theory, but if we look closer we will also find a rather spacious divide between European and North American approaches to the question of culture.

Although Aldo Rossi's *The Architecture of the City* appeared in the 1960s, the book was in many ways a response to the founding of the Congrès Internationaux d'Architecture Moderne (CIAM) in 1928. The organization from the start was dominated by a political agenda, and the language of the La Sarraz declaration, as Eric Mumford has noted, echoed the spirit of Marx's *Communist Manifesto*, particularly with its call for the collective control and ownership of land.[34] This political tone is also evident in the second CIAM conference held in Frankfurt in 1929, when several German architects joined the organization, yet the political edge lessened somewhat in the following year when a number of political hardliners—Ernst May, Mart Stam, Hans Schmidt, and Hannes Meyer—led "red brigades" of students to Russia to work on Josef Stalin's Five Year Plan. What did not change, however, was the rationalist and technocratic tenor of the organization. When Le Corbusier wrote *The Athens Charter* in 1943, it was a victory for his "Radiant City" proposal and in many respects for Weber's "iron cage" of modernism. Through a rigid set of propositions, the charter called for the reorganization of governmental agencies and the remaking of the city through its demolition, the separation of housing from traffic and working areas, high-rise buildings set far apart, and the subordination of private land to collective interests.

After the war, the politics of CIAM moderated. Germany, along with large parts of Europe, had been destroyed, and the Iron Curtain now divided the continent in two. CIAM's long-standing secretary, Sigfried Giedion, was struggling to make the organization again relevant, and in 1947 he allowed the organizational structure to be amended, at which time the first Italian architect—Ernesto Rogers of the Milan firm BBPR—was elected to the governing council. Italy had participated in the rationalist polemics of the late 1920s, but few architects had actually been involved with CIAM over the years. The reason was largely a cultural one. Italian designers generally preferred a more regional view of modernism, one more respectful of local or vernacular traditions and they were thus drawn to elements found in Le Corbusier's villas of the late 1920s, such as open-air terraces, rooftop gardens, and balconies.[35] Rogers followed in this lead, but the depth of this cultural divide—when Italian rationalism confronted the noetic rigor of CIAM's principles—became evident only in 1949 at the CIAM congress held in Bergamo, Italy. The Italian architect Bruno Zevi greeted the assembling delegates with an open letter in which he took the organization to task for its one-dimensional vocabulary and overly rationalist approaches.[36] He questioned why American and Scandinavian practice, as seen in the more regional approaches of Frank Lloyd Wright and Alvar Aalto, had been excluded from CIAM consideration. And as Zevi was unsettling the atmosphere of the Bergamo conference, Rogers, for his new position, was raising the same issues inside the conference halls.

The architectural context to Rogers's views, as it evolved over the next few years, was the "neorealist" movement in Italy, which, like the movement in Italian film, sought a modern vernacular language able to communicate directly with the people. Four years after the Bergamo conference, Rogers assumed the editorship of the relaunched journal *Casabella* and thus would have the opportunity to state his case in greater detail. His first decision, in fact, was to append the hyphenated word *continuità* to the journal's title to emphasize "historic awareness" and the need for "continuity" with Italy's cultural past, while rejecting "every manifestation of formalism" and rigid ideologies.[37] In one editorial of 1957, he called for respecting tradition without falling into the trap of historicism, and in the same issue, the journal reviewed favorably a design of Roberto Gabetti and Aimaro Isola for the Erasmus shop in Turin, a complex of offices, shops, and apartments notable for its compositional flair and local vocabulary of detailing.[38] In another issue, the journal praised Gardella's House on the Zattere in Venice, a seemingly timeless work that Manfredo Tafuri would later describe as a "commentary on the typology of the Venetian aristocratic palazzo"[39] (Figure 1.2). In 1958 Paolo Portoghesi proposed the appellation "neoliberty" for the new movement, designating it as a trend in design succeeding the previous phase of neorealism.[40]

It was at this point that a defender of CIAM's rationalist spirit stepped forth in the person of the influential English critic Reyner Banham. In the middle years of the decade he had been involved with London's New Brutalist movement and in 1959 he was completing his dissertation under Nikolaus Pevsner—published as *Theory and Design in the First Machine Age* (1960). Banham was strongly opposed to any hint of a regional modernism and he

FIGURE 1.2 *Ignazio Gardella, House on the Zattere, Venice (1953–58). Photo by author.*

made this point with considerable ferocity in a contentious article he penned for *Architectural Review* in 1959, in which he condemned Italy's flirtation with neoliberty as a "baffling turn" of events, as nothing less than "infantile regression" from the rational tenets of the modern architecture.[41] In the article he also criticized Rossi, who had reviewed the new movement favorably for *Casabella-continuità*.

Such is the polemical background against which Rossi's book appeared in 1966 as a belated response to Banham, yet there was a strong sociological undertone as well. It is a book that, as Peter Eisenman has noted, is not without a degree of ambivalence and sense of anxiety.[42] Rossi had the formidable task of defending the rationalist underpinnings of modernism (in particular Horkheimer and Adorno's notion of "resistance") against CIAM's more rigid interpretation of modernism, grounded in what Rossi would label its "naïve functionalism." His approach, as stated in the "Preface to the Second Edition," is one of constructing "a more complex rationalism than the schematic one offered by the historiography of modern architecture."[43] If the rationalism of modernism had failed, it was because, with its functionalist premises, it was insufficiently rationalist—that is, it did not succeed in purging itself of the "bourgeois" contamination of capitalist culture. Yet how does one construct a modernism that can resist such contamination?

Rossi's solution was essentially twofold. In his own design practice, and in following the lead of the painter Giorgio de Chirico, he empties form (including the forms of European high modernism) of all stylistic associations by reverting to a typological tool kit of Platonic solids (Figure 1.3). Akin to the "fixed structures" of linguistic theory, these "types" with their absence of human scale possess the status or quality of permanence—that is, they persist as primary elements or urban artifacts across generations and cultures, regardless of the human function or use. In a sense, they are the negative pole of Horkheimer and Adorno's dialectic touching upon nihilism. Only the socialization of the city, the ever-changing activity surrounding these types, endows them with animating substance or vitality.

Second, Rossi offers up a recipe for injecting culture into these types. In essence, the creation of cultural artifacts requires first a typological reduction that can classify the various types into which architectural forms and plans can be cataloged. Second, these types over time undergo a mediation, one that takes into account a multitude of things from the mythology of buildings and cities to their social content. Such a mediation requires a common cultural

FIGURE 1.3 *Aldo Rossi, Cemetery of San Cataldo, Moderna (1961–84). Photo courtesy of Bob Condia.*

basis that can recompose these types in new and revealing ways, but Rossi adds still one other qualification. Types ascend to cultural forms not from a conscious or heroic effort on the part of the architect (another critique of modernism), but rather from a collective psychology that gathers up these relationships over time, one in which collective memory, as it were, consumes the more traditional notion of history.

Within a few years, Rossi would even offer up a compositional technique to assist in this mediation. It is the notion of "analogy" or the "analogous city," which he illustrates with an eighteenth-century painting by Giovanni Antonio Canaletto. The painting depicts two buildings designed by Palladio (actually built and located in Vicenza), together with an unbuilt project for a bridge by the same architect—all situated around a nonspecific urban canal populated with boats and people. In 1765 Francesco Algarotti reported that many Venetians were interested in the painting and were curious to know what city it depicted. In essence, the painting became a cultural artifact displaced in time and place, but which nevertheless was perfectly accessible to culturally attuned eighteenth-century Venetians who viewed it as a real city. Rossi, in effect, translates the painting into a design process in which preestablished and formally defined elements are employed in a way in which they produce an "authentic, unforeseen, and original meaning of the work."[44]

The vehicle for Rossi that allows this living and ever-renewable analogy is a living culture, or a relational way of cultural thinking that draws upon both local and universal human attributes but at the same time is wedded to no particular place. "Analogy" is a term often used in literature and poetry in the sense of metaphor, but for Rossi it becomes the very typological foundation upon which architecture can construct the "memory" needed for a culture to thrive. And whereas many postmodernists would soon employ a strategy of historical eclecticism with quotations drawn from other places and times, Rossi's purified rationalism—his essentialist and self-proclaimed "focus on a rigid world, with few objects"—succeeds to the level of a cultural theory by virtue of the particular urban dimensions of geography, ecology, history, economics, politics, anthropology, and the social psychology of the place. Virtually all of these factors had been little emphasized in the planning tenets of CIAM, even less so within later currents of postmodernism.

Rossi's inflated model of urban or social consciousness, structured within the rationalist tradition of Weber, is fundamentally (if abstractly) cultural in its outlook, and the same can almost be said for Robert Venturi's view of design. The American architect first of all had strong cultural ties to Italy. He featured its architecture in his graduate thesis at Princeton in 1950 and four years later, as a Fellow at the American Academy in Rome, he met Rogers who was teaching a studio there.[45] Upon his return to Philadelphia in 1956, Venturi began work on *Complexity and Contradiction in Architecture*, the first draft of which was substantially complete in 1962. It did not appear until 1966, which may have something to do with his meeting Denise Scott Brown, a Zambian-born student who had come to the University of Pennsylvania to do graduate work under Louis Kahn. Her initial focus was urban theory and particularly from a sociological perspective. Between 1962 and 1964, the years during which Venturi was revising the book, he co-taught a course with her at Penn on architectural theory.

Daniel Bell likes to refer to the period of the early 1960s as a watershed moment in Western culture, when the idea of the "bourgeois" met its demise—that is, when Weber's notion of a unified social theory stretching across both the economy and the arts came to be seen as unattainable.[46] The reason, Bell argues, resided with the contradictions of modernism itself. The avant-garde art of the first years of the century had demanded "tension" between its values of "resistance" and the established values of bourgeois culture—the same tension that Horkheimer and Adorno later emphasized. By the late 1950s, however, this tension had all but dissolved because the presumed countercultural values of "radical chic" had in effect become institutionalized within the cultural media of museums, universities, and film. In other words, adversary or counterculture was now becoming the new cultural order. Artistic directions such as American Pop Art or British New Brutalism met no resistance because bourgeois standards of taste had already been eroded to the point of no return. The arts were now free to draw upon the objects of the everyday world: comic strips, billboards, advertisements, Hollywood starlets, and Coca-Cola bottles—or even past architectural styles. Art had become promiscuous in its cultural ransacking of artifacts of mass culture.

Pop Art was, of course, of great fascination to Venturi, but in the early 1960s a strong sociological direction had captured the architecture program at Penn, one that featured both a number of prominent planners (Edmund Bacon, Lewis Mumford, David Crane, Britton Harris) and a group of younger social activists, such as Paul Davidoff and Herbert Gans. Davidoff, for instance, was one of the founders of the advocacy planning movement, which brought the concerns of "the people" into play against the vested interests of the so-called establishment. Gans was a strong critic of urban-renewal programs, and for seven months in 1957–58 he lived in Boston's Italian West End, where he vehemently fought its "redevelopment" by the Boston Housing Authority.[47] In *The Levittowners* (1967), he again drew upon on-site observations to challenge the view that this lower-middle-class suburb was a social and cultural wasteland. In *Popular Culture and High Culture* (1974)—likely influenced by Venturi and Scott Brown—he once again attacked elitist assumptions and high culture's intense disdain for popular culture.

All of which brings us to *Complexity and Contradiction*. With all of the editing and reworking, the ten chapters and 253 images of the book read as two intertwined studies. One is the "high culture" text of an Ivy League architect: his firsthand work experience in the studios of Rogers, Kahn, and Aldo van Eyck at Penn, his intellectual fascination with Gestalt psychology, together with the painters Josef Albers, György Kepes, Robert Rauschenberg, Jasper Johns, and the literary criticism of T. S. Eliot, Cleanth Brooks, and William Epson. Collectively, these themes or sources are called upon to defend "the gentle manifesto," the argument that through a number of formalist devices—exploiting ambiguity duality, and contradictions—architectural design can be enriched and overcome "the puritanically moral language of orthodox Modern architecture."[48]

In its place, Venturi proposes to usher in "an attitude common in the Mannerist periods," that is to say, an enrichment of the language of modernism by the use of historically sanctioned strategies. If the classical Renaissance vocabulary, as the historian Heinrich Wölfflin once noted, had succumbed to the heightened visual tension of the Mannerist period, so too should the high-modern syntax now give way to a calculated ambiguity that allows greater tension and a measure of freedom for the architect, all in keeping with the greater complexity of modern life.[49] Otherwise, design will become stale and, in a reference to Mies van der Rohe, "Less is a bore."[50] There is also a visual and linguistic component to his argument, which is that architecture should fall in line with the other arts and explore its semantic dimensions.

It is when Venturi makes his pivot from the high culture of historical precedents to the low culture of "Main Street" that the second theme becomes evident, an argument expressing the "resistance" of the cultural wars of the 1960s. He starts the theme in his sixth chapter when—in alluding to the richness of the Italian street—he makes a case for using conventional elements ("old clichés") unconventionally. He offers it as a counterstrategy to the continual search for newness, including the modernist fascination with innovative technologies. He also rationalizes it on the grounds of simple economy and, more interestingly, as a form of cynical protest against "society's inverted scale of values."[51] It takes him a few more pages but the theme reenters at the end of his next chapter when he exalts the concept of the "honky-tonk" as the mean between the "endless inconsistencies of roadtown" (chaos) and the "infinite consistency of Levittown" (boredom). He obviously inclines more toward the former, as his later question—"Is not Main Street almost all right?"—makes clear.[52] He even takes the provocative step toward the end of the book of promoting these "seemingly chaotic juxtapositions of honky-tonk elements," drawn from "everyday landscape, vulgar and disdained," as the featured way to achieve a complex and contradictory architecture.

The contrast between the cultural visions of Rossi and Venturi is striking, as are their particular backgrounds. Rossi was quintessentially European in his cultural and scholarly bearing. He was a theorist in the rationalist tradition of

Weber, politically steeped in the perspectives of the Frankfurt School, and a political activist. His architectural vision may have seemed to some readers to be meliorist, but it was a tempered ideology lacking any genuine optimism. The political situation of Italy in the 1960s in fact demanded a degree of cynicism in response to the sociological vision of high modernism. And although he was often later described as a postmodernist, he is better viewed as an advocate of his version of rationalism.

Venturi, to the contrary, was bourgeois in his background, yet became brazenly countercultural and iconoclastic, liberal in his politics. Although his cultural outlook had little in common with the writings of Michel Foucault or Jacques Derrida, he nevertheless shared with them a flight from conventional ideology, the topical aesthetics of rhetoric, and the subversion of traditional cultural values. He left architecture with little cultural basis on which to appraise itself and, in this sense, he was a true postmodernist. In *Learning from Las Vegas* (1972)—a book that was received in Italy with considerable disdain—he and Scott Brown articulated the theme with a brashness signaling, in retrospect, the imminent demise of this period's fascination with cultural theory. Rossi and Venturi, however, do share one thing in common. Both were acutely aware of changing cultural conditions, and both saw architecture as a way to hasten along the demise of the old order. Whether either succeeded is, of course, another question—but it makes their efforts no less the practice or making of culture.

2

The Culture Wars

High-rise apartment buildings are less distressing to look at than slums but more disturbing to live in than much of what they replaced.

EDWARD T. HALL[1]

The social and political turmoil in the streets of the late 1960s was matched by no less contention within the academy, the field upon which much of the cultural upheaval played itself out. The problems coming to a head were seemingly insurmountable and publications within the human sciences rapidly burgeoned to numbers never before seen. As humanities departments were expanding, traditional fields were bifurcating into more specialized areas. What was often unquestioned, however, were the unspoken premises of the social science model—among them, the belief that all humans are born with blank-slate minds and that cultural training was the most important, if not the sole, factor in determining human behavior. The anthropologist Ashley Montagu made this point explicit in 1962 when he, in referring to the human race, noted that "instead of having his responses genetically fixed as in other animal species, man is a species that invents its own responses, and it is out of this unique ability to invent, to improvise, his responses that his cultures are born."[2]

Such a view, of course, carried with it a measure of philosophical anxiety or existential unease—given the massive devastation of recent wars. But then hopes were high that the blossoming of the social sciences would redeem or find an appropriate prescription for what ailed the collective human psyche. After all, as Montagu noted in another of his popular books, "human beings are not born with human nature," rather, they come into the world with only "potentialities for being human," which have to be culturally refined.[3] His point, arguably, is that all humanity really needs is better cultural training, and indeed this was a premise of B. F. Skinner's version of behaviorism so prominent in North America in the 1950s and 1960s. In dismissing both physiological and mental factors from psychological observation, Skinner intimated that it was cultural conditioning alone that best predicted human behaviors.[4]

Perhaps the most influential anthropologist in North America at this time was Clifford Geertz, whose book *The Interpretation of Cultures* (1973) assembled essays largely written in the 1960s. He had completed his dissertation after two-and-a-half years of fieldwork in Java and joined the faculty at the University of Chicago in 1960. He remained there for a decade before leaving for Princeton's Institute of Advanced Study. His intellectual background and interests were far ranging. He gained an appreciation of John Dewey during his years in Chicago. He was much influenced by the British school of language philosophers, chiefly Gilbert Ryle and Ludwig Wittgenstein, and he followed Emile Durkheim's insistence on viewing human behavior through larger social systems.

He was also drawn to the aspects of Weber's analysis. In fact, one of his definitions of culture derives from Weber's description of humans as animals suspended in webs of significance they themselves have spun. "I take culture to be those webs," Geertz responds, "and the analysis of it to be therefore not an experimental science in search of laws but an interpretive one in search of meaning."[5] He goes on to characterize culture as a "symbolic system" and his own approach as "semiotic," drawing some support from the methods of Claude Lévi-Strauss who also read cultures as "texts" to be interpreted.[6]

This view of culture as a symbolic language, of course, falls very much in line with the postmodern turn of the 1960s, which revealed itself across the humanities as well as in architecture. From Tomás Maldonado's seminars of the 1950s on semiotics at Ulm's Hochschule für Gestaltung to the writings of Christian Norberg-Schulz, Sergio Bettini, Giovanni Klaus Koenig, Renato De Fusco, Umberto Eco, George Baird, and Charles Jencks of the 1960s, semiotics or its sister field of semiology would become key underpinnings to the postmodern movement that roared into action in the early 1970s.[7]

What was less apparent to many anthropologists in the 1960s, however, were the weaknesses built into Geertz's cultural model, chief of which was his assumption that culture transcends or trumps our animal instincts. For him, culture is the mechanism that tamps down our biological instincts and is therefore "a set of control mechanisms" (plans, recipes, rules, and instructions) that order or govern human behavior. Geertz went so far as to argue that culture is essential to human conduct precisely because we are "the animal most desperately dependent on such extragenetic, outside-the-skin control mechanisms" for controlling our behavior.[8] In such a model, not only does cultural conditioning override our genes or natural instincts, but the biological brain of the newborn is little more than a programmable computer waiting to be instructed by the software of culture. As Geertz himself stated his position: "By submitting himself to governance by symbolically mediated programs for producing artifacts, organizing social life, or expressing emotions, man determined, if unwittingly, the culminating stages of his own biological destiny. Quite literally, though quite inadvertently, he created himself."[9]

Yet Geertz himself seems to have been somewhat uneasy with such a formulation, a disquiet perhaps raised by his interest in paleoanthropology. We can sense his foreboding in his discussion of the revised dating of the prehuman primate line *Australopithecus africanus*, whose appearance was changed in the 1960s from one million years ago to more than three million years. Geertz, in an interesting way, realized that a much lengthier human genealogy threatened his anthropological premise that enculturation (tool use, hunting, and social systems) took place rapidly and only in relatively recent times. If the human evolutionary line was shown to be lengthier, such cultural taming, as it were, opens the door to biological or genetic changes through natural selection. This coevolution of biology and culture, in turn, raises the very delicate issue regarding the presumed "psychic unity of mankind"—anthropology's most sacrosanct tenet for close to a century. For if cultural development is now intermixed with biological evolution, it is possible that some populations of humans, by virtue of their particular cultural/biological path of development, might be less equal than others in their cognitive development.

Geertz's response to this question—"phyletic differentiation within the hominid line effectively ceased with the terminal Pleistocene spread of *Homo sapiens* over nearly the whole world and the extinction of whatever other *Homo* species may have been in existence at that time"—is not only unscientific as a precept but oddly cavalier as a defense.[10] What is the evidential basis for concluding that evolution or biological adaptations ceased with the terminal creation of modern humans? And if indeed cultural programs created who we are as human beings, who created these cultural programs in the first place? Cultural theory, in this way, fails to explain its own premises.

II.

Robert Ardrey's *African Genesis* was a best-selling book with its appearance in 1962. A few years earlier this successful Hollywood screenwriter had put his career on hold to pursue his interests in anthropology—initially traveling to South Africa to meet Raymond Dart and inspect the fossils of *Australopithecus africanus* that had so fascinated Geertz. Ardrey accepted Dart's "killer ape" hypothesis, the idea that this potential human ancestor was a carnivore, and he argued on behalf of Africa (against Europe and Asia) as the birthplace of the human line. More importantly, he chose to take aim at anthropology's "Romantic Fallacy," which—going back to Rousseau—was the belief that humans in their pre-societal state were basically good and that the destructive impulses of aggression and violence were later societal abnormalities.[11]

Ardrey also emphasized the role that instinct still plays in our lives, and he argued that our behaviors today are not so very different from those of our primate ancestors. In his follow-up study, *The Territorial Imperative*, he stated his thesis in even bolder terms: "I can discover no qualitative break between the moral nature of the animal and the moral nature of man."[12]

Other studies soon followed suit. Konrad Lorenz's *On Aggression* appeared in German in 1963 and in English in 1966, and its central thesis is that aggression is not a destructive social principle after all, but rather one honed by evolution to fulfill a species-preserving function, along with such other instincts as hunger, sexuality, and flight. Animal aggression generally spreads out members of a single species evenly across a habitat, and thereby results in stronger parents to the benefit of their progeny. Aggressive instincts also better protect offspring from other species. Moreover, aggression creates patterns of movement or behavior that (even when they lose their original function during phylogeny or evolution) survive as ritualistic behaviors and ceremonies.

Lorenz's theme was taken up and expanded by his one-time associate Irenäus Eibl-Eibesfeldt. Often considered the founder of human ethology, he defined the field in 1971 as the study of "the functioning of those physiological mechanisms that influence a behavior pattern."[13] He laid out extensive evidence gathered from his own research that such behaviors as love, altruism, and aggression are indeed pre-programmed, as it were, by phylogenetic or evolutionary adaptations—that is, a set of instructions not culturally based but encoded in our genes. The peacock, for instance, undergoes a ritualistic dance when soliciting the favors of a peahen, and the male bowerbird constructs an elaborate nest to attract females to mate. Within species, these behaviors do not vary. He also suggested that aggression has become more dangerous to humans in the twentieth century not because of the instinct itself but because of the advent of more lethal weapons. The human race, he feared, has evolved into an anonymous mass society for which we are emotionally ill-equipped; our attitude toward traditions and authorities is more skeptical; the pressures of overpopulation have created nothing less than a situation similar to the penal conditions found in zoos.[14] In short, and to use Weber's analogy, we have become prisoners trapped within the iron cages of our cities and larger social patterns. It cannot be questioned, he concludes, that we come into the world with an ancient and still powerful evolutionary inheritance.

Perhaps the most popular book of the 1960s in this genre was Desmond Morris's *The Naked Ape* (1967), which carried the ironic but also informative subtitle "A Zoologist's Study of the Human Animal." In a reversal of vantage points, the primatologist examines human behavioral patterns against those of our presumed inferiors, the great apes. With seriousness yet with considerable irreverence, Morris argues that whereas some people may cling to the idea that culture has largely shaped human nature, the truth is the opposite: "it is the biological nature of the beast that has moulded the social structure of civilization, rather than the other way around."[15] Hunting has simply evolved into working, a forage base into a home, hunting grounds into places of business, pair-bonding into marriage, nest-building into architecture, and feeding into agriculture. If *Homo sapiens* has acquired a few new habits along its evolutionary way, the animal had lost none of its "earthy" old ones. Scarcely hidden beneath the respectable façade of modern culture resides the hairless ape:

> Optimism is expressed by some who feel that since we have evolved a high level of intelligence and a strong inventive urge, we shall be able ... to cope with the over-crowding, the stress, the loss of our privacy and independence of action ... that we shall control our aggressive and territorial feelings, our sexual impulses and our parental tendencies; that if we have to become battery-chicken apes, we can do it; that our intelligence can dominate all of our basic biological urges. I submit that this is rubbish.[16]

Morris's summary warning appeared six years before Geertz assembled the essays for his book, and by 1973 the issue of nature versus nurture had become a vexing one before a very interested public and scientific community, now with heightened if not simmering social tensions.

III.

Edward Wilson, with his reserved demeanor and quiet personality, would at first glance scarcely be taken for a revolutionary. His reputation today is that of a well-known conservationist and highly respected entomologist who in his early career had traveled to remote regions of the world in search of new species of ants and termites. Nevertheless, his book of 1975, *Sociobiology: The New Synthesis*, touched off a furor within the politically impolite halls of academe. Rather quickly, it escalated into the most heated biological debate of the second half of the twentieth century, although its main theme to this day remains uncontested.[17] It was simply a few details of his study that led to the donnybrook.

His main thesis is that neither cultural theorists (going back to Franz Boas and Émile Durkheim) nor evolutionary theorists (Ardrey, Lorenz, or Morris) had been successful in explaining human behavior. The answer, he explains, resides in the limitations of any single-disciplinary approach to appreciate the complexity of *Homo sapiens*. If we wish to pursue the issue of who we are with scientific rigor, he argues, we need new fields of interdisciplinary research, among them the merger of sociology with biology, or what he termed "sociobiology."

The book was formed within the context of the social and political debates of the 1960s, and therefore out of the concern for whether the human race was not drifting into dangerous social patterns, or whether this hardening of ideological perspectives would lead to "an eventual lessening of altruistic behavior through the maladaption and loss of group-selected genes."[18] We are at a pivotal point, Wilson laments, and we need more focused interdisciplinary approaches to understand better who we really are—that is, before we destroy ourselves altogether.

On this basis, Wilson begins a book that over the first twenty-six chapters is dense with charts and mathematical equations, as he discusses the behaviors of a number of species from simple cell organisms to the great apes. It is only in the last chapter that Wilson trains his sight specifically on "that very peculiar species" *Homo sapiens*, hypothetically and—in alluding to Morris—"in the free spirit of natural history, as though we were zoologists from another planet."[19] After a somewhat cursory glance at our evolutionary past, he begins with an extended analysis of human biological and social structures, many of which frequently conclude with questions. If humans, for instance, evolved an exceptionally large brain with respect to other primates, what percentage is due to the influence of phylogenetic factors and what percentage to culture? If group size and properties of hierarchy vary greatly in human societies, what is the reason for this social flexibility? In more general terms, why are there so many different types of social structures in human societies in the first place? He also punctuates his questions with descriptive observations on the division of labor within nuclear families, male dominance, mating behavior, and marriage—all of which would be greeted with less than acclaim within the contentious atmosphere of the period.

It is in the concluding pages of his massive study, however, that his message becomes ambivalent if not dispiriting in its scientific candor. On the one hand, he seems to suggest that problems such as modern warfare have grown so large as to require something akin to a Huxlean "brave new world" to take on the task, noting that to maintain the species into the future, "we are compelled to drive toward total knowledge, right down to the levels of the neuron and gene."[20] On the other hand, he sees sociobiology not as a form of biological determinism or behaviorist control (a "trap" that he forcefully rejects), but rather as something more akin to a humanistic investigation, the importance of which, as he later clarifies his position, "lies in its logical position as the bridging discipline between the natural sciences on the one side and social sciences and humanities on the other."[21]

In hindsight, Wilson was somewhat unprepared for the hostility with which his book would be greeted—by both serious scientists and political ideologues—but his call for interdisciplinary research to tackle these issues was not out of key with other voices attempting to mediate the competing viewpoints of biological and cultural theorists. In 1973 the anthropologist Eugene Ruyle offered the hypothesis that "individuals are the generating force behind the origin, spread, and transformations of sociocultural complexes," but these in turn are governed by selective pressures of natural selection.[22] In 1975 the anthropologist F. T. Cloak published the paper "Is a Cultural Ethology Possible," in which he also aligned cultural change with the processes of natural selection.[23] And one year later the British ethologist Richard Dawkins made a different yet similar case with his popular study *The Selfish Gene*. In singling out the "totally and utterly wrong" claims of Lorenz, Ardrey, and Eibl-Eibesfeldt, he argued that genes work not for the good of the species but rather for the good of the individual body in which they are housed.[24] Genes in effect lead animals to develop certain behavioral traits that increase the chance of survival and organisms are likely to reproduce these same genes-bearing traits in future generations. He even coined the word "meme" ("tunes, ideas, catch-phrases, clothes fashions, ways of making pots or of building arches") as a cultural corollary to the gene.[25]

The controversy surrounding Wilson's book had one redeeming value. His assault on the premises of cultural theory forced both biologists and anthropologists to acknowledge that evolution might be an outcome of both factors coming into play—genes and culture—and that only a composite model would do justice to these forces. These efforts, in fact, were already underway. In 1972 the Harvard sociologist Talcott Parsons called a conference of sociologists and biologists to explore the relations between social and biological theory, and in a follow-up conference he invited Wilson, the psychologist Karl Pribram, and the geneticist Stephen J. Gould to a round-table discussion with sociologists.[26] In 1976 the anthropologist William H. Durham published a paper entitled "The Adaptive Significance of Cultural Behavior," in which he argued that "human social behavior is a product of the coevolution of human biology and culture" and that "both biological and cultural attributes of human beings result to a large degree from the selective retention of traits that enhance the inclusive fitnesses of individuals in their environments."[27] Two years later, in response to the ongoing sociobiology debate, he expanded upon this proposal with a paper entitled "Toward a Coevolutionary Theory of Human Biology and Culture."[28]

By the early 1980s models of gene-culture coevolution became a hot pursuit within the academy. In 1981 the Stanford geneticist Luigi Luca Cavalli-Sforza joined with the mathematician Marcus Feldman in publishing a quantitative model of how gene-culture coevolution might work.[29] Wilson in the same year teamed up with the young mathematician Charles Lumsden to publish a parallel model. Although the mathematics of the both texts are daunting, their underlying tenet is straightforward. Coevolution, as Lumsden and Wilson define it, is "a complicated, fascinating interaction in which culture is generated and shaped by biological imperatives while biological traits are simultaneously altered by genetic evolution in response to cultural innovation."[30] What mediates this gene-culture interaction are what the two authors refer to as "epigenetic rules"—that is, genetically imposed "regularities" in the development of cognition and behavior that translate into patterns of culture. One example is the so-called Westermark effect, the fact that individuals generally have no sexual feelings toward those with whom they are closely related or raised in early life. Historically, incest has made it painfully evident that this biological mixing of similar gene pools does not produce a good result, and culture enforces this prohibition with such social sanctions as legislation and Oedipean tragedies. Lumsden and Wilson proposed a theory in which culture is free to evolve in many ways, but nevertheless is still "leashed" to biology through the interdependence of genetic and cultural exchanges.

In 1985 Robert Boyd and Peter Richerson published *Culture and the Evolutionary Process*, which took a somewhat different approach in that it was a model coauthored by an anthropologist and a biologist. The two professors have more recently defined culture as "information capable of affecting individuals' behavior that they acquire from other members of their species through teaching, imitation, and other forms of social transmission."[31] Information includes many of the traditional features of culture, such as knowledge, beliefs, values, and skills, but also specific traits that play a role in evolutionary theory. In this way, cultural evolution is not directly related to genetic evolution, but, from the perspective of population biology, it changes the way human evolution works because the reservoir of cultural information creates novel evolutionary trade-offs over the course of generations. They use the metaphor of a "recipe" for genes, which is then executed by the selection of ingredients and cooking temperature.

In many of these models, culture is akin to a human adaptation, a dynamic process that came about (probably during the rapid climate changes of the early Pleistocene era) because its mechanisms allowed people to respond more quickly to novel environmental conditions than natural selection could have done on its own. The interchange of culture and evolution is also seen as reciprocal. Cultural influences have led to less robust hominins, the development of language has altered the vocal tract, and the relatively recent implementation of dairy farming has changed the DNA enzymes for digesting milk among certain populations. These biological changes, in turn, alter the course of cultural development.

More recently, the idea of coevolution has been invested with a new urgency. Not only have new technologies greatly expanded the experimental reach of models, but major strides in our understanding of genomic expression, for instance, have also cast some issues in a very different light. Moreover, the conversation today is being enjoined by philosophers, psychologists, sociologists, aestheticians, and historians, which has greatly enhanced the level of discourse. Only architecture and its vaunted "theory" has so far remained aloof from these discussions. Architectural curricula remain one of the few programs in the humanities on campus without any serious examination of its underlying tenets.

IV.

The most eloquent architectural writer to suggest aligning architectural design with the progress made in the social and biological sciences was Richard Neutra, whose book *Survival through Design* appeared in 1954. This Austrian-born architect immigrated to the United States in 1924, worked under Frank Lloyd Wright at Taliesin and later in partnership with Rudolf Schindler in Los Angeles. His first important building of 1928, the Lovell "Health House," established what would be the most consistent theme of his practice. Four years later, he followed this production with the first version of his VDL Research House. It was an effort to design a low-cost, high-tech house with an emphasis placed on its interaction with human biology. During the war years, he continued along this path by experimenting with the design of several prefabricated communities in southern California as well as open-air schools and clinics in Puerto Rico, research that he published in 1948 as *The Architecture of Social Concern in Regions of Mild Climate*.

Neutra, like so many immigrants of his generation, anxiously viewed European political events and the Second World War, and he approached the essays of *Survival through Design* (many written during the war) with an air of pessimism. Since the days of "Sodom and Gomorrah," he opens the book, "organic normalcy has been raped again and again by man, that super-animal still struggling for its own balance."[32] Humanity will find its balance, he goes on to argue, only through research or "tangible observation"—that is, when architects realize that their role is the guardianship of the earth and its species and accept the serious responsibility entrusted to them. It is the baneful effects of the contemporary disorder and the sensory overload of our cities in particular that Neutra consistently opposes in strong if not ominous terms: "It is in this era of brain-physiological research that the designer, who wields the tools of sensory and cerebral stimulation professionally, can perhaps be recognized as a perpetually and precariously active conditioner of the race and thus acquire responsibility for its survival."[33]

Neutra's argument is biologically and psychologically driven. In citing research on genes in protozoa, for instance, he raises the specter of genetic "mutations more fateful than nature's" if designers continue "to operate accidentally," or remain trapped within "the pure aesthetics of a bygone brand of speculation."[34] He speaks of our multisensory interactions with the built environment: our sensitivity to minute sound reverberations, air currents, heat loss, aromas emanating from natural woods and exterior gardens, textures, the tactile resistance of a floor to our feet, and the comfort of our body's skin when sitting on an upholstered chair. He encourages the architect to become "a gardener of nervous growth," to recognize that "there are significant limitations to human brains and nervous systems."[35] He insists that good design "must turn from a commercial into a physiological issue," and it thus must take into account the activity of afferent sense receptors, proprioceptive muscles and tendons, visceral response from interoceptive organs, and teleceptives changes within the environment.[36] Neutra, almost eerily, intersperses his commentaries with predictions that have now come to pass: "Individual and social psychology will ultimately merge with BRAIN PHYSIOLOGY, TO GUIDE THE DESIGNER IN HIS OBSERVATION AND CREATION OF RESPONSE PATTERNS."[37]

For whatever reasons, Neutra's book seems to have had little influence on the direction of design education in the 1950s. European universities had scarcely recovered from the war years, and the idea that architecture might have an impact on the health and mental welfare of the human race had never had a strong foothold in architectural programs on the other side of the Atlantic. Nevertheless, scattered and isolated efforts in this direction appeared. In 1956 Lloyd Rodwin opened MIT's Center for Urban and Regional Studies, and in 1959 this school teamed up with Harvard University to offer a doctoral program under the auspices of the Joint Center for Urban Studies. Kevin Lynch was one of the early beneficiaries of this collaboration. In 1954 he, together with his mentor Gyorgy Kepes, received a grant from the Rockefeller Foundation for what would become a five-year research project to study how people understand the urban environment. His well-known book *The Image of the City* (1960) was a masterful research on how people form urban maps articulating paths, edges, districts, nodes, and landmarks—findings today supported in part by our understanding of how we neurologically navigate space.[38] In 1960 Lynch joined Rodwin in hosting a conference on *The Future Metropolis*, the publication of which was a sustained plea for further research on the urban environment.[39] Also in 1961 Jane Jacobs published *The Death and Life of Great American Cities*, which also was funded by a grant from the Rockefeller Foundation. It presented a strong counterpoint to the conventional view of urban renewal, and made a common-sense argument of preserving the social fabric and scale of existing neighborhoods.

Robert Venturi, as we have seen, profited from the sociology of Herbert Gans and Paul Davidoff, and another urban theorist later influencing both him and Denise Scott Brown was Melvin Webber, whose essay "The Urban Place and Nonplace Urban Realm" appeared in 1964. In it he challenged the basic tenet of traditional planning by offering a "communications systems" model of the future city, in which the inhabitants of which have many of their social and working contacts with each other through telephones or electronically, thereby eliminating the conventional need for a centralized urban core.[40]

The most prominent sociologist to engage with architects in these years was Robert Gutman. In 1965, he received a grant from the Russell Sage Foundation to explore the interactions between architecture and sociology, allowing him to take a semester in residence at Princeton University and the Bartlett School of Architecture to study the design profession "beset by a sense of crisis." He sought a common ground for collaboration between architects and sociologists, and in the summary of his study he suggests something of a compromise between the two fields: the introduction of more sociological coursework into architectural curricula and postgraduate programs in sociology departments to acquaint sociologists "with the culture and dilemmas of architecture."[41] The problem, of course, is what form this collaboration would take, and just how the sociologist could inform the designer beyond the initial programmatic stage. From its behaviorist perspective, sociology in the 1960s was little concerned with the deeper dimensions of human sociality.

The same is true for behavioral psychology in the 1960s and 1970s, albeit with a few exceptions. Robert Sommer's *Personal Space* (1969) was popular in design circles because it offered specific advice to designers mainly with the planning of interiors—based on his own research. In his follow-up engaging study, *Tight Spaces* (1974), Sommer expanded his interests in confronting the "hard architecture" of institutional and public buildings, which he defined by such features as their lack of permeability or social interaction with the outside, hard materials and furnishings, and cell-like interiors. In *Defensible Space* (1972), Oscar Newman drew upon Ardrey, Morris, and Lorenz to make the case for visibility and natural surveillance in the prevention of crime—thereby connecting the built environment with aspects of human behavior.

Highly influential were also Edward T. Hall's pioneering books *The Silent Language* (1959) and *The Hidden Dimension* (1966), which were also widely read within architectural circles. Hall was a well-respected anthropologist, having spent four years early in his career living among Navajo and Hopi populations in Arizona. He was one of the first critics to reject the use of high-rises for public housing projects and he touched upon many issues researchers are today revisiting. His notion of "tactile space" is a case in point. Drawing upon his own studies, Hall argued that our perception of "texture" in the world, when visually presented, is nevertheless appraised by tactile areas in the brain. If the artistic products of certain cultures, such as the works by medieval artisans or Japanese artists, are more sensitive to textural qualities than other cultures, the failing of modern industrial architecture, he goes on to argue, is precisely that "textures on and in buildings are seldom used consciously and with psychological and social awareness." This failing of modern architecture—its lack of tactile stimulation—is especially prominent in our cities, and he goes on to add: "Our urban spaces provide little excitement or visual variation and virtually no opportunity to build a kinesthetic repertoire of spatial experiences. It would appear that many people are kinesthetically deprived and even cramped."[42]

The high quality of the efforts of researchers like Sommer, Newman, and Hall aside—architectural interest in research was waning by the start of the 1970s. For one thing, the spectacular failure of the Great Society programs, in the United States at least, was underscoring the methodological weaknesses of then-current social science models. For another, a younger generation of architects were becoming attracted to the pastime of theory, and the particular theoretical turn toward semiotics and poststructuralism was drawing designers away from issues relating to their craft and toward a fascination with ideas.

V.

Empirical-based research, however, did not entirely disappear. One new area that came to the fore in the 1960s was environmental psychology, which had been pioneered a decade earlier by the psychologists William Ittelson and Harold Proshansky and their concern for the design of mental health facilities. The first book to appear under the title *Environmental Psychology* (1970) contained sixty-five essays, including contributions by Lynch, Rodwin, Jacobs, Gans, Alexander, and Webber.[43] Not unrelated to this field was the founding of Environmental Design Research Association (EDRA) in 1968, along with its journal *Environment and Behavior*. One can make the case that EDRA was the seminal phase to what would become known in the 1980s as evidence-based design. Its methods were first championed by researchers such as John Zeisel, but the turning point is better seen in Roger Ulrich's influential paper of 1984, "View through a Window May Influence Recovery from Surgery."[44] The latter was a study at one hospital of records of patients who had undergone gall bladder surgery between 1972 and 1981. Ulrich organized twenty-three pairs of patients of similar ages and health, yet with one difference. Those in one group had hospital beds looking out at the brick wall of an adjacent wing, while those in the other group had a view of trees in a meadow. The result was nothing short of spectacular for a surgical procedure then requiring up to nine days of hospital recovery. Those patients with the

THE CULTURE WARS

view of nature spent on an average almost one less day in the hospital, had fewer postsurgical complications, and requested fewer medications for pain. In the last three decades, the research efforts of evidence-based design have come to revolutionize the way in which healthcare facilities are today designed globally.

Christopher Alexander also began his research efforts in the 1960s. A native of Cambridge, England, he entered a doctoral program at Harvard in the late 1950s and participated in the Joint Center for Urban Studies. Formative to his interests was his association with the Center for Cognitive Studies, through which he published four papers between 1960 and 1964, three of which dealing with human perception. Alexander, under the lead of Serge Chermayaff, also contributed to the small planning guide *Community and Privacy* (1963), which, as the authors noted, advocated "the development of a Science of Environmental Design to supplement high purpose, creative ability, and technical skill before it is too late."[45] Alexander, who was just completing his doctoral studies, set out thirty-three design variables for prototypical mass housing, which he did with the aid of IBM computer. His dissertation was published in the following year under the title *Notes on the Synthesis of Form*, and here his intention was to create a design methodology by articulating a logical process for organizing pertinent data during design—the formation of tree diagrams, sets, and subsets of variables.[46] In 1964 Alexander joined the architectural faculty at Berkeley, and three years later he founded the Center for Environmental Structure, which would become the base for his research and practice.

The first project to emerge from the Center, coauthored with Sara Ishikawa and Murray Silverstein, was *A Pattern Language Which Generates Multi-Service Centers* (1968), a project funded by the National Institute of Health. Alexander and his team followed this effort one year later with another sociological exercise, *Housing Generated by Patterns*. It consisted of sixty-seven patterns for the design of a low-income neighborhood in Lima, a project funded by the United Nations and based on his own field research carried out in Peru. Neither his methodological interests or these early efforts were successful, but Alexander continued with his research and between 1969 and 1973 he and others at the Center for Environment Structure compiled what would become a best-selling trilogy of pattern books: *The Timeless Way of Building* (1979), *A Pattern Language: Towns, Buildings, and Construction* (1977), and *The Oregon Experiment* (1975).

The most popular of the three studies, *A Pattern Language*, consisted of 253 "patterns" covering everything from general principles of regional and town planning to the placement of windows in a house.[47] Each of the patterns begins with a statement of the problem, followed by a summary of research, and a proposed pattern or design solution. The research for the patterns, some specific and some not, was largely drawn from the social sciences of the 1960s, and they range from both general principles to specific design proposals. They were also intended to be recursive in the sense that they can be reused again with different solutions, and they reflect a laudable emphasis on the user's experience of the design.

Alexander brought a similar sensitivity to human experience and planning in his later study *A New Theory of Urban Design* (1987), which was based on a design studio at Berkeley. In the 1980s, he also began what would become his four-volume study *The Nature of Order* (2002–05). In it he combats, at a grander scale, what he believes to be the "mass psychosis" of political and cultural systems that produce buildings so aesthetically and ecologically "unfriendly" to people. His intention is "to show how architecture can be made whole again through a new picture of the nature of order, and through a new picture of the nature of matter itself."[48]

Paralleling the sociological perspective of Alexander is the work of Bill Hiller, which extends back to the 1960s as well. In his early article "A New Approach to Architectural Research" (1972), he and Adrian Leaman make a plea for rigorous research methodologies.[49] In a follow-up essay, "In defense of Space," Hillier embarks on an attack of the social sciences of the 1960s, which leads him to a condemnation of the repressive "social order" and rigidly defined schemes of spatial separation envisioned by early modern architects, in particular the urban schemes of Le Corbusier.[50]

The first presentation of Hillier's notion of "space syntax" appears in 1976. Hillier and colleagues at University College London—inspired by Noam Chomsky's notion of deep structure—proposed a "morphic language" of spatial organization, reducing the spatial patterns of complex buildings and urban settlements into eight major types. Spatial syntax is defined "as a set of related rule structures formed out of elementary combinations of the elementary objects, relations, and operations."[51] The reference to Chomsky is revealing. He was a leading voice in the linguistic debates the 1960s, arguing at the time that sentence structures are the outward expression of "deep structures" or grammatical trees generated by syntax, and he viewed human languages more broadly as variants of an innate universal grammar. Hillier's objective is to characterize the spatial structure as a morphological operation in itself (initially presented as a kind of symbolic algebra) and to tie it (in the manner of Durkheim) to the factual functioning of the collective social structure. Underlying it are such factors as man-to-nature relations, division of labor, and the social order. Hillier's book with Julienne Hanson of 1984, *The Social Logic of Space*, also brought his concern down to the level of the individual building and how its spaces influence social relations.

His reference to Chomsky's model notwithstanding, one of the more appealing aspects of Hillier's approach is his critique of architectural theory in the late twentieth century—that is, its tendency to borrow themes or structures from other disciplines and apply them to design. His own approach differs, he argues, in that he proposes hypotheses that can be tested and their shortcomings removed or accommodated. His starting point is the thesis that the pedestrian patterns of movement in both buildings and cities are generated by the plan's configuration or spatial grid. The innovation that he has brought to the task over the years are his increasingly sophisticated software programs, through which Hillier has sought to quantify the navigable nature of pedestrian spaces (such as convex, axial, shallow, and deep). His hypothesis is that spatial configurations create a field of probable encounters and co-presences of people affecting one another's behavior.

The works of Alexander and Hillier, together with that of researchers such as Neutra, Hall, and Ulrich, represent the best of twentieth-century efforts to integrate meaningful research into the design process, and the application of these methodologies into such areas will no doubt continue and expand with the newer tools that today's neuroscience can offer. Zeisel, for instance, has recently updated his book *Inquiry by Design* with a new chapter on neuroscience, which he believes will expand the range of present research "beyond the bounds of imagination."[52] The founding of the Academy of Neuroscience in San Diego in 2003, led by the efforts of John Eberhard and Allison Whitelaw, has stood in the forefront of these efforts, with its focus in such areas as wayfinding in building complexes and environments for assisted living for the elderly. Over the last two decades an abundance of research has been undertaken globally on how built environments might be better fitted to accommodate conditions such as cognitive decline.[53]

My interests in the present study, however, are directed to different issues that take us to the heart of the design process. They concern general questions such as how the human organism engages with the many facets of the built environment—how our perceptual and emotional modalities, the built environment, our inherent sociality, and cultural factors interact or mutually inform one another in composing the canvas of human existence. Questions can be raised today at every stage of the design process, and the insights and more sophisticated understanding of ourselves offered by the humanities and sciences afford us a fresh perspective and means to reexamine critically what it is that we really do as designers, and what exactly are the principles that should guide us. These questions can also at times be quite specific. How do we respond in an embodied manner to particular building materials, their scale, texture, and other qualities? How does the human body engage with space or with particular forms? How do we as human individuals define a sense of place? How does walking the alleyways of an Italian medieval town differ from walking the sidewalks of the concrete-and-glass metropolis? How much of nature should we bring into our urban environments and what are its measurable benefits? Today we can evaluate design in new ways because we have much enhanced tools at our disposal. Implicit in this endeavor is the recognition that the designed environment within which we are richly interwoven not only plays a role in human behavior but also, and perhaps more importantly, in our long-term capacity to thrive and prosper as organisms. We now have the knowledge and the tools to reconsider—in the most radical way—our living environments.

3

A Cultural Model for Design

Many of the things we do are shaped by behavioral predispositions, moods, emotions, and feelings that have a deep evolutionary history. These body states are not ghostly things flitting mysteriously through consciousness.

DANIEL LORD SMAIL[1]

The various disciplines within the humanities are today undergoing an upheaval whose proportions are difficult to appreciate fully. Fundamental premises are being revised and across multiple fields there are promises of new beginnings. When the historian Daniel Lord Smail made his controversial case above, he was pleading with colleagues, who have viewed their methods as autonomous and fixed in traditions, to connect "the humanities and social sciences with the physical and life sciences"—that is, by delving into "the neurophysiological legacy of our deep past," the biological mechanisms through which our habits and human actions have historically evolved.[2]

Our efforts in the present study are not dissimilar, because it is my belief that the design profession has to move beyond the conceptual limitations of twentieth-century thought and its reductive methodologies, and adopt a way of thinking in line with the newly gained knowledge about ourselves. If the objective of this study is to construct a way of thinking about design centered on the human experience of the built environment, it must encompass not just another conceptual paradigm or set of ideas but acknowledge the full range of our biological, affective, aesthetic, social, and cultural dimensions. And because the design arts and architecture traverse many boundaries of interests, this approach will of necessity be interdisciplinary. It is not that designers, as in the past, should borrow the strategies or methodologies of the humanities or the sciences—only that designers can and should be informed about areas of knowledge that have particular relevance to design. We therefore will consider design from the dual perspectives of how we engage with or enact the built environment, and conversely how the built environment in turn shapes us.

Defining the built environment through the medium of "experience," of course, is not a new idea to architecture or to art. Many architects over the years, from Steen Eiler Rasmussen to Steven Holl, have steered us toward the experiential and multisensory dimensions of the physical environment. Even earlier, one can point to John Dewey's *Art as Experience* (1934) and the emphasis that he placed on the physiological and emotional nature of perception. The last, for him, was not something gained through the senses and later processed by the mind, but the organism's active engagement with the world, a pre-reflective and emotionally driven moment of "heightened vitality" that takes command of our attentional systems.[3] Perception—he was one of the first to argue in modern times—is already imbued with meaning. Dewey goes on to define emotion as "the moving and cementing force," which "selects what is congruous and dyes what is selected with color, thereby giving qualitative unity to materials externally disparate and dissimilar."[4] Life is a dynamic flow of intentional acts enlivened with the sensibilities of a lived body, and experience thus becomes a holistic yet dissectible exercise of bodily rhythms. Our relationship with the world is radically an organismic one.

Dewey was not entirely alone in his day. Also in the same year of his artistic study, the biologist Jakob von Uexküll, in *A Foray into the Worlds of Animals and Humans*, expanded upon his earlier notion of the *Umwelt* and made the case that an organism's perception is always bounded by its own "surrounding environment," whose limits are defined by the sensory "carriers" of meaning particular to that organism.[5] Humans, for instance, may perceive a flower as an ornament, but an insect may perceive it as an impediment or a meal. Each organism, in effect, enacts its own world.

Operating with a similar premise, Kurt Goldstein, in *The Organism* (1934), made the case that human perception is not the faculty of a single sensory modality but a whole-organism event, because the perceptual experience is not exhausted by a simple sensory impression. A color, for example, is not a neutral element of someone viewing the composition of a painting, but one that induces a more pervasive "mood" or "atmosphere," which is the living essence of the perceptual experience. Moreover, every perceptual experience induces somatic responses as well, in particular "a certain muscle tension" corresponding to the experience.[6] What this means is that the biological systems of an organism, in responding to each and every stimulus, continually struggles "to be adequate to its environmental conditions."[7]

Phenomenology in the twentieth century pursued a similar track, albeit from a different vantage point. Edmund Husserl had initially put forth his introspective method of examining consciousness as a way to bring to light the inner and outer horizons of human experience—those elements that we bring to the perceptual act and how the environment or its context conditions what we perceive. For Husserl, perception is an active vitality in that it is always consciousness of something; it carries with it the weight of thoughts, memory, emotions, imagination, time, spatiality, and bodily kinesthetic awareness. Different phenomenologists later came to stress different aspects of experience. If Husserl saw phenomenology as a description of lived experience accessible to rigorous introspection, his student Martin Heidegger approached it in a more hermeneutic way as a fundamental process of interpreting our existential relationship with the world. Maurice Merleau-Ponty, who drew much from the fields of psychology and biology, emphasized the embodied nature of human experience.

The insights of Merleau-Ponty are today greeted with renewed interest in philosophical and neuroscientific circles. If traditional metaphysics viewed the mind as something "mental" yet housed in a carnal body, Merleau-Ponty broke down the distinction between mind and body as well as between the body and the surrounding world. Perception, for him, is an embodied, organismic event filled with gestures, attitudes, and meanings. When we move through a room, for instance, we are always aware of what is forward and backward, and we generally move with intentions and motivations. Architecturally, we experience our habitats both kinesthetically and viscerally. We are immediately aware of the narrowness or vastness of the spatial field in which we move; we inwardly bend toward the outward conditions to which we are attracted. We know what is distant or close by our touch as well as by our vision. We perceive space not as a geometric abstraction but through the experiences of a living, motile organism. Perception is not a sensory awareness of things in the world; it is always an integrating and creative composing of things of "autochthonous" significance, whether personal or social.[8] In his last unfinished manuscript, Merleau-Ponty even described our relationship with the world with the German term *Einfühlung*.[9]

The idea of *Einfühlung*, or "empathy," as we noted earlier, is today frequently invoked in the humanities and life sciences. The idea has a rich history in perceptual and aesthetic thought going back to the last three decades of the nineteenth century. It has the literal meaning of "feeling into" something, and originally it referred to the physiological and psychological processes through which we connect with or perceptually engage people and things, including art and architecture. The term played a pivotal role in the development of German modernism in the first decades of the twentieth century and several historians have made the case that it was an important aesthetic underpinning to the foundation of the Weimar Bauhaus.[10] The reason that the idea of empathy has been resurrected within so many fields today is because scientists, with the aid of neuroimaging technologies, are now observing the specific neurological processes involved with perception. The term has also become a focus of the new field of social neuroscience, which—in adopting the commonplace meaning of "empathy" in English—examines the neurological processes by which we socially relate to others. Some neuroscientists, in collaboration with philosophers, have built models of intercorporality around the idea of empathy and its expression through embodied simulation.[11]

Also informing current models of perception has been the work by James Gibson. Already in 1966, the psychologist pointed out the composite and interwoven nature of perception in *The Senses Considered as Perceptual Systems*. In his follow-up study *The Ecological Approach to Visual Perception* (1979), he recast the idea of *Umwelt* in terms of "affordances"—the fact that we perceive the objects of our environmental fields not as entities to which we assign a name but already as terrains, shelters, water, fire, tools, and human interactions. Vision, for instance, entails the moving body (made possible through the activity of musculature and vestibular nerves), the body's support of an environmental ground, the body's spatial reference with respect to the ground, and the constructive cognitive engagement of the organism's neural mechanisms with the environmental field. The environment is not just the exterior backdrop to these processes; it is the medium that affords respiration, locomotion, the detection of vibrations and diffusing emanations, the larger frame of reference, and the illumination allowing vision. The organism and the environment are therefore reciprocal in their connectedness.

As Gibson's work was unfolding in the 1970s, cognitive neuroscientists were pursuing the idea of perception from another direction.[12] One model of "action-oriented perception," for instance, operates on the hypothesis that one can characterize perceptual systems—highly selective in their acts of seeking information—not as ends in themselves but through their ongoing courses of action or potential actions. In the perception-action cycle, for instance, an organism may gather a perceptual "schema" of information, which sets in motion possible courses of action within the motor cortex, based on the anticipation of how to take on or accomplish a particular goal. These plans of action are ever being modified. In this way, as Michael Arbib has noted, "the brain must be able to continually modify the schema assemblage so that the schemas remain appropriate to the corresponding objects and tasks, though such changes are relative and may involve remappings of input (sensory) and output (motor) pathways."[13] Arbib has illustrated his action-oriented perception cycle by citing the way that Peter Zumthor lures the visitor's movement through thermal baths at Vals by means of an ever-changing array of sensory values:

> Zumthor's design manages the visitor's movement though the space, merging from one sensory experience to another. Different sensory modalities can be engaged. In one room there are fragrant flowers in the water to engage the sense of smell; elsewhere a heavy leather curtain may engage a sense of tactility and heaviness in the action of moving the curtain aside.[14]

II.

One of the definitions of a "niche" in *Merriam-Webster's Collegiate Dictionary* is "a habitat supplying the factors necessary for the existence of an organism or species." Architecture can certainly be defined as the art of constructing niches or habitats, because its creations provide inhabitants with the features necessary to survive and enhance their well-being. Yet the idea of building a niche has recently taken on a larger ecological significance. In the 1990s three biologists—F. John Odling-Smee, Kevin Laland, and Marcus Feldman—proffered a new field that would deal with the complexity of our ecosystems. "Niche construction," they defined, "investigates the evolutionary impact of the modification of the environments by organisms"—that is, the impact that their environmental alterations have on the natural selection pressures of the species.[15] Much early work on this area was focused on animal species and their physical habitats, but the idea of "ecological inheritance" today encompasses the role that human environmental and cultural actions (including architectural design) may play in changing human living patterns, the interaction of genes and culture, and how these exchanges may speed up or slow down the processes of natural selection.

If, as is now being demonstrated, environmental and cultural changes bring about neurological and other microbiological alterations in organisms, then organisms can no longer be viewed as fixed carriers or vehicles for genes, as in the past. This is the case because organisms, as they are modifying their environmental variables, are at the same time altering the expression of their genomic structures. Estimates of the number of human genes that have undergone a rapid evolution (by conventional natural selection standards) have ranged from a few hundred to several thousand, and one biologist has suggested that as much as 10 percent of the human genome may have been modified within the last several thousand years.[16] Such changes are much faster than earlier genetic models would have predicted, and the reach of culture, particularly in the last 40,000 years, is today seen by some as more consequential than inheritance in bringing about these genomic alterations. Because humans, in particular, are born into a world massively altered by previous generations, with a legacy of farms, houses, cities, cars, and nations, "niche construction and ecological inheritance are thus likely to have been particularly consequential in human evolution."[17] Such a statement, by three prominent biologists, raises an obvious question: Do we really know what we are doing in designing our houses and cities?

More recently, two neuroscientists have extended the idea of an "ecological niche" of organisms and environment into a triadic model of niche construction, one incorporating the domains of *neural* alteration and *cognitive* development.

For instance, in their experiments with monkeys, they have shown that when a primate learns to master a tool, it not only enlarges complexes of neural circuits in sensorimotor regions of the brain but also enhances the monkey's cognitive powers in other ways. In applying such a principle to humans, our evolution can now be seen as a holistic terrestrial ecosystem (ecological, neural, cognitive), involving successive stages of acquiring and expanding our sensorimotor skills, which in turn alter our neural circuits and enhance our cognitive skills within a positive feedback loop.[18]

Again, there is much in this model to stir the designer's imagination. The advent of primate bipedalism has long been known to have had significant biological and physical consequences in the development of the hominin body and brain. Moreover, the transition from tree tops to the open plains, with the introduction of fire, clothing, and shelters, began a hominin pattern of adapting to different terrains and climates often demanding major changes in manners of acting and thinking. Language, the arts, agriculture, and urban settlements—all fed the pace of cultural change, just as today automobiles, airplanes, televisions, and computers are presumed to be affecting changes of behavior at an accelerating pace. If these cultural innovations in the long run have led to a loss of tactility and olfactory systems, a more gracile skeleton, and weaker musculature, they have had numerous advantages as well. The human species is unique in its behavioral flexibility and has a higher degree of neural plasticity, population diversity, and lifestyle opportunities than our primate cousins.[19] Neural plasticity has in turn resulted in a greater appreciation of novelty and creativity, once again a feature largely unique to human cognition.

Yet what does the idea of niche construction say about the human habitats that we design? Here we seem to be entering difficult terrain, because such questions can only be explored through experimental testing. Some evolutionary psychologists, in making the case for biophilic design for instance, have argued that the industrial materials and monochromatic severity of the modern metropolis are not particularly well suited to human perceptual systems—those sensory systems that evolved in natural terrains. Some experiments have even shown that our denatured cities and air quality may be inhibiting or diminishing the cellular populations of the human immune system, weakening our resistance to certain cancers and coronary problems.[20] Other researchers have questioned the effects of social congestion, ambient noise levels, foul air, and profound sense of placelessness as we stand in the shadows of our ubiquitous generic towers. We have long known that rates of alcoholism and schizophrenia are generally higher within urban settings than without, yet are there other lessons to be learned here? Should we step back and fundamentally rethink the nature of urban life? At a smaller scale, what does niche construction say about the organization of a working space, a living room, or their ambience?

None of these issues can be answered without serious investigation, and because niche construction is a relatively new field, little work has been done specifically in relation to design. "'Who are *you*,' said the Caterpillar. This was not an encouraging opening for a conversation. Alice replied, rather shyly, 'I–I hardly know, sir, just at present—at least I know who I *was* when I got up this morning, but I think I must have changed several times since then.'"[21] Notwithstanding Alice's dilemma, the central tenet of niche construction can be framed for designers in succinct terms—*just as we design our built environments, so do our built environments reconfigure who we are.*

III.

Let us further consider the idea of a "niche." The most basic task of constructing an environment is to provide a shelter or habitat with an optimal climate of light, temperature, and humidity—long-accepted values of design. When we speak of the idea of a "niche," however, the term suggests multiple systems of interacting relationships. In addition to these homeostatic variables, there are a host of perceptual, neural, social, and cultural factors that play into the cognitive performance of an environment. In entering a room or stepping onto a terrace, for instance, our perception may fix upon its noise or silence, its warmth or coolness, its color or blend of textures, or the atmospheric effects that we deem to be pleasing or unpleasing—such as the way a table is set, how much we might enjoy the fragrance of a plant, or the smile of another person standing within the room. All of these sensory events may change over the course of a day or during the seasons of the year. In this way, the overall character of any niche or environment is never determined by any one factor but of many, and perhaps the most important are the intentions or emotional responses that we bring to the experience itself.

If we do not wish to be reductive when thinking about design, we must first recognize the great complexity of the human organism in its interactions with the physical and social environments. The complexities are brought about because we are in fact biological organisms, and we now know, for instance, that natural and built environments can effect changes in our organismic systems at cellular, neurological, emotional, perceptual, and cognitive levels. In this way, the complexities of design multiply. A second task, then, in opening up the horizons of this field to designers is to bring some order to the process.

In constructing a way of thinking about design, what we find in the number of variables composing this complexity is not dissimilar to the issues raised during the sociobiology and coevolutionary debates of the 1980s—questions of how to bring together and structure these biological and cultural variables. Newer genetic models and their philosophical interpretation provide us with some assistance in this regard. Traditional genetic theory, for example, viewed the gene and its DNA sequences as a privileged master program that was transmitted to organisms from generation to generation; only after birth did these organisms become modified further by epigenetic or environmental influences. A number of critics from both the sciences and humanities stepped forth during the sociobiological debates to argue that this dualistic model (genes and environment) was an oversimplification of far more complicated processes that cannot be so simply stated.

One of the more prominent of these critics was the philosopher Susan Oyama, who proposed the alternative model of "developmental systems theory." Drawing upon newer genetic models, her basic argument is that all organismic forms, rather than being transmitted or directed by genetic programs, are better seen as reconstructed in a developmental process that continues throughout the life of the organism with the input of multiple systems. As she characterizes the issue: "What is transmitted between generations is not traits, or blueprints or symbolic representations of traits, but developmental *means* (or *resources*, or *interactants*). These include genes, the cellular machinery necessary for their functioning, and the larger developmental context, which may include a maternal reproductive system, parental care, and other interaction with conspecifics, as well as relations with other aspects of the animate and inanimate worlds."[22] In short, no organism is ever complete or finished at any point within this developmental process, but is continually reconstructing its genetic structure, cellular system, neurological circuits, and bodily forms as all of these factors come into play over the course of a lifetime. From such a perspective, there is no single controlling variable such as a gene in human behavior. The same might be said of the design process.

Such a perspective enlarges the conventional idea of inheritance by drawing upon multiple interacting factors affecting development: genetic, epigenetic, behavioral, and cultural. It also views inheritance not as an atomistic process, but as a systemic and interactive one stressing the interdependence of the organism with the environment. In this way, Oyama attempted to solve another seemingly entrenched problem of late twentieth-century thought—by breaking down the wall between nature and nurture. As she made the case, the two are not contraries but rather "nature is the *product* of the *processes* that are the developmental interactions we call nurture."[23] They are one and the same system and thus there can be no fixed human "nature" because the developmental processes of interactions within organisms are continually taking place.

I am not suggesting that developmental systems theory as a philosophical critique has any application to design. I raise the idea as an analogy to underscore the complexity of issues with which the designer must contend when considering design through the experience of the user. Oyama, however, goes on to make one other argument that draws a little closer to our theme.

Whereas most people generally contrast sciences such as biology with social fields such as cultural history—human history, she argues, is in fact "fully biological" when viewed developmentally, "not because it is predestined, but because it is the chronicle of the activities of living beings."[24] The mistakes that many cultural historians make in discussing cultural change, she goes on to argue with another design metaphor, are the subtleties of how such changes come about: "What comes of the chemical, mechanical, social-psychological resources an organism inherits depends on the organism and its relations with the rest of the world. It makes its own present and prepares its future, never out of whole cloth, always with the means at hand, but often with the possibility of putting them together in novel ways."[25] In a follow-up volume on developmental systems theory, the three noted architects of niche construction placed their model within the context of developmental-systems theory by noting that "niche construction organisms not only shape the nature of their world, but also in part determine the selection pressures to which they and their descendants are exposed."[26] Niche construction and natural selection are therefore not only operating in parallel but also interacting in a developmental manner.

Let us bring this matter still closer to design. A cultural theorist who has considered Oyama's argument with architecture in mind is the anthropologist Tim Ingold, who makes the distinction between the "building perspective" and what he terms the "dwelling perspective." The building perspective, he notes, "is the architect's perspective: first plan and build the houses, then import the people to occupy them."[27] The "dwelling perspective" reverses this logic by thinking of a house as something that arises "within the life process itself."[28] Ingold points out that a house has to be connected with the developmental processes of what takes place inside the house, and what this means "is that the forms people make or build, whether in their imagination or on the ground, arise within the current of their involved activity, in the specific relational contexts of their practical engagement with their surroundings."[29] Here, once again, the emphasis of design is placed not on the built structure, but on the experience or activities that take place within the building.

The cultural theorist is making an important point here, which is that designers should be viewing their efforts within the developmental context of people's living activities, or how they experientially connect with their environments. Such a perspective, as we noted earlier, is not new to architectural thinking. It has been acclaimed over the years by voices as distinct as Alvar Aalto, Aldo van Eyck, Christopher Alexander, as well as by a number of phenomenologically minded architects.[30] Ingold, as well, is similarly critical of the abstractions of so much of twentieth-century architectural theory. "It is true that human beings—perhaps uniquely among animals—have the capacity to envision forms in advance of their implementation," he goes on to say, "but this envisioning is itself an activity carried on by real people in a real-world environment, rather than by a disembodied intellect moving in a subjective space in which are represented the problems it seeks to solve."[31]

Another philosophical perspective that draws close to Ingold's position and our theme is that of *enactivism*. The seminal text in this regard is *The Embodied Mind* (1991), and its three authors—Francisco Varela, Evan Thompson, and Eleanor Rosch—were, respectively, a biologist, philosopher, and psychologist. The interdisciplinary nature of this collaboration reflects the transforming intellectual climate of the 1990s.

One theme that appears throughout the book is that "perception is not only embedded within and constrained by the surrounding world; it also contributes to the enactment of this surrounding world."[32] In other words—and in parallel with the idea of niche construction—the organism both shapes the environmental field and at the same time is continually being shaped by it. Merleau-Ponty made a similar point as a philosophical observation, but the authors draw upon a number of experimental studies demonstrating, for example, that we are not born into the world with a visual cortex able to see objects; rather, the visual cortex does not form inside the brain without the motor activity and contextual bases to activate such systems. Motility, experience, and enculturation are therefore crucial to our perceptual systems from the start.

Another key point in their study is the importance they place on embodied sensorimotor activity during human perceptual activity, although not to the exclusion of other systems. The term "sensorimotor" refers to the sensory and motor cortices, the areas of the neocortex through which we have a sensory awareness of our bodies and move ourselves. In this regard they highlight two points: "first, that cognition depends upon the kinds of experience that come from having a body with various sensorimotor capacities, and second, that these individual sensorimotor capacities are themselves embedded in a more encompassing biological, psychological, and cultural context."[33] This context is at the same time providing feedback to the developing perception, and thus the organism is continually rebalancing or recalibrating the meaning of its worldly interactions. Cognition is therefore enacted through our history of coupling with the environment, and organisms and habitats are mutually specified and codetermining units of the same biological system.

The Embodied Mind proved to be a pivotal work and within the next two decades there appeared a score of studies centered on the themes of embodiment and enaction.[34] Such a perspective was even integrated into a number of proposed models for social cognition and artificial intelligence.[35] Phenomenologists, in particular, were drawn into the discussion. In 1996 Varela wrote a paper, "Neurophenomenology: a methodological remedy for the hard problem," in which he made the case that the "hard problem" of a philosophy of consciousness—"the structure of human experience itself"—could be better approached by employing the new tools of neuroscience.[36] Varela set out to collaborate with Thompson in this endeavor, but with his passing in 2001 the project fell to the philosopher, who in 2007 published *Mind in Life*. It defined in more precise terms the meaning of enactivism, but of greater importance for our topic is the fact that Thompson, from the perspective of a philosopher, explored the ramifications of the new perspective with regard to human emotion, empathy, and culture.

Emotion comes from the Latin verb *movere* (to move) and traditionally it is defined as the response of an organism to a stimulus. Yet when one considers the workings of emotion from an enactive perspective, it is less a "response" to sensory input than an endogenous activity at the front end of the experience—that is, an ongoing activity or movement within the organism that is present from the start. Thompson characterizes emotion as "a prototype whole-organism event because it mobilizes and coordinates virtually every aspect of the organism."[37] He means by this that emotion operates not only the major cortical and subcortical areas of the brain but also the molecular networks of the nervous, immune, and endocrine systems. In a phenomenological sense, Thompson equates emotion with Husserl's notion of intentionality—the stretching forth of the organism toward an aspect of the environment in preparation for some future activity. Emotion is therefore not a response or a reflex, but, in Thompson's words, "sensorimotor processes modulate, but do not determine, an ongoing endogenous activity" of emotion; rather, the latter "infuses sensorimotor activity with emotional meaning and value for the organism."[38]

Emotion for Thompson, similar to the observations of Dewey, is therefore a welling up of an organism's intrinsic vitality involving not only emotion's traditional dimensions (arousal, action preparation, bodily expression, attention, and mood) but also what are often deemed to be cognitive dimensions (perception, attention, evaluation, memory, planning, and decision making).[39] We shall also make the case throughout this study that the "prototype whole-organism event" of emotion is also central to the experience of architecture, and it has been a factor much undervalued by the attenuated emphasis of theory in recent years. In this regard, the notion of "empathy" will also play a key role in our analysis.

Thompson considers "empathy" under the theme of enculturation. It is therefore his intention to use the emotional underpinning of empathy as a bridge to Husserl's notion of intersubjectivity. He conceives empathy as the emotional means through which the organism projects itself toward and engages with the sociocultural environment, and it does so in two ways. First, it is the primary basis underlying our intersubjective experience with others—that is, how the "self and other enact each other reciprocally through empathy." Second, culture invests empathy with another layer of meaning, in his words, how "human subjectivity emerges from developmental processes of enculturation and is configured by the distributed cognitive web of symbolic culture."[40]

Again, from a phenomenological perspective, empathy is "a unique form of intentionality through which we engage with another's experience," and it is an immediate one: "we experience another human being directly as a person—that is, as an intentional being whose bodily gestures and actions are expressive of his or her experiences or states of mind."[41] This empathetic process unfolds in time. In addition to pairing with another living body, we may have an imaginary movement or transposition into another's place, or the understanding of someone as "another" to me. We also have the moral perception of another as a person with ethical standing. What brought the idea of empathy into philosophical and psychological circles in the 1990s was the discovery of "mirror neurons," which, as we will later discuss, began to reveal the biological workings or the sensorimotor and emotional mechanisms through which empathy arises.

Thompson goes on to draw one other implication of empathy that is germane to our topic, which is that human nature cannot be reduced to what simply goes on inside the head because "human mental activity is fundamentally social and cultural"—that is, culture "is no mere external addition or support to cognition; it is woven into the very fabric of each human mind from the beginning."[42] He is speaking of enculturation here in the sense of Merlin Donald's notion of "deep enculturation," the idea that literate culture, and the more recent memory devices of books and computers, has led human evolution into a stage of "superplasticity," whereby the forces of our digital culture, over generations, have accelerated the processes by which the brain effectively rewires its neural connections to accommodate itself to new tasks.[43] Such a view, of course, is a vastly different one from cultural models of a half-century ago, and especially in the understanding that enculturation has changed the way we think, or more fundamentally our human natures. The developmental processes of the human organism and the physical and cultural environments are continuously shaping one another—in Thompson's words, reconstructing themselves "from generation to generation by way of myriad independent causal pathways on multiple levels—genetic, cellular, social, and cultural."[44] In this way, it is no longer possible to see a crack of philosophical light between biology and culture. By virtue of their intricate interlacing, they cannot be construed as separate developmental domains.

In our analysis related to the design arts, we will use the term "empathy" in both its perceptual and social senses. On the one hand, empathy, through the sensorimotor operation of mirror or sensorimotor mechanisms, is the biological process by which we perceptually and aesthetically engage with or enact the built environment. On the other hand, social empathy, whose neural circuits are today becoming better known, is the particular mirror mechanism by which we connect with others.

IV.

On the basis of what we have discussed thus far, we can begin to lay out a framework for our study, which will attempt also to provide a fresh consideration of issues related to design. This approach will encompass both the many recent breakthroughs of the human and biological sciences as well as the considerable interpretative literature that in recent years has been constructed around the themes of perception, emotion, empathy, sociability, and enculturation. We must stress that the crafting or detailing of the built habitat will always remain the centerpiece of design, and that the themes of metaphor and narration are often integral, although not always essential, to this process. Central to our view, however, is the idea that architecture is at heart a phenomenal experience, one in which the built environment can no longer be considered *apart from the user's experience of it*. We mean by this that the practice of architecture is more than the process of form making, and that the designer has to accommodate the perceptual and social dimensions of design with more than a vague sense of those who will inhabit the work. The designer's responsibility in fact unfolds along three interrelated poles of action.[45]

First, design is the homeostatic fitting of the architectural gown to the body's sensory and nervous systems across its multiple levels of organization. This is simply the recognition, long understood, that the built environment biologically conditions human health and behavior on many levels. If we gravitate toward the natural light of a window when entering a cool room, it is because we are animate organisms seeking warmth and the beneficial effects of solar radiation.

Second, because our conscious engagement with the built environment initially and cognitively takes place during the perceptual experience, we should give greater attention to this dimension. Perception is historically seen as some kind of prereflective activity, or as something that takes place prior to the cognitive acts of judgment. Yet contemporary research is eroding the wall separating the two. "Gut feelings," for instance, are not "ghostly things flitting mysteriously through consciousness," as Smail pointed out; they have an evolutionary and physiological grounding and are, in effect, experiential shortcuts or early stages within the ongoing reasoning process.[46] The perception of the built environment involves the operation of the nervous, endocrine, and sensory systems, as well as the many other factors of human experience. Only on multiple levels does the human organism come to terms with or create meaning from its processing of light refractions, textures, forms, materials, and spatial qualities of the designer's creation. Perception is therefore a continuous process of enacting the built environment that of necessity unfolds over time and is conditioned by one's experience.

The third level on which the designer's responsibility resides are its social or cultural dimensions. We must bring these issues back into design consideration, only in a far more rigorous way than earlier efforts allowed us to do so. In this realm, too, we have an abundance of insights gained from the new models of the humanities and sciences, which can inform the designer—in ways often unconsidered in the past. Ultimately, these insights hold out the possibility that the field of design can reclaim a larger social ethos, one that historically has always been fundamental to a thriving culture. In summary then, we can model the design experience in the following way:

(1) *The biology of the design experience, or our body's homeostatic adjustments to and orientation within the built and natural environments;*
(2) *The perceptual and aesthetic experience of design, or the dynamics of how we engage with the built and natural environments; and*
(3) *The social and cultural experience of the built environment.*

How we structure these realms is less important than the larger point that we need to expand upon the way we think about design. From the perspective of today's human and biological sciences, we are living in lively and provocative times. Vast new domains are now opening for designers to explore.

4

New Models of Perception

It might well be thought that, as a fine art, architecture works for the eye alone, but it ought primarily—and very little attention is paid to this—to work for the sense of movement in the human body.

JOHANN WOLFGANG VON GOETHE[1]

Elephants, dolphins, sea lions, several primates, and Eurasian magpies have all passed the so-called mirror test, in which an animal displays a self-awareness in front of its own image. Alfred Hitchcock exploited the suspicion (and fear) of many that crows are cleverer than we think, and male bowerbirds—the most notable architects within the avian world—construct elaborate nests, some close to three meters tall, to attract females for mating. Those species who construct the most elaborate nests have considerably larger brains than others within the genus. If the human brain and its vast neural network is distinct from others, it is because evolution has shaped it in curious ways. Yet where does perception end and thinking begin? Or can we even pose such a question today?

Although it weighs on average only 1,350 grams or three pounds, the human brain is anything but a simple organ. It is estimated to house close to 100 billion nerve cells or neurons, each of which is potentially capable of as many as 10,000 synaptic connections with other neurons. A neuron consists of a nucleus or cell body, from which emanates an axon (sending electro-chemical signal to other neurons via a synapse) and dendrites (tree-like appendages receiving signals from other neurons). Both environmental factors and genetic expression are essential for normal brain development, and deficiencies along either front will have profound effects on the developing organism.

The different modules of the human brain were also anatomically constructed over many millions of years. The oldest part is the brain stem, consisting of three bulbous extensions atop the spine. At the rear of the brainstem is the cerebellum, another ancient brain module that coordinates muscles, balance, posture, and motor learning. Sitting atop the brainstem, in each lobe, is the thalamus, which occupies a central position within the skull and is, among other things, the main routing station directing the incoming sensory input to processing areas. Connected to and wrapping around each thalamus are a group of subcortical limbic modules, such as the hypothalamus (coordinating homeostatic systems and linking the nervous system to the endocrine system), amygdala (emotional responses), and the hippocampus (memory). All areas are central to our discussion. The hippocampus, for instance, is also involved with the processing of place, spatial navigation, and perception of buildings.

The area that most people associate with the brain, the neocortex, is the outer mantle of the brain, split down the middle into hemispheres. The neocortex is a thin membrane of brain cells, six layers collectively between 2 and 4 millimeter or 1/8 inches in depth. Beneath this mantle are the axons (white matter) connecting neocortical brain cells with each other and with the subcortical regions.

Each hemisphere, wrapping around the limbic modules and brain stem, is divided into four lobes (Figure 4.1). The frontal lobe in each hemisphere projects forward and folds under and inward behind the eyes. The underside of this lower projection (part of the prefrontal cortex) is the orbitofrontal cortex (OFC), which is one center of cognitive performance and the experience of pleasure. The furrows and ridges in the neocortex are the result of evolutionary growth of cortical tissue within limited skull

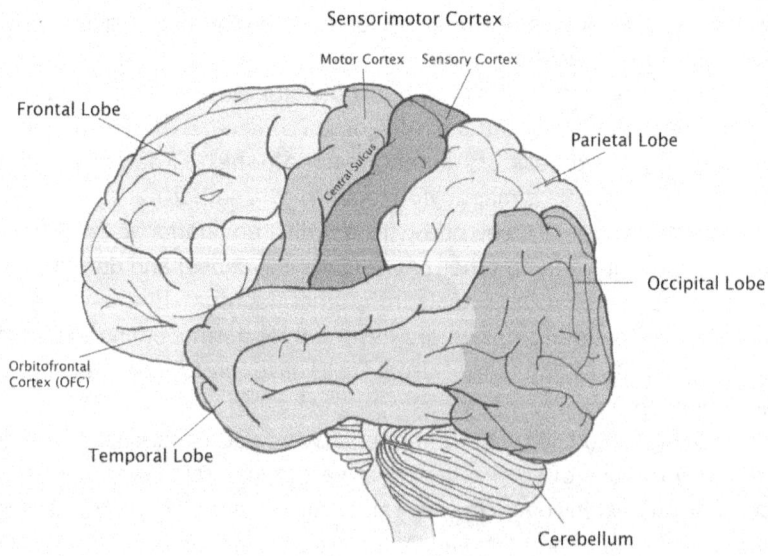

FIGURE 4.1 *The Neocortex. Image courtesy of Dan Costa Baciu.*

space, anatomically fixed by size of the birth canal. The frontal lobe in each hemisphere is the front half of the neocortex. On each side in the central and rear portions of the brain are the temporal lobes, and at the lower rear of the brain's neocortex are the occipital lobes, largely the seat of vision. Rising upward from them, between the temporal lobes, are the two parietal lobes, which meet the frontal lobes at the central sulcus. Two parts of the neocortex, to which we will often refer, lie horizontally (from ear to ear) along this central sulcus: the motor cortex at the rear of the frontal lobe, and the sensory cortex (also called somatosensory cortex) at the front portion of the parietal lobe. Together, they are called the sensorimotor cortex and are the areas controlling bodily movements and corporeal sensations. Both are central to the new models of perception.

II.

Important to our topic is the idea of neural plasticity—the way in which we shape our neural circuits and connections. Learning affects the size and configuration of individual neurons or how they connect with each other and how they become linked to distant populations of neurons. When two neurons fire with each other, the electrical charge passing through the synapse sparks growth and, with repeated firings, a circuit is formed. The effect of our physical and cultural environments in shaping these circuits is strong throughout our lives but especially powerful in our childhood years when the basic circuits are forming. Notwithstanding, a variety of factors and adult experiences—learning, drugs, hormones, diet, disease, stress, aging, and the built environment in which we live—also affect neuronal health and connectivity.[2]

Neuroimaging and other investigative tools today allow us to study these changes. Early musical training, for instance, has been shown to increase gray matter (brain cells) and thickness in the auditory cortex (in the temporal lobes) and cerebellum, enhancing sound discrimination and the processing of rhythm. The fine motor skills of learning to play a violin enlarge the area of motor cortex involved with the movement of the four fingers of the left hand. These circuits are most malleable around the age of five or six, the age by which almost all virtuosos have begun their training.[3] Yet learning to play an instrument at a lesser level of proficiency also has positive structural effects within the brain. Studies have shown that music training before the age of seven increases the size and number of connections between the two hemispheres, as well as spurring growth of gray matter in the motor, auditory, and visual-spatial regions of the brain.[4] Musical training also seems to have a small but lasting effect on a child's overall IQ and powers of abstract reasoning.[5] Numerous studies report that practicing a musical instrument enhances verbal ability, improves nonverbal reasoning, and leads to changes in frontal-parietal networks.[6] One thinks in this regard of both Frank Lloyd Wright's musical training and the spatial ability he likely cultivated from his play with Froebel blocks.

Neural plasticity or the sculpting of brain circuits is largely conditioned by experience. Social or environmental deprivation, for example, can inhibit the normal development of cell growth, decrease their metabolic demand and neuronal activity, and restrict connectivity. One of many environmental connections that has been established by research, for instance, is that between the impoverished home environment and attention deficit hyperactivity disorder.[7] Conversely, enriched environments can excite social and cognitive development by promoting neuronal and vascular health. The integration of networks is similarly affected by abnormalities within these systems. A condition of blindness, for instance, will cause other sensory areas to rewire themselves to accommodate the abnormality.[8] Culture has a similar effect on our neural structures. Learning to read or do arithmetic, for instance, can "invade" older brain circuits and take over their structural organization.[9]

Environmental deprivation, of course, takes place in other ways. The effects of "seasonal affective disorder," created by prolonged exposure to darkness or artificial light during the winter months, are well known. The slowdown in the activity of human stress hormones (vitamin D) results in depression, mood swings, and a general feeling of fatigue. Similar effects are found with those experiencing extended periods of spatial confinement, restricted social contact, and environmental monotony, such as experienced by sailors, submarine crews, oil-rig workers, and astronauts. Scientists enduring the seven-month austral winters of Antarctica, for instance, are prone to sleep disorders, depression, headaches, increased anxiety and irritability, social withdrawal, and lessened cognitive performance.

The effects of total sensory deprivation—anxiety, anger, depression, cognitive decline, and hallucinations—were shown by experiments in the middle years of the twentieth century. The classic studies in this regard were carried out by two Nobel Prize winners in the 1970s. In one instance, they sutured-shut one eye of kittens shortly after birth and then studied the extent of neural damage in the visual cortex. The critical period for the development of the visual cortex in kittens is between the fourth and eighth week after birth. If one eye is deprived of vision, there is a rapid and sharp decline in cell activity in both eyes, and three months of monocular deprivation can permanently damage parts of the deprived retina, as well as areas of the optic nerve and visual cortex.[10] Another early study with kittens demonstrated that neurons within the visual cortex specialized in the processing of the orientation of lines and edges are determined by visual experience.[11] For instance, if one eye is exposed only to horizontal lines during the growth window, the visual cortex cannot later process lines of other orientations. Other studies of rodents raised in sound-proof conditions have shown that they have a lesser ability to discriminate certain auditory patterns, while those raised in darkness lose some depth perception, are less able to locate visual events or orient themselves in certain lighting conditions, or transfer signals from one modality to another.[12]

Equally debilitating to brain development is social deprivation. This fact was first demonstrated in the 1930s when the psychologist Harry Harlow carried out his experiments on maternal deprivation with a colony of Rhesus monkeys. He constructed two surrogate "mothers" who would dispense milk to the newborn: one a wire cylinder with a box-like head, the other a cylinder clothed in a terrycloth robe with the head of a teddy bear. The newborns overwhelmingly preferred the clothed surrogate, clinging to it even when it had no milk, and only approached the wire surrogate for feeding. These experiments were carried out in an era when hospital nurseries were sterile in appearance and mothers were discouraged from having much contact with their infants beyond feeding times. Harlow suggested that a mother's milk was not the endgame but rather the means for providing the "contact comfort" essential to the normal social development of the newborn.

Today we are beginning to understand why this "contact comfort" is essential. Rat pups deprived of their mother's physical nurturing have shown stress responses ranging from variations in body temperature and heart rates to emotional instability and growth retardation across different parts of the anatomy. One study has shown that removing a ten-day-old pup from its mother for one hour results a 50 percent drop in its growth hormone release and protein synthesis.[13] Hormone production picks up immediately when the pup is returned to its mother, but repeated or more extensive periods of maternal deprivation will have long-term physiological and psychological consequences, ranging from depression, anxiety, and eating disorders to alterations in gene expression, impaired spatial learning and other cognitive abilities, and psychological disturbances similar to schizophrenia.[14]

With human neonates, regular fondling or tactile contact with a mother facilitates brain growth and behavioral organization across infancy. Pregnancy produces neuropeptides and hormones such as oxytocin within a mother's cellular and vascular systems, which are passed to the child in the womb. Regular maternal contact after birth leads to the production of these same chemicals. These receptors are concentrated in the dopamine-rich areas of the brain associated with the "pleasure circuit" and their production is crucial to the expression of love.[15]

Sensory or environmental enrichment also has its short- and long-term consequences. One early study divided groups of rats into two cage conditions: one with reduced illumination and with no contact with other animals, the other in larger cages with assorted toys and mazes. Postmortem studies of their brains revealed that those raised in the enriched environment displayed greater synaptic development and "significantly greater" weight of neurons or gray matter.[16] In the last half-century, this experiment has been repeated dozens of times. Enriched environments, which should be defined as an optimal rather than a maximum level of environmental stimulation, have been shown to have numerous neurological consequences.[17] They stimulate sensory, cognitive, and motor functions in almost every area of the brain. Novel and complex environments arouse and assist learning and memory, as well as reduce levels of anxiety.[18] Enriched environments also lead to long-term enhancements in cellular and hippocampal (memory) networks related to cognition.[19] In one study of marmoset monkeys sheltered in an enriched environment for only one month, researchers found an increase in the complexity of the dendritic tree (neuron receptors) and healthier synapses in both the hippocampus and prefrontal cortex.[20] What is striking in these studies is how significantly the quality of the built environment affects the brain's chemistry, functioning, and density of neurons or gray matter.

Our knowledge of sensory deprivation and enrichment has spawned new biological models. We now know, for instance, that the genome in itself does not determine a specific behavior; it rather provides the framework for the cellular machinery that supports behavior—but only if the organism develops within an appropriate environment. Behaviors thus arise from interactions between organisms and environments (physical, social, and cultural), and interactions within organisms (cells, cell assemblies, neural systems). The neurobiologist Gilbert Gottlieb has proposed a model for these interactions that he calls "probabilistic epigenesis," which "emphasizes the reciprocity of influences within and between levels of an organism's developmental manifold (genetic activity, neural activity, behavior, and the physical, social, and cultural influences of the external environment) and the ubiquity of gene-environment interaction in the realization of all phenotypes."[21] The central problem for architects and planners, in view of this knowledge, is to define better the quality of built environments, but this also depends on an up-to-date understanding of how we perceive things.

III.

We experience life with the totality of the human body, whose activities are more deeply implicated with each other than we might first suspect. When our ancestors descended from the forest canopies into the African savannahs some four million years ago, the upright body underwent profound anatomical changes as well as major perceptual and cognitive transformations. Erwin Straus, many years ago, noted that the upright posture and its counteraction to the forces of gravity led to an increase in learning, activity, attention, and wakefulness, as well as the creation of distance from the ground and from objects. The upright carriage ushered in not only the possibility of individuality and promoted face-to-fact encounters with our fellow humans but it also led to the development of the hand and arm as sensory organs and productive tools, the ability to transform our surrounding spatial framework, and the anatomical change of the animal head into a human jaw and head, allowing the development of language.[22] In addition, it resulted in a major redesign of our systems related to movement.

We are born, as the Maxine Sheets-Johnstone has observed, as animate organisms defined by our movements, and "wherever there is animate movement, an individual of whatever order is not just doing something—'acting'—but is experiencing it kinesthetically and/or proprioceptively."[23] From our very first movements within the womb, our movements express the vitality of a living being. Because we are animate, our consciousness is kinesthetic. Therefore, "locomotion, not cognition," as Tim Ingold has phrased it, "must be the starting point for the study of perceptual activity."[24]

Walter Freeman regards perceptual activity as a "semi-autonomous generator of goal-directed behavior," the intentional activity of an organism actively enacting its surroundings.[25] Cognition, from this perspective, is not reasoned problem solving but rather a skillful coping with the world. When we move, we experience the world on many levels: articular (skeletal), muscular, vestibular, cutaneous, visual, olfactory, and aurally. Motion already implies time, and in orienting ourselves within a room we extend our boundaries and engage the space around us. In such a way, movement is a proprioceptive act of discovery and thought. Oliver Sacks has defined proprioception as "the inner sense by which the body is aware of itself."[26]

Movement takes place on many levels—from the ceaseless cellular activity of our body's chemistry or movements of our eyes to the locomotion of a large corporeal mass against the forces of gravity. In the last regard, the "sixth sense" of the vestibular system is paramount to the maintenance of posture and skillful mobility within any environment. In addition to performing several perceptual and cognitive functions related to the voluntary control of movements, it also seems, as a recent study has shown, to have its own cortical processing area in the lower parietal cortex.[27] Yet the effect of the built environment on the vestibular system, although noted by several writers on architecture over the years, remains much underappreciated.

This sensory system is situated just inside the inner ear and attached to the auditory sac that transmits vibrations into the cochlea. It consists of two liquid-filled sacs and three semicircular canals, all of which respond to gravitational forces, our bodies in motion, and to the movements of the head, allowing us both to maintain a sense of balance as well as spatial orientation. The three semicircular canals, roughly placed at 90 degrees to each other, allow us to define the three axes of spatial orientation, and collectively the system serves as a compensating device both to keep the body coincident with gravitational forces and to remain oriented (right and left, forward and backward) with respect to the environment. Spatial disorientation, for instance, is disorientation within the horizontal plane, whereas seasickness is caused by the vestibular fluids repeatedly being raised and lowered. The vestibular system, in addition to cortical areas, also has connections to the eyes, the autonomic systems within the brains stem, and the spinal cord.

Yet the coordination of a body in motion and its reciprocal muscular contractions is once again a complex sensory activity involving, in addition to vestibular information, numerous inner muscle spindles and tendons. Roger Sperry underscored this fact with his early experiments recording the neuronal activity of humans simply moving one body part. The "neuromuscular coordination" involved with raising the arm, he noted, is not a modest exercise:

> Changes in speed, changes in the angle of the arm with respect to gravity, changes in the weight of an object held in the hand, changes of the angle between arm and shoulder and other shifts in general posture, all cause extreme variations in the physiological patterns underlying what, from an unanalytical observation, might appear to be a fairly constant simple response.[28]

The act of hitting a golf ball, as the neuroscientist Lutz Jäncke has noted, is a complex ballistic movement, achieved by numerous simultaneous and sequential movements of the arms, hands, legs, feet, shoulders, head, and hips, using different clubs varying in shaft length, weight, and head size, all orchestrated toward striking a small ball with a high degree of accuracy.[29]

Multiple experiments have underscored the complexity of the body's balance and control systems. In one study, researchers applied vibrations to different parts of the soles of the feet of a standing person and recorded responses. They found that the whole body tilts in the opposite direction to the slightest simulated pressure increase, demonstrating the nerve sensors of the feet form a "dynamometric map" able to code every pressure exerted against the sole.[30] In another experiment scientists monitored the neural network effects of motor responses across the body and concluded that proprioceptive information from neck and ankle muscles work together in maintaining balance control and body orientation.[31] In still another study employing virtual illusions of a hand's movement, researchers demonstrated that visual, tactile, and muscular proprioceptive inputs together enhance the quality of the perception, a result that discounts the traditional anatomical distinction between the exteroceptive senses (vision and touch) and the muscular aspects of proprioceptive movements.[32] What we can extract from this research is how strongly we physiologically experience the space in which we move. The slightly angled ramps of New York's Guggenheim Museum make us aware of our bodies walking.

Another aspect of the proprioceptive body is our haptic interface with the world through our skin. It is not only the earliest sensory realm to come on line (functioning in the womb only a few weeks after gestation) but also the largest and most transparent organ of the human body. Possessing 16 percent of the body's weight, our skin not only "reads the texture, weight, density and temperature of matter," as Juhani Pallasmaa has noted, but it also "traces spaces of temperature with unerring precision, the cool and invigorating shadow under a tree or the caressing sphere of warmth in a spot of sun."[33] Our skin reveals our emotional state of mind and often our state of health. Dogs have been trained to sniff out ovarian cancer from the smell emanating from the skin. The kind words of someone can "touch" us with joy. Bernard Berenson, in reflecting how early Florentine painters portrayed movement, viewed their innovation as a play upon our "tactile imagination, only here touch retires to a second place before the muscular feelings of varying pressure and strain."[34]

By some accounts there are as many as twenty kinds of skin receptors responding to touch, texture, pressure, weight, vibration, temperature, humidity, pain, and bodily movement. Meissner's corpuscles lie just beneath the skin, and because they are concentrated in the lips, fingers, and erogenous zones, they are most sensitive to light touch. Golgi tendon organs reside in muscle fibers and respond to the tensing and relaxing of muscles. Pacinian corpuscles respond to vibrations and deep pressures in the skin, the gut, or around the joints. In the last location, they are proprioceptors that inform us about the location of the joints and work together with Ruffini corpuscles, which are sensitive to the stretching of the skin. When a receptor is stimulated, it passes information along nerve fibers that collect in the spinal cord and are ultimately conveyed to the sensory cortex, which is apportioned spatially by the number of receptors coming into it. The largest areas are given to the processing of hand and face sensations. The sensory cortex and the surrounding area are seen as key to our multimodal body integration, linguistic understanding, and action processing because of their connections to the visual, auditory, and motor cortices.

Research today is expanding Edward Hall's concern with "tactile space" that we mentioned earlier. Worn cobblestones, for example, have long been admired for their pleasing textural effects, but they also seem to have benefits beyond simply stimulating the touch receptors of our feet. One study carried out of elderly people demonstrated that repeated sessions of walking on cobblestone mats not only improved their physical balance but it also significantly reduced their blood pressure—that is, when measured against control groups of people walking on smooth surfaces.[35] Sarah Robinson reports that many villages in Taiwan have pebble paths on which people walk daily to stimulate the touch receptors on the soles of the feet, which they believe will also enhance their overall well-being.[36] Some European studies have shown that people who regularly walk on cobblestones live longer, perhaps in part due in part to better proprioceptive skills.

Ingold has commented the "groundlessness of modern metropolitan life." Walking surfaces within the city, he points out, are generally paved with hard and smooth surfaces, and the limited grass within urban parks is often not to be trodden upon but only visually admired. His argument is that we need to have a more "grounded" approach to our urban life to reverse our continuing slide toward sedentary habits.[37]

Even the words that we speak or hear generate tactile responses, as numerous neuroimaging studies have shown. Saying the words "lick," "pick," and "kick," for instance, activates areas of the motor cortex involved with the movements of the mouth, hands, and feet.[38] Employing a textural metaphor in a sentence (e.g., "she had a rough day" versus "she had a bad day") recruits activity in the domain-specific area of the sensory cortex related to textural processing.[39] When we see someone being touched, we map the feeling of the touch onto our own sensorimotor system, on the basis of which neuroscientists and philosophers have proposed models of intercorporeality or intersubjectivity.[40]

Perhaps the most interesting of these tactile studies dealt with the cinematic metaphor of a scene from a James Bond film, in which the spy is awakened from his sleep by the movements of a tarantula crawling across his chest. People often shudder at the scene, and thus the question posed by researchers was, why would simply watching someone else being touched have such a powerful effect on our own bodies? They had participants lie in a scanner and watch a video of someone being brushed on the leg, another video of a stroking movement ten inches away from someone's leg, and a third condition in which the subjects had their own leg brushed. In a second phase of the experiment, they viewed people touching rolls of paper towels and binders. The experience of having one's own body touched activates circuits in the secondary and primary areas of the sensory cortex, and earlier textbooks explained the activity of the secondary areas as the processing of oneself being touched. Yet the finding of this study was that the secondary area became active both when one's own leg was being touched and when inanimate objects were touched.[41] Thus what the shuddering viewers of the James Bond film are experiencing is not the work of their imagination, but an actual *neurological simulation of a tarantula crawling across one's own skin*. But if we respond neurologically to the touch of animate or inanimate objects that we observe, would we not also respond to architectural materials and forms touching one another?

IV.

What this previous experiment demonstrated, as one of its authors concluded, is that "mirroring is a rather general principle of brain function"—that is, "we seem to recruit those brain regions we would use to experience the same state, be it an action, an emotion, or a sensation. The exact brain area activated changes from motor areas for actions, emotional areas for emotions, and somatosensory areas for sensations, but the principle remains the same."[42] What the term "mirroring" refers to here is the discovery of "mirror neurons."

The discovery, which took place in a laboratory at the University of Parma in the 1990s, was made by a team of scientists who had inserted electrodes into the brains of monkeys and were observing their motor responses to certain sounds and actions.[43] The team discovered two types of neurons active in the perception of objects and actions. "Canonical neurons," in premotor areas of the brain, fire during motor movements, such as grasping an object, but also during the presentation of objects for potential motor interaction. In effect, they demonstrated James Gibson's idea of affordance, the fact that we perceive objects not as neutral events (forms, colors, shapes) but in relation to the potential actions or meaning they have for the perceiver. A peanut, for instance, may evoke the response within the premotor cortex of how to squeeze the fingers to open the shell. In a related way, "mirror neurons" in premotor and parietal areas of the brain became active when the monkeys were executing certain actions and when they were perceiving other monkeys performing a goal-directed action. They responded not to the object itself, but seemed to encode the intentional goal of the action of another. In other words, we mirror or simulate the actions of others in our own brains and thereby understand the intentions behind the actions (Figure 4.2).

Within a few years, scientists began to understand that the human brain possesses a complex mosaic of "mirror mechanisms" that becomes active in all of our visual, auditory, tactile, and social processing. In effect, we perceive the world through our sensorimotor potentialities for action, the dynamic field or *Umwelt* surrounding our bodies. "Empathy" is one term by which neuroscientists refer to these mechanisms. The term has its roots in the

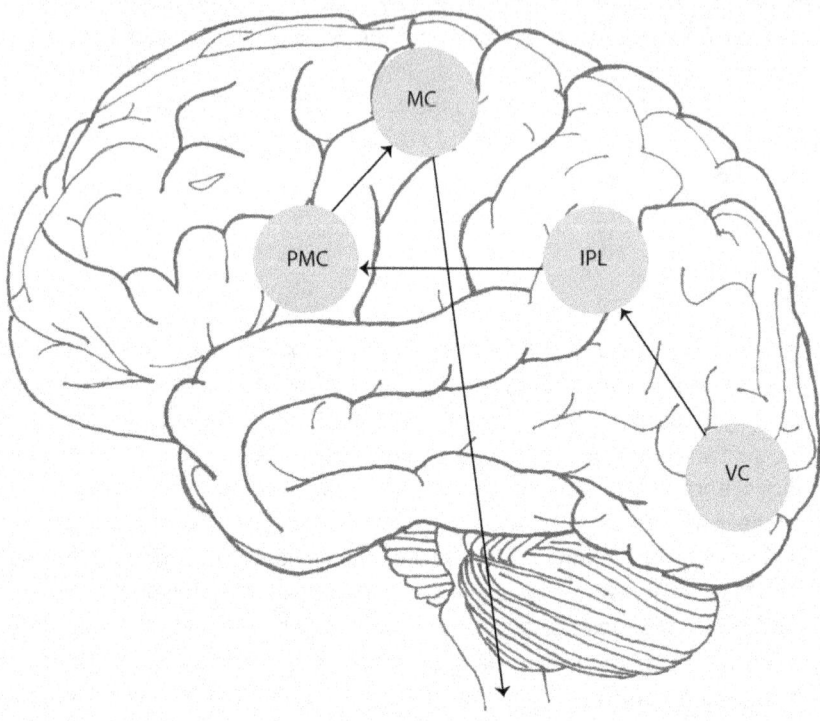

Motor Evoked Potentials

FIGURE 4.2 *Pathway of the mirror-neuron system in visual action-perception. Visual input processed in the visual cortex (VC) activates mirror areas in the inferior parietal lobe (IPL) and premotor cortex (PMC), and ignites Motor Evoked Potentials (MEPs) in the motor cortex (MC), preparing the body for action in response to what it is seeing.*

nineteenth-century concept of *Einfühlung*, a "feeling-into" something, which, as Robert Vischer once observed, induces sensorimotor responses from "stimuli that affect the whole body."[44]

The fact that much of this mirror activity takes place within the sensorimotor system is the kingpin of the newer models of perception, which are based not on single modalities, such as vision, but on our larger multisensory (brain/body) enactment of the world. Every motor action is initiated in the motor cortex and the secondary motor areas anterior to it. Among these areas, located on the side of each frontal lobe, is the premotor cortex, which is involved in a number of functions, such as the sensory guidance of our hand and body movements, particularly in the space surrounding the body. Experiments have also shown that the premotor cortex becomes active around 350 milliseconds before the motor cortex displays activity or when we may consciously decide to move our limbs. This pre-activity, as it were, indicates that a readiness potential for action (perception-action) is present before we consciously decide to move a part of our bodies.⁴⁵ The premotor cortex is also involved with speech production, an adjacency that again is not coincidental because we know that words also stimulate these areas and are often coincidental with hand gestures—all of which demonstrates that gestures very likely preceded spoken communication.⁴⁶

Mirror mechanisms have also been found in the secondary areas of the sensory cortex. What this means is that the sensorimotor system is a highly complex network of circuits involving not only the haptic senses but also the integration of all of the senses and bodily actions. Moreover, these areas are connected to other areas involved with our visceral awareness (our internal organs) and emotional responses.

The process through which mirror mechanisms operate has been called "embodied simulation."⁴⁷ The basic idea is that in watching or listening to someone perform actions, we are, within our sensorimotor systems, continually simulating the actions that we see, feel, and hear. One neuroimaging study, for instance, had musicians and nonmusicians lay in a scanner actively (with a silent keyboard) and passively (without moving their hands) listening to piano pieces. They found motor activity during the active phase of the study, yet in the passive portion of the experiment the musicians displayed a "transmodal mirror system," comprising the premotor and parietal areas known to have mirror populations as well as an auditory area of the temporal lobe involved with language understanding. The musicians were in fact neurologically performing the auditory experience while listening to the music—that is, without igniting activity in the motor cortex, which would actually move their fingers.⁴⁸

In another fMRI study related to movement, researchers observed mirror activity of twenty-four participants watching dancers. The participants were naive in the sense that they were untrained in dance, and they watched a set of movements twice, once without instruction and a second time when they were evaluating the dance movements artistically. In both instances researchers found mirror activity in the right premotor cortex, but this activity was stronger with whole-body movements in the aesthetic portion of the experiment. The scientists concluded that the aesthetic response of the mirror system was driven "by the specific kinematic details of the movements observed," the simulation of movements, as well as their speed and direction.⁴⁹ What this seems to imply is that in watching a dancer on stage, we take aesthetic pleasure in projecting ourselves—to use the expression of Vischer—into the body of the dancer as we simulate the actions being perceived in our premotor cortex. The more experience we have in moving our own bodies in such a way, the stronger is this projection.

Neuroimaging studies have now shown that there are also mirroring mechanisms involved with the perception and understanding of another's emotions, and one plausible explanation that we, by simulating the facial expressions of others, self-generate the same emotion.[50] Mirror mechanisms therefore have major implications for our understanding of how the mind works in general. The "meaning" of an experience can no longer be construed as an abstract mental process; rather, it is a creative process through which one, through the process of embodied simulation, actively constructs experiences out of one's own biological activity, and this cortical sensorimotor system is in fact an integral part of our cognitive systems. From this perspective, the line between what might call the real world and the imagined world is much less sharply drawn than conventional wisdom allows. Both perceptions and their memories utilize similar neural circuits, as we will later discuss. Space, objects, and the movements of others are apprehended directly. Christopher Tilley once noted that totemism and animism are particular modes of thought characteristic not only of the "savage" mind but are also "present within all of us, a concrete and sensuous rather than abstract logic of the human mind by means of which we relate to the world."[51] The animating force of empathy is also, as we will argue, an important foundational stone to the experience of architecture.

V.

It was in the early years of the Second World War that Sigfried Giedion, in the opening pages of *Space, Time and Architecture*, famously bemoaned the divide between "thinking and feeling," the split personality of an unbalanced civilization plunging the world into war.[52] It was a divide especially prominent in architectural circles in the first half of the twentieth century, when the moniker "rationalist" was proudly accepted as a mark of distinction. The split was also prominent in the 1960s, when the rationalism of both semiotics and poststructuralism carried the day. The divide that Giedion lamented in 1941 has by no means been repaired in the intervening years. The idea that architectural forms invoke within us a particular feeling or emotion, for instance, has virtually disappeared from architectural discourse.

Giedion was a self-proclaimed disciple of the famed art historian Heinrich Wölfflin, and the former no doubt remembered the day when the rationalist tenor of theory had not been so unbending or dismissive of the tight connection between human feelings and perception. Wölfflin had opened his doctoral dissertation of 1886, "Prolegomena to a Psychology of Architecture," with a simple question: "How is it possible that architecture forms are able to express an emotion or a mood?"[53] The dissertation was conceived as an expansion and correction of Vischer's notion of "empathy," but the question was framed within the larger debate taking place within architectural circles about the need to disregard historical styles. This belief that architectural forms in themselves could be accessible to psychological analysis was an entirely original one.

The divide between thinking and feeling is a classic Cartesian distinction. It is also prominent in the foundation of psychology in the first half of the nineteenth century, as seen in Johann Friedrich Herbart's self-described "improvements" to Kantian thought. Herbart's aesthetics was predicated on the "formalist" notion that the arts, including architecture, are emotionally experienced through the elementary relationships of lines, planes, colors, and sound. Within a few years, the question of how we aesthetically perceive the world came under the investigative scrutiny of a number of physiologists and psychologists. Hermann Helmholtz, for instance, was very much concerned with the dynamics of perception, particularly auditory and visual perception, while Gustav Fechner proposed an "experimental aesthetics" that would—through mathematical modeling—correlate the value of a stimulus with its emotional effect.[54] Wilhelm Wundt, who in 1879 opened the first laboratory dedicated to psychological research, initially made the case that we react to forms through our motor systems—that is, through the physiological impact that they have on our bodies. And in 1890 William James published his *Principles of Psychology*, which again underscored the sensorimotor underpinnings to our cognitive activities. In parallel with the Swedish physiologist Carl Lange, he argued (in what is today known as the James-Lange model of emotion) that physiological arousal instigates the experience of emotion, and not the other way around.

The newer models of emotion are not too distant from these early observations. The role of the body in emotion, and the neurology and chemical activity that accompany emotion are now well accepted. Jaak Panksepp has shown "that affective states arise from the intrinsic neurodynamics of primitive self-centered emotional and motivational systems situated in subcortical regions of the brain."[55] Others have stressed the dynamic or kinesthetic nature of emotion. Evan Thompson, as we have seen, defines emotion as "a prototype whole-organism event," one that "coordinates virtually every aspect of the organism."[56] Sheets-Johnstone argues that "affective feelings and tactile-kinaesthetic feelings are experientially intertwined"—that is, emotion and proprioception entail a "postural attitude" or "corporeal readiness to act in some way or other."[57] Giovanna Colombetti makes the case that because all living systems are sense-making systems, emotion pervades cognition through and through, and emotion "is thus integral to both perception and action."[58]

Note the locutions invoked here: "primitive self-centered emotional and motivational systems," "whole-organism event," "corporeal readiness," and "sense-making systems." The divide between reason and emotion has today become antiquated because emotion is now seen as the essential underpinning to the human organism's reasoning process. With the emphasis on emotion's dynamic and preconscious readiness to act, it is also important to stress, as Colombetti reports, that sensory stimulation does not initiate perception and action; rather, "sensory stimulation reaches a brain that is already motivated and action oriented and uses information about the world to modulate motor activity relative to its intentional orientation."[59] In this way we can define emotion in architecture, on one level at least, as *the biological process through which the human organism enacts or engages with a built environment.*

The psychologist Lisa Barrett has noted that in having a novel perceptual experience, we first experience a "core affect," an initial state of pleasure or displeasure arising from the experience and its potential impact on the organism's vital condition. This core effect is then routed through the limbic system and cortical areas along two neurological pathways. One evaluates the preliminary value of the stimulus and its impact on homeostasis; the second modulates the autonomic, chemical, and behavioral responses to the stimulus.[60] Much of this activity takes place preconsciously.

Nevertheless, the preconscious nature of emotion already implies a bodily self-awareness—that is, not only does the initial emotional activity take place before we reflect on things but emotion is the homeostatic medium through which we become conscious of our bodies. This corporeal awareness is particularly evident in the body's proprioceptive response to ambient environmental conditions. Upon entering a room, for instance, we rapidly know its temperature and level of humidity, the touch or feel of the floor material, the presence and warmth of natural light, the room's acoustic resonance and overall ambience, the hand of fabrics, the smell of materials, and the room's spatial dimensions—all of which we assimilate before, little by little, we stand back and reflect on the experience, and consider why we like or dislike particular aspects of it.

Such a view of emotion also has important aesthetic implications. If we limit ourselves to proprioception, let us consider how the design of a staircase affects us emotionally. Barbara Montero observes that the beauty we perceive in a dancer's movement is conditioned by how we kinetically simulate what we see. If we view the movements of a dancer to be graceful, it is because "if I were to move in this way, these movements would feel graceful."[61] She attributes this understanding in part to the activity of mirror mechanisms, and, in later teaming up with the neuroscientist Jonathan Cole, she makes the case that "affective proprioception" likely also draws on "small afferents arising in the muscles and joints," which are linked with the sensory and insular cortices, the areas of the brain that monitor bodily sensations and feelings. These afferent pathways become active not only when viewing the movements of others but also when we move in some graceful or athletic way, "the feeling of effortlessness, of the body moving almost on its own without any need of conscious direction."[62] If this is the case, then our emotional experience of a staircase would manifest itself in the comfort of ascending or descending the tread and risers—that is, how well they allow us to move gracefully and with little effort.[63]

Other studies have shown the presence of multiple afferent systems. For instance, in one study researchers had participants watch dancers perform skilled movements, and images of other irrelevant or low-skill movements. They found similar activity in both the visual stream and the premotor cortex, but also activity in areas related to the perception of form: "We found that the degree of whole-body movement is a major driver of aesthetic evaluation of dance, and also has reliable consensus correlates in sensorimotor and visual form processing areas in the human brain."[64]

There are several important things for the designer to take away from these new models of emotion. All environments are kinesthetic, holistic bodily events affecting muscles and nerves, heart rate, endocrine systems, opioid release, posture, and facial expressions—therefore emotional activity is present in every architectural experience. In a room, affective proprioception emerges in a different way than it does with dance. Here we experience spaces by attempting to move in a graceful way, all the while being aware of our body's physiological condition while moving through the environment. When we enter a grand space, such as the hall of Exeter Library or the nave of a Gothic cathedral, for instance, we tend to slow down or stop, stand erect, and lift the head with deepened respiration. There is no mystery to these responses. People for centuries have commented on the emotional dimension or sense of awe found in the grand architectural experience. Sarah Robinson has characterized the way in which people have traditionally shaped their buildings with their own bodies as "nesting."[65] Pallasmaa has noted that "a real architectural experience is not simply a series of retinal images; a building is encountered—it is approached, confronted, encountered, related to one's body, moved about, utilized as a condition for other things, etc."[66] We measure the length of a room by our footsteps; we open a door by the force of our arms, legs, and body.

Nowhere can this be better demonstrated than with the feeling of *pleasure* or the so-called pleasure circuit, an emotional experience initially born not of reflective thought but the operation of specific neural circuits that can now be recorded with a scanner. Pleasures, of course, come in many forms, but the interesting thing about them is that they share many of the same neural circuits in triggering the release of opioids, cannabinoids, and neurotransmitters (such as dopamine), which flood the brain and produce the feeling of delight. Many of the "hotspots" of these circuits have now been identified but their names are less important than the process itself—a vital force springing up from the brainstem along very ancient circuits, and once arriving at the OFC and other cortical areas, manifesting itself in the values of beauty, love, and social bonding.[67]

VI.

With this backdrop in view, we can now see that individual sensory modalities are not isolated phenomena operating alone but skillful, multimodal experiences, drawing upon and integrating themselves within larger motor-emotional networks. The knowledge recently gained of the visual-processing system reinforces this point.

The visual system, to begin with, is grounded in its evolutionary history. The hominin line split off from the great apes more than six million years ago, and the *Homo* genus appeared around three million years ago. The geographical places for the vast proportion of our visual development were the savannahs of northern Africa with their particular landscape features. The colors, lines, and textures of this landscape shaped the organizational and functional properties of the human visual system. Even with our large-scale constructed environments of the last ten thousand years, we nevertheless remain at home with natural light, natural forms, earthly tones, and naturalistic patterns. Rectilinearity, as Ernst Gombrich once noted, almost seems to be a peculiarly human act of defiance, and yet, as the neuroscientist Thomas Albright has said, even in our built structures we take a particular delight in certain shapes, scales, and patterns that have mathematical relationships, such as the strands of a cable bridge or the delineation of a rose window in a Gothic cathedral. Why is this the case?

The answer is still not clear. At least one neuroscientist has suggested that certain forms and proportions fit better with the cellular buildings blocks of the visual system.[68] Others have proposed the importance of fractal-like properties and their relation to natural scenes, which in their view provides a "sparse coding" for sensory input, through which "an artist creates a work of art so that it induces a specific resonant state in the visual system."[69] Albright attributes such preferences to the fact that they display "visual patterns in which there is a statistical regularity between adjacent contour orientations," such as we find in the natural world.[70] Other studies have focused on contours, and a large number of studies have shown that humans prefer curved shapes over those with sharp angles, presumably for the reason that sharp contour transitions in nature convey a threat or injury to the body.[71]

Vision also has two fields of action, which has architectural implications as well. The central 5 percent of our visual cone is directed or focused vision.

It allows us to focus on details of particular concern. The remainder of the visual cone is peripheral vision, which is both less focused and at the same time equally essential to maintain a stable frame of reference. A building from a distance is simply an object, a landmark within the scene of a visual field. When inhabiting or walking through a building, however, our awareness of it might shift to peripheral vision, and for this reason Pallasmaa has referred to peripheral vision as the rightful domain of architecture, the perception that "transforms retinal images into a spatial and bodily involvement and encourages participation."[72] Kevin Rooney has made the similar argument that the conceptualizations of design in recent years has resulted in an undue emphasis on focused vision at the expense of peripheral vision. The latter, much of which is nonconscious, takes in the holistic atmosphere of the experience and therefore more strongly resonates with our bodies.[73]

Still another feature of the visual system is the parallel way in which it functions. We tend to think of visual processing as a kind of feature analysis in which we focus on the details of any scene. Yet we discern the "gist" of any novel scene or situation almost immediately, even before the aspects of the scene come into focus.[74] In effect, we first seize upon coarse global features of a scene—a threating bus heading toward us or the overall ambiance of a room—employing circuits different from those in focused perception. Much work is being done in these areas today.

Visual processing is not a simple activity also for the reason that so many parts of the brain and body participate. Light passes through the pupil and focusing lens of the eye and is refracted to the retina at the rear of the orb. The retina has three layers of nerve cells, of which the third layer, along the rear wall, are the photoreceptive cells of rods and cones. Somewhere around 100 million rods are active in dim light, while about 10 percent of that number are concerned with color and fine details. A higher density of cells at the center of the retina inform focused vision, while fewer cells process peripheral vision. Focused vision is also highly attention-dependent, which makes it open to "change blindness"—that is, when observers fail to detect major changes in overall scene when they are focusing on specific parts. This fact disputes the conventional view that the brain creates an internal "representation" of the world. One alternative explanation is the "sensorimotor account" of vision, which regards vision as an active "mode of exploration of the world that is mediated by knowledge"—that is, a *making use of certain capacities* to interact with the environment.[75]

Upon leaving the eye, the retinal stimuli from each eye crosses over at the optic chiasm, where the signals are divided between the two hemispheres. A little farther on, the two optic nerves pass through the two thalami, where some preliminary neural screening takes place. From there the signals pass into the visual cortex located in the occipital lobes at the lower rear of the neocortex. The two optic nerves (one in each lobe) lead into general processing areas (V1 & V2), which then passes the signals to other areas of the visual cortex for more specialized processing.[76] The area V3, for instance, assesses the orientation of shapes and lines, while the majority of cells in V4 process color. The cells of area V5 are highly sensitive to motion.

The complexity within these specialized areas of the visual cortex should also be noted. In the V3 area, for instance, single cells or columns of cells are highly selective in their response to the orientation of lines. Some respond only to vertical lines, others to horizontal lines, and still others to subtle variations of diagonal lines. Because no cells have been found to process curved lines, it is likely that we perceive curves by rotating among cells that are responding to small changes in diagonals. Cells in the V3 area seem to have a bias toward vertical and horizontal lines, which some have interpreted as an evolutionary adaptation to savannah environments, while others argue that it is conditioned by the vestibular system of the inner ear, which maintains our sense of balance.

Some of the cells in the V4 area also respond only to one color, or to one color placed against a specific background. Furthermore, colors, as every painter knows, are highly variable in relation to the context in which they appear. Edward Land's experiments in the middle decades of the twentieth century demonstrated that we evaluate the wavelength of light in a visual field not only against its immediate backdrop but also against the other wavelengths of the surrounding field. Colors, in a strict sense, are not really "out there" in the world, but are a product of the brain's algorithmic accounting. The same is true of the so-called chiaroscuro effects that painters such as Rembrandt mastered with such effectiveness. The perceived brightness of light arises not only from the intensity of light at a given point in space but also by the contrast between this point and the lighting levels of the surrounding areas.[77]

Another feature of visual processing is that the activity of each of these areas has varying times. The location of objects is perceived before color, which in turn is perceived before the recognition of the object's shape and motion. Nowhere is an "image" ever assembled or brought together in one place of the brain, and the issue of how we eventually bind the activity of these different processing areas together is perhaps too complex for us ever to know. In any case, the visual cortex only does the preliminary work in the formation of the perception. The visual signals leave the visual cortex along two relatively well-defined processing pathways, generally referred to as the "Where" stream moving upward into the parietal lobe, and the "What" stream moving horizontally along the lower occipital and temporal lobes.[78]

The "Where" stream, according to earlier models, tracks the object's movement and location in relation to an egocentric or bodily spatial perspective (Figure 4.3). Yet the matter seems to be more complex. The parietal lobe also processes language and abstract causal relationships and it can therefore be viewed as a hub for multisensory integration. Giacomo Rizzolatti has proposed that the "Where" stream actually consists of two different streams running in parallel.[79] One stream evaluates skillful motor actions in real time, while a second stream leading into the inferior parietal cortex "is responsible not only for the organization of actions directed towards objects, but also for space and action perception."[80] The latter stream also connects with the premotor cortex in the frontal lobe, which (like the inferior parietal cortex) houses populations of mirror neurons. Spatial perception and action recognition, in this way, are not two separate activities after all because both are predicated on our motor and cognitive experiences with the world.

The lower "What" stream attends to the recognition and discrimination of objects, as neuroimaging technologies have shown. Basically, it consists of a necklace of areas specialized in recognizing things such as faces, bodies, and places, which it does by employing a bottoms-up (purely sensory) and top-down (drawing upon attention and experience) processing. In 1997 a team of scientists led by Nancy Kanwisher discovered an area of the lateral occipital cortex that processes basic shapes through contours, textures, or other depth cues.[81] Further along the "What" stream, the same team identified an area they called the fusiform face area, which specializes in reading faces.[82] Nearby is another area specialized in processing human bodies.[83] These discoveries were first seen as evidence for the brain's specialization or cognitive

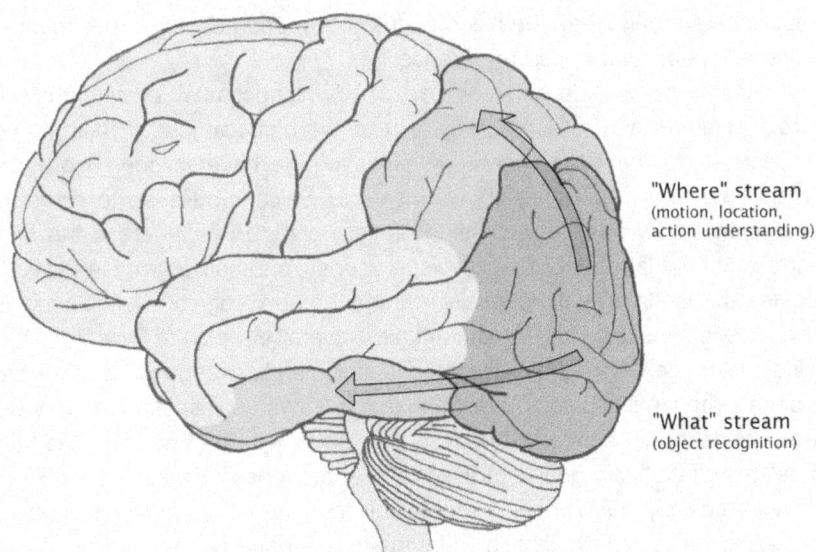

FIGURE 4.3 *"Where" and "What" streams. Image courtesy of Dan Costa Baciu.*

modularity, yet later studies showed that the face area, for instance, is also active in the recognition of species of birds and brands of cars, especially for those with expertise in these two areas. Thus, another view is that these areas are general-purpose stations specializing in categorization and therefore dependent on acquired expertise.[84] Still further along, another area attends to the texture and properties of objects and building materials, their texture and weight.[85]

Proceeding along the "What" stream into the inferior temporal lobe is an area that is active in the processing of buildings and scenes. In 1998 two teams of researchers competed for this discovery. In one study, researchers, drawing in part on Kevin Lynch's earlier efforts, identified an area specialized, among other things, in the "perception of buildings." The authors concluded that while buildings may today fulfill the role of landmarks in an urban setting, this particular area may have a broader sensitivity toward large natural features of the terrain or visual "scenes" in general.[86] A second paper in the same year identified a region that researchers called the "parahippocampal place area" (PPA). The parahippocampal gyrus is an older cortical tissue lying along the inferior temporal lobe—adjacent to the hippocampus. In their initial study, the researchers described the area as encoding features of the local environment, particularly scenes depicting spatial layouts such as buildings, streets, empty rooms, and large landscape features.[87] This area becomes active in the perception of environmental features that have orientational value. Some believe that the parahippocampal cortex, with its connections to the "Where" stream in the parietal lobe, promotes the construction of stable cognitive maps by translating between egocentric (body orientation) and allocentric (world perspective) frames of reference.[88]

Another area considered to be part of the hippocampal formation is the retrosplenial cortex (RSC), also adjacent to the hippocampus. It has strong connections to the body-orientation areas of the parietal lobe. Scores of papers have been published about this area, which is believed to serve as a complementary spatial processing station to the PPA. Whereas the PPA responds to the landmarks of local visual scenes, neuronal activity in the RSC situates the landmarks directionally within a broader cognitive map, such as when one locates the Eiffel Tower within the overall city plan of Paris. The RSC helps determine where we are located in space and its response is therefore stronger with familiar places, indicating that it draws upon spatial memory. As one scientist has described it, the RSC allows the "you are here" and the PPA translates it into "your goal is to the left."[89] Another has noted that the RSC is active particularly "when environmental information is not directly available to senses, and is localized within a wider imagined spatial context."[90] Still others make the case that the visual system is but a neurological and corporal mosaic of widely distributed and overlapping systems, mediated by affordances but also by "ideas of 'executability and desirability.'"[91] Today's views, in any case, are quite different from those of only a few years ago, which saw visual perception as series of processing stations.

What is also interesting in light of these discoveries is that all of this spatial activity takes place around the hippocampus, a limbic module that, in addition to spatial processing, is involved with learning and memories, and it is also the one area of the brain today known to manufacture new brain cells.[92] Memories, as we will explore in a later essay, very much affect the processing of images and therefore the connections of these areas with early processing stages become important because learning modifies the manner and speed by which information is evaluated.[93] Connections of these areas with other areas of the brain also coordinate emotion and plans of action with the developing perception. What is therefore emerging today is the recognition of the enormous complexity of the visual-processing system: its sensorimotor, affective, and imaginative components, all of which are grounded in and conditioned by memories. Vision is intrinsically synesthetic.

VII.

One of the more eventful biological discoveries concerning the hippocampus was that of "place-cells," first revealed by John O'Keefe in his studies of rats in 1971. These cells fire only when an animal is in a particular place within a spatial field, a feeling that need not be conscious. They provide positional information (an episodic memory) about where we are, and they fire independently of our behavior or attention to our location, or of the direction in which we are facing. If we move into a different room and alter the spatial field, the place cells remap themselves onto the new field by drawing upon higher-order sensory inputs, such as landmarks, boundaries, and the spatial context.[94]

In the following decades scientists detected "head-direction" cells in the cortical and limbic areas surrounding the hippocampus.[95] They become active when the head is pointing a certain direction, regardless of one's location and even when one is asleep. They likely serve as an internal compass for place cells, and they are anchored to local reference points or visual cues in the surrounding environment.[96]

In 2005 a group of researchers discovered spatially active cells in rats in the part of the hippocampal gyrus known as the entorhinal cortex, which they called "grid-cells."[97] Together with the place cells and head-direction cells, grid cells impose a hexagonal or triangular grid on space, one in which cells fire when the animal crosses vertices. The measuring grid may be anchored to external cues, yet the grid remains constant and persists when the cues are removed and it even fires in a condition of total darkness. Moreover, the grid is active even in a novel environment, suggesting that grid cells form part of an overlapping and "generalized, path-integration-based map of the spatial environment."[98] The existence of grid-like neuronal activity has been found in the entorhinal cortex of humans, and in 2008 two teams of researchers also found, in the same area, the presence of "border-cells," which become active when we approach or near a boundary, such as a wall of room.[99]

All of these specialized cells—effectively what might be called a place-mapping system—work directly with the hippocampus, although the latter is not always involved. Traditionally, two different strategies of navigation have been noted: egocentric and allocentric. The former, a directional awareness of where my body is, uses kinesthetic and episodic memory of traveled routes, whereas allocentric navigation employs a cartographic knowledge of a building's plan or a city's layout. The two are not entirely independent and people in their navigation commonly switch between the two strategies. In 1997 researchers in London scanned the brains of experienced London taxi drivers as they were imagining moving along highly complex routes across the city. The scan revealed that not only do the areas around the hippocampus became active during the imaginary drive, but also the fact that their right hippocampus was found to be enlarged in taxi drivers with respect to those of the general population. The scientists concluded that the right hippocampus is recruited for complex, large-scale spatial environments, and the enlargement of the hippocampus suggests the role that experience plays in our spatial skills.[100] In another study recording individual cell activity in humans undergoing invasive brain surgery, researchers deduced that the areas surrounding the hippocampus extract "allocentric spatial information primarily from salient visual landmarks, to form a coarse representation of space," while the hippocampus provides these spatial features "with context to compute the flexible map-like representations of space underlying navigation."[101]

Perhaps the major architectural insight to be gained from these studies is the central role of the hippocampus, a part of the brain known to be crucial for the formation of memories. The idea of "place" seems to be key to these memories—that is, *memories seem to be bound to the places in which events take place*. Yet why are places and memories so connected?

Jennifer Groh answers this question by suggesting that "spatial locations may be the filing system of the brain, keeping related memories grouped together and retrievable *where* you need them"—that is, we understand places through our senses but more importantly through the memories of our emotional consciousness.[102] Such an understanding, of course, supports a number of classical scholars, such as Cicero, who argued that in training one's memory one should associate facts with images of places.[103] Ubiquitous or generic environments with few sensory connections or cues, it would seem, lack any life-enhancing stimulation, yet every place that we visit over the course of a lifetime has a topographic or spatial signature.

Moreover, the memory capacity of the hippocampal formation seems to be unlimited. We can from our earlier years remember the smell of a rustic cabin, the particular hand of a sofa, or the ambience of a particular room from our childhood, and these sensory associations and spatial maps seem to be the underlayment on which our larger cognitive map is drawn. We may associate a room or a city with a positive or negative event, and we may hesitate to walk down a certain street or enter a particular public establishment because its character does not "feel right." We do not necessarily think of why this is the case, but we immediately respond to a place or landscape with a sense of its potential impact on our well-being. We order our lives by the places in which we have lived, and we also know that each place carries with it a particular mood.

The significance of the hippocampus, which incidentally is rich in opiate receptors, is perhaps more far reaching. Various studies have pointed out that remembering the past and imagining or simulating the future share a common brain network.[104] In proposing a "scene construction theory," two scientists have proposed that the hippocampus is crucial not only to memory but also to imagination, thinking about the future, or what we might call design. In their words, the hippocampus "facilitates the construction of atemporal scenes allowing the event details of episodic memories and imagined future experiences to be martialed, bound and played out in a coherent spatial context. In this way, scene construction is held to underpin not only episodic memory and imagining the future but also cognitive functions such as spatial navigation, and perhaps even mind wandering and dreaming."[105] If this is indeed true, it would seem that one of the designer's primary roles should be both scene construction and place making—that is, composing the diaphanous colorations of a place's mood and atmosphere, its temporality, and the associated physiognomic impressions and cultural rituals.

VIII.

For many years now architectural design has been taught as if it were purely a visual art, and this focus comes with a sizable sacrifice, which is the exclusion of consideration of the other sensory dimensions of the built environment. There have, of course, been exceptions within design literature, but this trend today seems to be reversing.[106]

Car designers have long known the importance of the "new car" smell, but architects without complaint accept "conditioned" air as a fact of life, even when climate temperatures and humidity are benign. Edward Hall in the 1960s lamented the extent to which some cultures have divorced themselves from this "powerful communication channel"—the aroma of freshly baked bread, "the smell of coffee, spices, vegetables, freshly plucked fowl, clean laundry, and the characteristic odor of outdoor cafés," those things that "help to locate one in space but add zest to daily living."[107] Neutra once observed that "a certain faint smell may make a room almost uninhabitable," but then he goes on to remark that "the smell of a natural cedar paneling has a nose distinct from that of varnish and paints."[108] Aside from the use of natural materials, the easiest way to make a room appealing to the olfactory sense, as Neutra suggested, is simply to open the building up to the outdoors, to allow "that accidental precious whiff of nature's perfume, varied as the seasons unroll, thanks to the blooming lilac bush, the night jasmine, or the pittosporum in the neighbor's garden."[109]

Yi-Fu Tuan once noted that odors lend character to places and instill them in our memories, a fact that Zen poets and good writers have for centuries exploited.[110] The most cited passage of Marcel Proust's *Remembrance of Things Past* is the madeleine that the protagonist eats, soaked in lime-blossom tea, which recalls for him his childhood house and the Sunday ritual of his aunt. In many ways, olfaction is perhaps the simplest of the sensory systems. As a primal part of the brain, the olfactory cortex sits near the very center of the brain and directly in front of the thalami. The initial processing, however, takes place in the olfactory bulbs, which extend forward into the nasal cavities and gathers electrically transmitted information from as many as 1,000 olfactory receptors in the nose. The receptors evaluate molecules from the air and can distinguish as many as 20,000 types of smell. The dynamics of this system are of lesser importance than the strong relationship of smell with architecture.

Sound is another neglected element of our sensory life, and here we should follow the distinction of J. Douglas Porteous between a soundscape and a noisescape. If the latter, which has been the object of abundant research, relates to the unwanted noise (a word, incidentally, derived from the Latin *nausea*), a soundscape relates to the human perception of sound in both positive and negative senses.[111] Porteous makes the case that with the proliferation of technological noise, we are losing our capacity for soundscape complexity.

For many years, the perception of sound has been viewed as a mechanical process. The vibrations of air molecules strike the eardrum, behind which a series of tiny bones called ossicles transmit the vibrations, via the vestibular sac, into the cochlea, whose organ of Corti transforms them into electrical signals and passes them down to the cochlear nuclei of the brainstem's medulla. From there, the signals are routed through the thalami and into the auditory cortices, located in the temporal lobes just above the ears. Yet here we run into a problem that no mechanical explanation of the auditory system can answer. How does the brain transform a series of competing and often ambiguous molecular vibrations with multiple frequencies (pitch) and varying amplitude (loudness) into an understanding of what is taking place in the physical world?

The psychologist Daniel Levitin explains the process as one of extraction and integration. The brain extracts certain features from a sound by using highly specialized networks "that decompose the signal into information about pitch, timbre, spatial location, loudness, reverberant environment, tone durations and the onset times for different notes. This bottom-up processing of elements occurs in the peripheral and phylogenetically older parts of our auditory system. Next comes a process called integration. The auditory and frontal cortex receive the basic features from lower brain regions and work top-down to integrate them into a perceptual whole."[112] This too, as Levitin would agree, is something of a simplification. The auditory cortex consists of primary, secondary, and tertiary areas that deal with different issues—such as frequencies, harmonies, rhythms, and integration—processes that, as with visual processing, take different lengths of time and yet come together to form a perception.[113] Again, there are other widely distributed cortical and subcortical networks that support such activities, including the play of emotion, auditory experience, and cultural training. And finally, there is the issue of the attention one gives to the auditory stimulus, in which the primary and secondary auditory cortices also play a major role.[114]

Historically, the perception of sound has been one of the more important aspects of architecture. The philosopher Don Ihde has observed that upon entering the Parisian Cathedral of Notre Dame for the first time, one experiences the monumentality of the high, arching, dark interior, the shuffle of countless tourist feet, but only with the ghostly sense of a civilization past. Yet later, "I return, and a high mass is being sung: suddenly the mute walls echo and reecho and the singing fills the cathedral. Its soul has momentarily returned, and the mute testimony of the past has once again returned to live in the moment of the ritual."[115]

R. Murray Schafer, who has long studied the soundscape, has made the similar observation that "when architectural historians begin to realize that most ancient buildings were constructed not so much to enclose space as to enshrine sound, a new era in the subject will open out."[116] He points out that the high reverberation levels of Gothic and Renaissance churches (6–8 seconds) have the consequence of slowing down the modulation and gravity of both music and speech, whereas today's smaller rooms result in the faster pace of speech. The "small, dry spaces" of the contemporary office building, he laments, are "similarly suited to the frenzy of modern business."[117] Schafer's observation is a perfect illustration of niche construction. In changing the character of our environments, we also change the way we speak and hear.

Nevertheless, sound plays an extraordinarily important role in how we perceive a room, a space, or an urban environment. Neutra has noted that "whether we are conscious of it or not, the constructed environment either appeals to us or harms us also as a complex auditory phenomenon and is often effective even in its tiniest reverberations."[118] The touch and resonance of materials, the temperature or reverberation of the room, or the embodied interchange of multiple sensory events—all play into our overall perception of a built space. In *Atmospheres*, Peter Zumthor has noted how the "the sound of a space" is amplified by "the shape peculiar to each room and with the surfaces of the materials they contain and the way those materials have been applied."[119]

Schafer, in 1977, praised the acoustic knowledge of Vitruvius but came down very hard on modern architects, whom he accused of "designing for the deaf."[120] If buildings of times past were designed for acoustic as well as visual spectacles, where orators, thespians, and musicians could showcase their work, the ventilation, lighting, elevators, and heating systems of modern buildings not only destroy the acoustic quality of the interiors but their fans and exhaust systems also "disgorge staggering amounts of noise into the streets and onto the sidewalks around the buildings themselves."[121] As designers of soundscape, we seem to have made little progress in the last half-century.

5

Aesthetic Perception

It is in this more complex world, as we see it in the light of current organic research, that the coming designer must operate, not in the pure aesthetics of a bygone brand of speculation.

RICHARD NEUTRA[1]

For someone to raise the idea of "aesthetics" within architectural circles today almost borders on an affront. The reaction is understandable. Although the idea and its association with "beauty" has enjoyed a lengthy pedigree and a generally exalted position with the history of architectural thought—from the erotic undertones of Vitruvian *venustus* (derived from the goddess Venus) to the celestial harmony of Albertian *concinnitas*—the term strikes many today as unserious. People in their everyday language may speak of a spectacular sunset or the unworldly beauty of their romantic partners, but architects and other elites within the arts generally shy away from such terms. When architects do make an aesthetic judgment in a design studio or in a presentation to a client, they inevitably do so with a bad conscience. They more often than not approach the matter of aesthetics with a sense of guilt.

One could trace the reason from the architect's discomfort back several centuries, but much of the blame, it must be said, resides with the twentieth century. The break with historicism and efforts to define a "modern" architecture at the start of the century demanded a new aesthetic standard, or at least a new metaphor for one. The problem was that few could agree on what the metaphor should be. For Otto Wager, the new architecture was sartorial: "someone dressed in clothing from the Louis XV period" would look out of place in the industrial setting of a modern train station or sleeping car.[2] Adolf Loos, another critic known for his mantled elegance, similarly likened the new style to replacing the blue cloth and gold buttons of the dress coat of 1800 with the black cloth and black buttons of the modern dress coat.[3] For him, the exterior of a building should be as inconspicuous as the well-tailored dinner jacket.

Hermann Muthesius took a different tack. He labeled the "superfluous ornament or linear show" of his day as an act of political incorrectness—that is, out of character with middle-class ideals and values of *Sachlichkeit*. The ethos of the last term demanded "simple forms of pure practicality."[4] The buildings of Peter Behrens and Walter Gropius in the first decade of the century were often described as having a "factory" aesthetic. The German Werkbund in 1914 rudely fought the matter of aesthetic standards to a standstill at the Cologne Exposition of 1914, just as armies were amassing across Europe in preparation for the First World War. I am not sure that the juxtaposition of hostilities was entirely coincidental.

At the conclusion of the war, three schools of thought—Dutch De Stijl, Soviet Constructivism, and the Bauhaus—were seriously pursuing the idea of a new aesthetics across the arts, predicated on the primary elements of colors, lines, and forms, yet these efforts were soon overtaken. By the second half of the 1920s, the majority of European practitioners, as with the purveyors of artistic theory more broadly, began to shy away from using the word. The new scripture sanctioned design as an act of social or political intervention in service to simplicity and the industrial values of modernity. A new metaphor was called for. Le Corbusier famously decreed the house to be a "machine." Walter Curt Behrendt proclaimed the "new realities" of the modern style to be our "new tools, new machines, and new methods of construction," and J. J. P. Oud described the new aesthetics as one of "constructive functionalism."[5] Sigfried Giedion, in 1928, went so far as to encourage the architect to renounce the "artistic bombast" of the title and refer to oneself as a "constructor."[6] It is therefore not surprising when, four years later, Henry Russell Hitchcock and Philip Johnson, in speaking on behalf of the newly founded Museum of Modern Art, reduced the aesthetic "principles" of the International Style to the three: volume, regularity, and the avoidance of applied decoration.[7] By this date anyone venturing to suggest an aesthetic rationale for the practice of design was deemed to be a miscreant or simply suffering from a form of madness.

Notwithstanding, around the start of the new millennium the idea of "aesthetics" made something of a comeback, at least outside of architectural parlance. Serious scholars like Hans-Georg Gadamer and Elaine Scarry wrote eloquently on the topic of beauty, reviving and distilling the aesthetic traditions of Plato, Plotinus, Augustine, Aquinas, Dante, and Botticelli.[8] Roger Scruton, in an oration on the theme presented to the BBC in 1993, defined beauty as a "universal need of human beings."[9] The poet Joseph Brodsky characterized beauty's "fusion of the mental and the sensual" as "the purpose of evolution."[10] Evolutionary psychologists argued that our appreciation of beauty is not an idle luxury of taste but a biological adaptation very much written into our genes. Some anthropologists and neuroscientists even went so far as to suggest that there are indeed "aesthetic universals."[11]

Is it now safe for us to raise the issue of aesthetics inside the architect's parlor? I think the answer is yes, even imperatively so, yet first we need to redeem the meaning of the word from its recent past.

II.

The word "aesthetic" first appears in modern languages in the eighteenth century. The concept is intimated in the writings of many writers near the start of the century, but the actual word was first invoked by Alexander Baumgarten in a dissertation published in 1735. Fifteen years later, he developed the theme more extensively in his two-volume study carrying the Latin title *Aesthetica*. The Greek word *aisthētikos,* from which the Latin term originated, means "perception, feeling" or the activity of the senses. Baumgarten, in making the distinction between the logical standards of reason (the domain of philosophy) and the less trustworthy standards of the senses (the domain of taste), defined aesthetics in 1735 as the science of what is sensed or imagined, and he emphasized in particular its emotional coloration. In his tome of 1750 he defined aesthetics more succinctly—and for our purposes more correctly—as the "science of sensible cognition."[12]

Around this time, the idea of "taste" had become a featured topic in many philosophical circles. The theme was raised by the Select Society of Edinburgh in 1754, and it attracted contributions from Allan Ramsay, David Hume, Robert and James Adam, and Lord Kames. It also received a belated response from the Irish politician Edmund Burke, who in 1757 held back his introductory essay "On Taste" from the first edition of *A Philosophical Inquiry into the Origin of Our Ideas of the Sublime and the Beautiful* in order to respond to Hume's essay of the same year, "Of the Standard of Taste."[13]

The most comprehensive exposition of the idea, however, came from Immanuel Kant, who devoted a lengthy book, *Critique of Judgment* (1790), to answering the issues raised by Baumgarten, Hume, and Burke. The first part of his study was entitled "Critique of Aesthetic Judgment" and, as with his earlier philosophical writings, Kant began with the premise that the mind possesses an a priori or internal structure through which it relates to the world. If our cognitive faculty of understanding, for instance, knows the world through the a priori principle that nature is always lawful, the faculty of aesthetic judgment should also have its governing principle. For judgments of taste, he chose the abstruse German term *Zweckmässigkeit*, which, following Ernst Cassirer, we will simply translate as "harmony."[14] The German word (its root word *Zweck* means "purpose") carries with it connotations of practicality and functionality, and it is often translated into English with the ponderous if not impenetrable term "purposiveness."

Yet Kant did not intend the word in any functional sense; in fact, it was just the opposite. For him *Zweckmässigkeit* was a heuristic or mental standard by which we make aesthetic judgments—that is, we make judgments of taste on the basis of a work's purposiveness or harmony of form, which, in this sense at least, is not far removed from Alberti's conception of *concinnitas*. Artistic works are judged beautiful when their forms resonate harmoniously with our inborn aesthetic sense.

The question for Kant next becomes, how does one describe the impression that a form may have on us? Is it some kind of "feeling of pleasure or dislike," as he suggested at the start of his work, or is it some idea or attribute that we attach to a work?[15] For instance, he believed certain arts, such as music, appeal to us directly through their formal elements, while other arts, such as architecture or sculpture, seek to express a higher ideal or concept. Kant, however, never worked out the solution. For him art's association with "feeling," as with Baumgarten, devalues it with respect to the higher cognitive faculties of reason, and feeling at the same time seems to allow emotion into the aesthetic judgment, which Kant went to great lengths to deny.

At one point Kant sought refuge in the notion of "aesthetic ideas," or those ideas involving the imagination without any "definite concept," but a few pages later he flatly contradicts himself by invoking Epicurus, who had insisted that "all pleasures, at heart, issue from a bodily sensation."[16] Toward the end of this section, Kant even makes the argument that "all pleasures," even those that evoke aesthetic ideas, are "animal" (today we might say biological)—that is, they reside in corporal sensations without damage to the "*spiritual* feeling of respect for moral ideas."[17]

If Kant could not work out the problem of aesthetics within his conceptual framework, our task today is somewhat easier. Our focus lies not with the qualitative standard of the built "object" apart from the human occupant; it is grounded in the sensorimotor coupling of the human organism with the environment, or with the *experience* of the built environment itself. In this way, we can return aesthetics to its original meaning of sensible cognition—or better, to the idea of *perception*, now stripped of all reflective standards of judgment. Aesthetics, in fact, is no longer bound to the shape of form or its mathematical regularity, as Kant intimated. The aesthetic pleasure of a formless starlight night or the transitory quality of a glowing sunset is powerfully attractive, even without the stability of form.

Biological models today lend further support to such an approach. The fact that the hedonic or pleasure circuit of the brain becomes active not just with music or other works of art but also with a good meal or a romantic relationship suggests that, as Steven Brown has noted, "such a system evolved first for the appraisal of appetitive objects of biological importance, including food sources and suitable mates, and was later co-opted for artworks such as songs and paintings."[18] In other words, aesthetic perception within the course of human evolution has its roots in more mundane survival needs and only later came to appraise such social and emotional needs as community rituals and individual expression. Brown refers to this perspective as one of "naturalizing aesthetics," which is a worthy goal. One may still speak of a touching musical lyric or a profound architectural experience, yet our interest in this essay is with the perceptual experience of these sensory events—that is, the privileging of what Vittorio Gallese refers to as "the sensorimotor and affective features of our experience of perceptual objects."[19] Judgments about what is beautiful will naturally come later when we begin to consider the social use of the term.

III.

All of which brings us to the newer models of perception, with which philosophy today is much concerned. Alva Noë, like many others, approaches perception through the idea of action: "Perception is not something that happens to us, or in us. It is something we do." It is a bodily skill that is determined by our experiences or what we are ready or prepared to do: "we enact our perceptual experience; we act it out."[20] Evan Thompson draws our attention to Edmund Husserl's perceptual notion of "appresentation," the fact that every perception carries with it content that is already present within the perception.[21] If I walk by a house, for instance, I see much more than the two façades on my retina. I perceive the house as whole and with four sides, because of my previous experience with or memories of a house. Andrea Jelić interprets these hidden profiles to mean "that the way we perceive, experience, and engage with architecture depends on the particular kind of body we have and the possibilities for body-environment interactions that are inscribed in terms of the motor or skillful knowledge as potential for action."[22]

If aesthetic perceptions are at some level prereflective, it is because this is the way we actually experience things—although admittedly prereflectivity is a difficult term to define. One study timing the responses of people to "beautiful" artworks and landscapes found some activity in the "executive" areas of the prefrontal cortex less than a half-second after the stimulus onset.[23] This would suggest that an appraisal of some kind is already built into the perceptual process almost from the start. If this is the case, when does prereflectivity end and reflectivity begin? For our purposes, I will refer to reflectivity only in a vague sense as a deliberative and later stage of the experience. In the example of the house, I may at some later time reflect on its historical style or place it within a specific neighborhood; in another instance, its historical style may be the very feature that attracts my initial perceptual attention.

Because aesthetic perception is selective in what it attends to within the sensory bombardment of stimuli, it is an act inherently meaningful or imbued with significance. Perceptions are not only tightly correlated with action and meanings but also with the emotional circuits through which they are expressed. In this way, perception is already an act of cognition, and the divide that plagued so much of philosophy over many centuries between thinking and feeling has today been recast in a very fundamental way. Perception, emotion, and cognition cannot really be considered apart from one another.

The connection of perception with emotion needs to be highlighted. In *Art and Experience*, John Dewey made the point that artistic experience is in many ways immediately understood, and his understanding of human biology is remarkably close to contemporary models. Foreshadowing Merleau-Ponty and more recent phenomenologists, Dewey placed perception at the front of the cognitive process, as when he underscores both the primacy of perception as a meaningful activity in itself (without recourse to symbols) and our lives as a dynamic flow of intentional acts enlivened by the sensibilities of a lived body. He referred to emotion, as we have seen, as a "moving and cementing force" that brings unity to our perceptual experiences.[24] For Dewey the artistic experience is a corporeal interaction with an environment in which energy gathers and is released, bodily rhythms fluctuate, anticipation and suspense mount and decline, and when fulfillment comes it leads to a "heightened vitality" that "reaches to the depths of our being—one that is an adjustment of our whole being with the conditions of existence."[25] Such a reading reverses eighteenth-century theories of sensibility, because, as Dewey insists, perception and emotion are not processed through the senses but are present in the initial expenditure of energy. The beholder, particularly in viewing something novel, is aroused and at the same time actively constructs the experience in what amounts to an act of perceptual surrender, the loss and reestablishment of the equilibrium with one's surroundings. Action, feeling, and meaning are one. The aesthetic experience speaks to us directly.

The contemporary philosopher Mark Johnson makes Dewey's focus on "meaning" the central theme of his own interpretation of artistic experience, and under it he lists the meanings of form, expression, communication, qualities, emotion, feeling, value, and purpose, among other things.[26] More recently, Johnson has called attention to "one of Dewey's most radical ideas," which is that aesthetic meanings are always marked off by a "pervasive unifying quality," one that is neither emotional, practical, nor intellectual.[27] Again, this would suggest that the aesthetic perception is grounded in the experiential processes of living, and is similarly defined by a heightened vitality. It also implies that the aesthetic perception resides not with objects alone, but rather with the constructive interaction or the organism (and its experiences) with the social and cultural environments.

Dewey's view of art as an "experience" also shares many things in common with the hermeneutics of Gadamer, who characterized art as something that "transforms our fleeting experience into the stable and lasting form of an independent and internally coherent creation."[28] The philosopher speaks of the artistic experience on two levels, defined by two German words *Erlebnis* and *Erfahrung*. The term *Erlebnis* (lived experience), he notes, was coined by Wilhelm Dilthey in the late nineteenth century to refer to the "immediacy with which something real is grasped."[29] When Gadamer speaks of an "aesthetic experience" in this sense, he reports how "the power of the work of art suddenly tears the person experiencing it out of the context of his life, and yet relates him back to the whole of his experience" (*Erfahrung*). It is through one's personal experience (*Erfahrung*) that the lived experience is mediated with historical consciousness.[30]

The psychologist Giovanna Colombetti also emphasizes the emotional character of experience. Affectivity (emotions, moods), she argues, resides not in fleeting events within an otherwise blank mind; the embodied mind and human experience are "constitutionally affective" from the beginning—that is, you cannot remove affectivity and still have a mind or the experience. All organisms share this "primordial affectivity," that is, "all living systems are *sense-making* systems, namely (and roughly for now), they inhabit a world that is significant for them, a world that they themselves enact or bring forth as the correlate of their needs and concerns."[31] This activity does not just take place inside the head, because action is always a function of the whole body moving within in an environment. Emotion is built into the perceptual or cognitive experience, coevolves with it, and is already an appraisal of a bodily event, or, as Colombetti and Thompson have made the case, "emotions are simultaneously bodily and cognitive-evaluative, not in the familiar sense of being made up of separate-but-coexisting bodily and cognitive-evaluative constituents, but rather in the sense that they convey meaning and personal significance as *bodily meaning and significance*."[32]

Affectivity is therefore not a response to an event that has just happened. It is both visceral and at the same time an appraisal of an environmental valence by the organism. It is immediate or built into the perception from the start. Ioannis Xenakis and Argyris Arnellos have described this anticipatory and preparatory nature of perception with the term "interactive affordances," through which "aesthetic perception allows an agent to normatively anticipate interaction potentialities, thus increasing sense making and reducing the uncertainty of interaction."[33]

It is our contention that the enactive experience with the built environment should first be considered at this bodily emotional-anticipatory-action level, because it is here that we first understand how the experience both conditions and is drawn into our existence. To reduce architectural spaces and forms to their geometries or objective properties is not only to demean or decouple the organism from the environment but also to ignore a whole range of nonquantifiable elements of a design that endow a human habitat with life, vitality, decorum, and pleasing atmospheric qualities. The features of a design, of course, may have their symbolisms and other stories to tell, but these are better considered through a more critical understanding of the underlying aesthetic perception itself.

IV.

The idea that every artistic and architectural experience entails a loss and reestablishing of equilibrium within the organism leads us to the idea of novelty, not simply limited (as normative aesthetics directs us) to the specific features of the object. Once again, it is something that resides within the constructive experience. Novelty has always been a cornerstone of architecture practice. Giorgio Vasari extolled the works of Renaissance masters for their design innovations. Claude Perrault and François Blondel vigorously debated the relevance of novelty to Vitruvian classicism. The picturesque theorist Richard Payne Knight lauded novelty as "one of the most universal passions" for creating "new trains of thought" and for "multiplying and varying the objects, the results, and the gratifications of our pursuits beyond the bounds of reality."[34] Edmund Burke opened his treatise on the sublime and beautiful with a section on novelty, and labeled its pursuit "the simplest emotion which we discover in the human mind," contrasting it with the "loathing and weariness" of habituation. Early twentieth-century modernists believed their design efforts to be a search for novel forms and expressions, and the idea of novelty became the veritable calling card of many late twentieth-century architects seeking to eradicate or deconstruct any semblance of the metanarrational order.

More recently, however, the search for something strikingly novel seems to be losing its efficacy within architectural circles. Many critics view the rootless anarchy and perpetual newness of forms—allowed by and sometimes emulating the software algorithms that make them possible—as leading to a new kind of dampening uniformity or "gratuitous novelty."[35] Robert Lamb Hart has cautioned that yesteryear's "promise of discovery, originality, and relief from the rigidity and authority of exhausted ideas" often reduces itself to the impulse of skipping over "years of accumulated learning and the sophistication of past generations. The result, of course, has been novelty and diversity with as many failures as successful breakthroughs."[36] Design today seems to have lost its cultural moorings and the aesthetic theories of yesterday are too vitiated to find new ones.

Novelty, of course, comes in many shades. The eighteenth-century intuitions of Knight and Burke have in recent years received considerable support from researchers. The developmental model of the human nervous system suggests that health and efficient functioning are predicated on novel stimulation and continual learning. Jaak Panksepp has labeled novelty's keepsake—curiosity or seeking—as one of seven endophenotypes or core emotional circuits active in all mammals, and "these circuits appear to be major contributors to our feelings of engagement and excitement as we seek the material resources needed for bodily survival, and also when we pursue the cognitive interests that bring positive existential meaning into our lives."[37] Novel events and what we extract from the encounter alter our neuronal circuits—the process of neural plasticity that is a hallmark of organic vitality. Pleasing novelty, as everyone would agree, is important to overcome habituation, and is therefore conducive to our cognitive health and well-being.

Perhaps the better question to pose is what constitutes pleasing novelty, and here is where the issue takes on a different coloration, in that it returns us to the action-perception cycle and the structure of the brain itself. In the limbic regions of the brain, we have noted the importance of the hippocampus and the surrounding areas for memory and place construction. Adjacent to the hippocampus is the amygdala, which receives information from all sensory modalities and responds to the salience of a stimulus. The amygdala is active in all novel situations, and therefore works as a kind of emotional primer or early-alert system.[38] It is particularly active with events of negative valence and high arousal values, such as environmental threats that might evoke the fight-or-flight response. Effectively, the hippocampus and amygdala work in tandem.[39] With any novel event—say one's arrival in a new city or a summer hike into the backcountry of Yellowstone National Park—the amygdala becomes active. As the hippocampus with its memory banks works to discriminate and contextualize the city or landscape as nonthreatening, the amygdala's response will lessen and go silent.

One obvious issue in this regard is that not all built environments are viewed positively. People with fear of heights, for instance, may have little desire to live in a high-rise, and complex buildings demanding shrewd way-finding skills produce anxiety for those lacking such abilities. Facilities such as hospitals or dental clinics are almost always approached with a high level of anxiety, suggesting, as some neuroscientists have noted, the need to restrict novel stimuli that may intensify the situation.[40] Moreover, some buildings seen as novel and exciting at first inspection, rapidly become jaded with subsequent visits. The effects of novelty can therefore quickly wear off, as many expensive museums and other cultural institutions have over the years demonstrated.

Yet the workings of the amygdala seem to be subtler. Numerous studies have shown that objects with sharp or pointed edges, including room furnishings, activate the amygdala, alerting us to be cautious around them.[41] Many argue that there are evolutionary reasons for this. The designer may think that a pointed chair or an angled building is entirely novel and therefore appealing as a "new" form, but some research suggests that we may be biased against such forms. Drawing upon this research, Oshin Vartanian and a team of scientists used neuroimaging to undertake "an exploratory study" of the architectural environment. They had participants view a series of curvilinear and rectilinear rooms with varying ceiling heights. Not only did the subjects perceive curvilinear spaces to be more "beautiful" than the rectilinear ones, but the curved spaces alone activated the anterior cingulate cortex, which is implicated in the pleasure circuit and responds to the emotional salience of objects.[42] In a follow-up fMRI study evaluating people's responses to ceiling heights and perceived room enclosure, researchers found that rooms with higher ceilings or with more openness were more likely to be seen as beautiful. Moreover, closed rooms with few means of egress were likely "to elicit exit decisions" and activated a part of the mid-cingulate cortex receiving direct input from the amygdala, which "suggest that a reduction in perceived visual and locomotive permeability characteristic of enclosed spaces might elicit an emotional reaction that accompanies exit decisions."[43]

The second study followed upon earlier experiments of Arthur Stamps, who had shown that we respond very directly to the "permeability" of space (the degree of movement it allows) both visually and proprioceptively. His premise was that our safety within an environment, again conditioned by our evolutionary past, is dependent on the ability to see and move through a space, and escape when it becomes dangerous. Through a series of experiments in which rooms had differing levels of visual permeability and exiting options, he found that people are generally attracted to more permeable and better-lit spaces and shy away from those with fewer possibilities for exiting.[44]

All of these studies should rightly be seen as "exploratory" and they cannot be interpreted to mean that all architectural spaces need to have degree of openness or curvilinearity. The coziness of a room might reside on the fact that it lacks openness, and curvilinearity might be a novel, and therefore an interesting, solution in response to the general rectilinearity of our built environments. One must also keep in mind that the major limitation of neuroimaging and virtual-reality constructions is that participants view images of rooms rather than the full multisensory and spatial experience of one, and the material and atmospheric qualities of the spaces are therefore considerably lessened. Detailing and other effects of scale and texture, for instance, would seem to be very powerful tools for achieving a successful outcome with architectural environments.

Nevertheless, a few studies have tackled the issue of novelty from a perceiver's perspective. The psychologist Colin Ellard, for instance, has made the case that sensory richness and variety are important parts of successful architectural and urban environments, and that their contrary—boredom—has the adverse biological effect of creating stress.[45] There have also been studies in the areas of product and industrial design that focus on this play between the "tension-heightening" effects of novelty and the "tension-reducing" effects of the familiar, as Paul Hekkert frames the issue. He argues that people prefer the optimal combination of the two. They prefer novelty so long as it does not mitigate feelings for the familiar and typical, and familiarity so long as it does not work to the detriment of novelty.[46] He also makes the case that we not only enjoy the sensory aspects of novelty but also enjoy looking at things that, with minimum means or in a cognitively efficient way, facilitate the organized perception—that is, support "navigation and identification."[47] One way to achieve this principle in design, he argues, is to design a product with maximum effect and minimum means. In this regard, he cites Herzog and de Meuron's Dominus Winery with its stacked gabion walls as an illustration of this approach (Figure 5.1). "This simple solution results in a range of effects," he notes, "the fit is easily established, the construction is cheap and very solid, the thick walls bring about a cool and constant inside temperature, and above all, the sunbeams that peep through the walls cause a poetic pattern of dancing lights. The net result is one of high aesthetic quality."[48]

What we are beginning to understand about imagination is also revealing of the interplay of novelty and familiarity. Imagination, as we noted earlier, shares a similar brain network with remembering the past, thereby drawing in neural circuits utilized in perception, emotion, and motor control.[49] In some ways, imagination can be viewed as a variation on the model of mirror mechanisms and embodied simulation. If mirror circuits allow us to perceive the actions or emotions of another by activating many of the same neural circuits we would use in performing the action or experiencing the emotion—imagination follows a similar process. Imagining a musical phrase, for instance, prompts similar circuits of the auditory cortex that are used when listening to a piece of music. And if the primary and secondary areas of the auditory cortex of the right hemisphere extract musically relevant stimuli from a tonal sequence, the secondary auditory cortex becomes active when people, without auditory prompting, imagine a familiar melody.[50] Stephen Kosslyn has similarly shown that with visual imagery we re-create or re-present many of the same circuits of the visual cortex used in related perceptions. Therefore, imagination "not only engages the motor system, but also affects the body, much as can actual

FIGURE 5.1 *Herzog & de Meuron, Dominus Winery, Napa (1995–98). Photograph by author.*

perceptual experience."[51] Such a position would seem to support the play between novelty and familiarity.

Kosslyn's body of work also falls into line with various studies relating to creativity, which suggest, quite unequivocally, that imagination operates from no unitary system of neural circuits but always works from distributed networks built upon smaller neural subsystems related to functional tasks. It seems obvious that the imagination or cognitive ability suited to solving a complex mathematical equation would be different from that of writing a musical composition or designing a building, but imagination in all instances is characterized by distributed networks, which, of course, are mediated by experience.

In the late nineteenth century, William James already observed that the divide between imagination and the perceptual sensation is less than we might think, and that "the imagination-process differs from the sensation-process by its intensity rather than by its locality."[52] Writers such as Arthur Koestler and Anton Ehrenzweig have made the case that the artistic structure of creativity is essentially polyphonic—that is, "it evolves not in a single line of thought, but in several superimposed strands at once. Hence creativity requires a diffuse, scattered kind of attention that contradicts our normal logical habits of thinking."[53]

Various cognitive neuroscientists have framed the issue of creativity as a conceptual process grounded in the lateralization of brain functions, but the holistic task of the designer—one integrating the corporeal and emotional foundations of the architectural experience—would seem to add an inscrutable layer of complexity to the problem.[54] The traditional venues for enhancing architectural creativity, such as travel, sketches, journals, and firsthand experience with the atmospheric qualities of different environments, remain essential tools of architectural training today, not only to broaden one's cultural horizons but also (and more importantly) to instill memories with a palpable corporeal vitality. The philosopher Hans Ulrich Gumbrecht, among others, has emphasized that aesthetic experience—in addition to its reflective meaning—entails the component of "presence" or the bodily involvement of "haptic vision."[55] "Presence," it would seem from our earlier discussions, is an excellent word to bring into architectural discourse.

The one key element that is emerging from today's research, and one that has been stressed repeatedly in this book, is that all focused and unfocused neural processes (perception, action, emotion, imagination, and conceptualization) are grounded in actual bodily states. The "mind" is not a "logical thinking" software program placed within the hardware of a body; its mental processes always emanate from the experiences of the anticipatory and moving body engaging with environments, and specifically in terms of the actions afforded. It has been argued, correctly I believe, that Louis Kahn's often stunning play with light owed much to his pastel sketches of ancient monuments that he visited during his stay at the American Academy in Rome.[56] Because imagination is the act of a mindful body, experience and a sense of presence are key to the efficiency and strength of the imaginative process. The architect Ester Sperber has summarized this idea for designers by noting that "the architect's creativity depends on the ability to utilize multiple modalities of the human mind and body," and that "the freedom to utilize a wide range of mental and physical methods in order to elaborate an imagined idea is what allows these fantasies to become realities."[57]

In its perceptual operation, the human nervous system craves stimulation and information, and when something novel and interesting appears, it may touch off a rush of opioids implicated in the pleasure circuit. Pleasure in itself may not be the goal of good design, but we should take account of the fact that we prefer experiences that are both novel (new and without previous interactions) and richly interpretable.[58] Novelty without such an experiential grounding tends to be shallow, and current models of embodiment are now building more complex approaches to aesthetic perception.

6

Feeling-for-Form ... Feeling-for-Space

How did Casals derive his precise shape? What is the meaning of the function of such purity of expression in relation to the central nervous system?

MANFRED CLYNES[1]

The German language has a characteristic that is less apparent in the Romance languages, which is the tendency to form new words, and indeed new concepts, by combining words. The partly Germanic English language, among many other languages, has this characteristic, yet to a lesser extent. For instance, designers may speak of floorboards, but floor plans, floor lamps, and floor treatments are generally given the visual luxury of a spacing. The German word *Formgefühl* is a good example of Germanic word construction. The noun *Form* is the similar word in both English and German, but the noun *Gefühl* means "feeling." Literally, the word means "form-feeling," but this rendering has a certain ambiguity when translated into English. In my earlier life as a translator, I rendered the word as "sense of form," but this translation also has its limitation in that it tends toward abstraction. The word within aesthetic literature is perhaps best rendered as "feeling-for-form," in this case the feeling that a particular form induces within us.

Conceptualizations also have philological ramifications. One minter of new words in modern German history was Johann Gottfried Herder, who in 1774 coined the term *Einfühlung* (feeling-into-something) as a hermeneutic tool to suggest how a historian might better interpret and understand—free of bias—the nature of a people or their culture.[2] The term suggests a certain compassion or empathy with one's subject: the sense, for instance, that someone's culture is not inferior to one's own. A century later Robert Vischer recast the word *Einfühlung* in artistic terms by employing it to describe the process by which someone is drawn into (feels-one's-way-into) an artistic object, in his words, projects one's "own bodily form—and with this also the soul—into the form of the object."[3] He entitled his doctoral dissertation "Über das optische Formgefühl"—perhaps best rendered as "On the Optical Feeling-for-Form."

The idea *Formgefühl* is also a prominent term in Heinrich Wölfflin's dissertation of 1886, which, as noted, was focused on the question of how a building evokes an emotional response in us.[4] If he accepted Vischer's thesis that a building does so through our physiological responses, he did so by emphasizing even more the corporeal underpinnings to our feeling-for-form. He noted that not only do the building's mass and details have strong sympathetic and vestibular effects on our "internal organs," but also the heaviness, balance, and hardness of these forms have expressive values for us because we have bodies and are therefore familiar with the laws of mass and gravity. In a physiognomic way, we internalize artistic forms and if a building displays a rusticated "brow," or its composition produces an unbalanced effect, it creates within us a sense of bodily unease. It is therefore through our body's internal processing of the perceptual event that architectural forms generate emotional responses.

It is not coincidental that Wölfflin's concern for our emotional responses to architectural forms was voiced in 1886—at a time when architects were discussing the need to discard stylized forms and replace them with others more suited to the changing lifestyles of the industrial age. Toward the end of his dissertation, he even raised the question of why, in fact, do architectural forms or styles change at all. He attempted to answer it by making the rather daring leap of expanding the individual's *Formgefühl* or feeling-for-form to the larger cultural "mood" of a people or nation as a whole. He even went so far as to align the attenuated features of Gothic architecture with the "Crakow shoes" and pointed facial features seen in scholastic paintings, in which "the bridge of the nose becomes narrower; the forehead assumes hard vertical folds; the whole body stiffens and pulls itself together; all restful expansiveness disappears."[5] This cultural observation became the leading theme of his first book, *Renaissance and Baroque* (1888), in which the soon-to-be-famous art historian considered the formalistic or stylistic changes in Italy during the stylistic transition from Renaissance to the Baroque forms.[6]

As is often the case historically, Wölfflin was not alone in this thinking. In fact, his book on the Baroque owed much to the efforts of Adolf Göller, a professor at the Stuttgart Polytechnikum. The German architect, like Sullivan in Chicago, was similarly immersed in the psychological theories of his day, and in an essay of 1887 he posed the question, "What is the cause of perpetual style change in architecture?" Göller offered up a two-point hypothesis of stunning simplicity. First, architecture, unlike painting and sculpture, is not a representational art but a geometric and formal one. And if architecture could be considered outside of its representational or historical values, it would more correctly be seen as "the art of pure form," whose aesthetic appreciation would therefore reside in "an inherently pleasurable, meaningless play of lines or of light and shade."[7] Second, the explanation for these changes of forms or styles resides in the predictable psychological process whereby, over the course of one generation or two, a culture constructs collective "memory images" or formal preferences, which, in succeeding generations, are then subject to the process of "jading." In Göller's view, this jading effect would lead first to a "baroque" phase of a style, whereby forms are refitted with new profiles, but eventually the variations or manipulations of forms would be used up and a culture would begin the process of creating entirely new forms. Göller followed in the same year with a lengthier presentation of his ideas, and one reviewer late in 1887—Cornelius Gurlitt—praised his two "remarkable books," although he found one fault. Göller, the reviewer believed, had not realized that if architectural styles could be stripped of their representational content and be reduced simply to forms, so could the arts of painting and sculpture![8]

II.

It has scarcely been appreciated how this new focus on the physiological perception of "form," as we find in the writings of Vischer, Wölfflin, and Göller, laid the foundation for German architectural modernism. This focus was carried into the new century through the empathy theories of Theodor Lipps and Wilhelm Worringer in particular, but the thematic focus on form was also of interest outside of Germany. In 1896 the American artistic connoisseur Bernard Berenson, from his Tuscan estate *I Tatti*, began to speak of the "tactile values" found in many Florentine painters of the Renaissance.[9] As R. G. Collingwood has interpreted his meaning, "tactile values" for Berenson did not refer to the "texture of fur and cloth, the cool roughness of bark," but rather to "motor sensations such as we experience by using our muscles and moving our limbs."[10] One member of Berenson's Florentine circle, the writer Vernon Lee, was equally impressed with the motoric premise of the new psychological aesthetics, a subject that she embraced in the late 1890s. In collaboration with the painter Clementina Anstruther-Thomson, she embarked on a series of experiments attempting to measure the muscular and breathing responses to form—in one instance, by monitoring someone viewing Alberti's facade for the Church of Santa Maria Novella. When Lipps, from Germany, criticized Lee and Thomson for the naiveté of their efforts, the two energetically countered with the idea that "our motor activities rehearse the tensions, pressures, thrusts, resistances, efforts, the volition, in fact, the life, with its accompany emotions, which we project into the form and attribute to it."[11]

Geoffrey Scott, another figure connected with Berenson's Florentine circle, also emphasized our embodied and empathetic relationship with architectural form in his book *The Architecture of Humanism* (1914), yet the English writer most successful in placing the new idea of "form" before the public was Clive Bell, whose book *Art* appeared in the same year.

Bell wrote the book to provide his English audience with a way to understand the new techniques and themes of abstraction that were appearing across the arts and particularly in painting, and he began his study with the premise that all of the arts—pictures, sculptures, buildings, ceramics, carvings, textiles—share one thing in common, which is that they induce "aesthetic emotion," indeed a deeply rooted emotion that seems to be independent of culture and learning. Aesthetic emotion is also a response to a "common quality" that, if found, would solve the central problem of the new aesthetics:

> What quality is common to Sta. Sophia and the windows at Chartres, Mexican sculpture, a Persian bowl, Chinese carpets, Giotto's frescoes at Padua, and the masterpieces of Poussin, Piero della Francesca, and Cézanne? Only one answer seems possible—significant form. In each, lines and colours combined in a particular way, certain forms and relations of forms, stir our aesthetic emotions. These relations and combinations of lines and colours, these aesthetically moving forms, I call "Significant Form"; and "Significant Form" is the one quality common to all works of visual art.[12]

One aspect of Bell's notion of "significant form" is that while the experience of form is subjective, it is also deeply rooted in human perception—that is, it is not something gained through learning or intellectualization but something emotionally felt and therefore stands outside of everyday affairs.

One could trace the importance of significant form within aesthetic theory over the first seventy years of the twentieth century, but it would add little to our theme. Notable toward the end of this period was the work of Rudolf Arnheim and Ernst Gombrich, both of whom approached the idea of form with some scientific rigor. In *Art and Visual Perception* (1954), for instance, the Gestalt-trained Arnheim defined the perception of form as "the outcome of an interplay between the physical object, the medium of light acting as the transmitter of information, and the conditions prevailing in the nervous system of the viewer."[13] In other words, people do not simply perceive forms visually; perception in itself is a creative or constructive act and several factors manipulate what we see. In *The Dynamics of Architectural Form* (1977), he defined form in a pure Gestalt sense of a system of forces conditioned by human frames of reference and the brain. If the Baptistery in Pisa is visually problematic for him because of its weak base, Bramante's Tempietto in the courtyard of San Pietro in Montorio succeeds architecturally because the cupola is visually supported by tall columns and the larger base of the peristyle[14] (Figures 6.1 and 6.2). In many respects this reading of form owes much to Wölfflin.

FIGURE 6.1 *Bapistry of Pisa (1152–1363). Photograph courtesy of Jan Drewes. Creative commons.*

FIGURE 6.2 *Donato Bramante, Temple in the Courtyard of San Pietro in Montorio, Rome (1502). Courtesy of Angelo Hornak, Getty Images.*

Gombrich goes further than Arnheim in making the case that the "sense of order" that we apply in our design or composition of forms is intrinsically a biological feature of our organic systems. In his books of this title, which appeared in 1979, he notes that not only does "the tablet on which the senses write their messages have certain inbuilt properties" but also that, like iron fillings in a magnetic field, "the nervous impulses reaching the visual cortex are subject to forces of attraction and repulsion."[15] In defending his book against a reviewer in 1979, Gombrich stated his biological thesis in more specific terms: "I claim that the formal characteristics of most human products, from tools to buildings and from clothing to ornaments, can be seen as manifestations of that sense of order which is deeply rooted in man's biological heritage."[16] Gombrich, on occasions, also resorted to the concept of *Einfühlung* to explain his sense of order. "This doctrine," he notes, "relies on the traces of muscular response in our reaction to forms; it is not only the perception of music which makes us dance inwardly, but also the perception of shapes."[17]

The perceptual ethologist Christa Sütterlin, in reporting her experiments of people responding to complex patterns, has recently brought support to Gombrich's thesis: "Evidently, our eyes are somehow able to see through the superficial pattern and discover the secret order behind, and exactly these 'cognitive' properties of our vision seem to be at the origin of aesthetic pleasure. We are tuned to recognize regularities—even hidden ones—because our memory is based on standardized experiences (templates)."[18] Order in this way becomes the brain's projection of itself into the world.

The neuroscientist Semir Zeki, the founder of neuroaesthetics, has recently returned to Bell's idea of "significant form" and—with a few definitional modifications—has wondered if our current neurological understanding of perception might support aspects of Bell's observations.[19] Zeki cites numerous neuroimaging studies that have shown there are neural circuits that are always active in pleasurable aesthetic perceptions, which are the reward circuits culminating in the OFC or orbitofrontal cortex. Moreover, these studies demonstrate that the intensity of the artistic experience is correlated with the intensity of this cortical activity. Zeki proposes extending Bell's thesis across the arts by making two definitional changes. He replaces the term "aesthetic emotions" with "aesthetic perceptions," and the idea of "significant form" with "significant configurations." The latter accomplishes two things. First, it characterizes aesthetic perceptions across the arts, and second, it helps to transform the aesthetic experience from a purely visual into a multisensory experience. Aesthetic perception, for Zeki, does not reside simply in lines, colors, or sounds, for instance, but in how we create the holistic event.

Drawing upon his own fMRI research, Zeki puts forth the hypothesis that there must be a spark, as it were, within the different sensory maps of the brain that ignites the reward circuits of the orbitofrontal cortex. For the visual arts, he points to one area of the parietal lobe that has been shown to be involved with the grouping of signals related to form, and in certain situations with significant configurations of form. It is perhaps this area, he reasons, that sets off the pleasure circuits of the orbitofrontal cortex.[20] As he summarizes his hypothesis:

> The mysterious laws that the artist taps into become, then, his or her capacity to create forms that activate the relevant visual areas either optimally or specifically, by which I mean activate them in a way that is different from that obtained by stimuli that lack significant configuration. Perhaps only when so activated are the 'sensory' areas of the brain able to arouse the aesthetic emotions.[21]

It might be of interest to consider this hypothesis of significant form with an architectural example, say, Francesco Borromini's Church of San Carlo alle Quatro Fontane—but more on this later.

III.

Let us return to the idea of *Einfühlung*, which has the meaning of feeling-one's-way-into the artistic event or object. The German term was much popularized in the writing of Theodor Lipps around the turn of the twentieth century, and in 1909 the psychologist Edward Titchener translated the term into English as "empathy," which has become the standard translation in the years since. The choice of this particular English word is not incorrect, particularly if one takes its meaning back to Herder, but it is also somewhat problematic. Empathy, in English, carries the connotation of compassion or sympathy, which the German term does not always have. For Vischer, at least, empathy was not simply an emotional expression but rather the psychophysiological process by which we relate to or find pleasure in artistic forms.

This point is important because empathy is today widely used throughout the neurosciences to signify the neurological processes through which we relate not only to objects but also emotionally to other human beings. Whereas these meanings emerged around the turn of the present century, an interesting foreshadowing of this viewpoint was voiced in the 1970s by Manfred Clynes and his notion of "sentic forms." Clynes, a concert pianist, neurophysiologist, and friend of Albert Einstein, demonstrated through his empirical studies that all elegant artistic forms—from the phrasing of a cello piece performed by Pablo Casals to the line in a Raphael painting—convey a "touch of emotion," which Clynes in fact attempted to record with a machine of his invention. Our haptic sensitivity to form, he went on to argue, unfolds in degrees from simple mimicry to a sympathetic involvement with form, and then to complete empathy, as when we project ourselves into the artistic work. This emotional "contagion" of empathy, moreover, is social in that it is also present in our daily meetings with others, such as when we read another's facial emotions or understand their intentions.[22]

These mirror or sensorimotor mechanisms, as we discussed earlier, are systems of multisensory neurons that fire in response to objects, actions, or to other events within our perceptual fields. As I approach a staircase, for instance, mirror mechanisms within my premotor cortex are already preparing for how and when I might modify my gait and lift my foot to begin the ascension. If I meet a close friend, I am immediately aware of how they are feeling by reading their posture or facial expression. These sensorimotor mechanisms, as some have argued, are the means by which we conceptualize or understand the world around us in a more general way.

Giacomo Rizzolatti, the lead scientist in the discovery of mirror neurons, has spoken of mirror systems in terms related to James Gibson's notion of *affordance*. In the latter's ecological psychology, an affordance—the primal recognition of things as shelters, water, fire, objects, tools, and human interface—is the manner in which we perceive or connect with the world. Rizzolatti points out that mirror mechanisms are highly selective in when and where they fire. If mirror mechanisms in the premotor cortex are highly sensitive to movements or actions, those in the posterior parietal areas (closer to the processing stations of the visual cortex) are sensitive not only to objects but also to the particular size, shape, orientation, and use of objects. A pointer and a pencil, to give one of his examples, can both be used for pointing and therefore have similar affordances, but we hold them in very different ways and mirror neurons in the premotor cortex respond to them in the manner by which they are held. "Once we have discovered," he observes, "how to conjugate the different kinds of motor acts with specific visual aspects relative to objects, which therefore become object affordances, our motor system will be able to perform all the transformations necessary to carry out any act, including that of picking up a cup of coffee."[23] He was one of the first to refer to this process as embodied simulation.

Today we are beginning to understand the importance of embodied simulation and sensorimotor activities in the perception of the built environment, although so far only indirectly as to date little research has been devoted specifically to architecture. Researchers at Delft University, for instance, suggest that the architectural experience is an enactive one played out through a host of "image schemas," such as containment, spatial orientations, balance, forces (interactions of energy fields), and motion. In their view, the "container" schema becomes active in our movements within and out of spaces, and the particular sense of security they convey. We may evaluate a chair, for instance, by how well it envelops and conforms to our body, while we evaluate a domestic environment by how well it keeps us safe from inclement weather or allows us to feel at home. The "balance" schema is the means through which we read the stability, stillness, or unbalanced tension of certain environmental features that may affect our body's posture and functioning.[24]

Schemas are also cross-modal, and they explain how our sensory modalities are formed. Infants, for instance, rely heavily on seeing, grasping, and even licking an object to understand its shape, spatial and textural properties, and it is through this multimodal process that they form spatial and material categories. In one study exploring this relationship between touch and vision, researchers had adults examine complex three-dimensional shell shapes separately on the basis of visual and tactile cues. They found that not only was "the haptic modality on a par with the visual modality in recovering the topology of the physical space" but these same "highly congruent perceptual spaces" relied on the same cognitive system.[25] Another neuroimaging study in which people viewed classical sculpture with an aesthetic attitude showed activity in the emotional areas, as well as mirror activity in the premotor and parietal areas—suggesting that we not only read the emotional expressions of the sculptures but also simulate the movements portrayed.[26] A later study of people viewing paintings also found activity in emotional circuits, but only when the subjects viewed them with an aesthetic attitude. When participants were asked to describe the paintings for their visuo-spatial characteristics, entirely different areas of the brain related to spatial processing were active.[27]

The tactile and mirror dimensions of architecture are also discussed in a paper published in 2007 by the art historian David Freedberg and neuroscientist Vittorio Gallese. The paper "Motion, emotion and empathy in esthetic experience" compiled a number of neuroimaging studies related to vision and the activation of mirror mechanisms. On this basis, the two authors offered a hypothesis with far-reaching implications for design: "We propose that a crucial element of esthetic response consists of the activation of embodied mechanisms encompassing the simulation of actions, emotions and corporeal sensations, and that these mechanisms are universal."[28] If, for example, we read someone's handwriting by simulating the hand action within our own sensorimotor systems, would we not also simulate the brush strokes in an abstract painting or the tactile qualities of an architectural surface with our tactile circuits? In viewing a stucco wall or a stainless-steel lamp, for instance, do we not understand their material qualities and touch to the hand? Do we not also feel into the qualities of the elements in a building, or the composition as a whole, in a similar way?

For Freedberg and Gallese, an important part of aesthetic perception is the grounded activity of both emotional and mirror systems. In viewing one of Michelangelo's *Prisoners*, for instance, people respond with the simulated activation of muscles seen in the sculptural work, the struggle of the figures seemingly trapped within the constraints of the marble. They respond as well to perceived blows of the chisel and hammer. Another example they give are the paintings of Jackson Pollock, in which paint is thrown onto the canvas with force. Here viewers have a sense of the energy invested to the drippings by the physical traces of the paint. If this were true, would we not also have a tactile response, as Gottfried Semper once noted, to the weight, hardness, and pounded chisel marks of rusticated blocks of stone?[29] The one architectural example given by Freedberg and Gallese is that in viewing a twisted Romanesque column we may tense up in a visceral way by simulating our own bodies being twisted.

The pivotal point made by these authors is really twofold. We empathically relate to works of art and architecture first by simulating the movement, intentions, and values imparted to the work, and second, on an emotional level, by engaging directly with the atmospheric qualities, details, and materials employed (Figure 6.3). If the plastic forces of a Borromini façade, for example,

FIGURE 6.3 *Francisco Borromini, San Carlo alle Quattro Fontane, Rome (1638–41). Photograph by author.*

might convey for us a sense of movement, force, or embrace, so might we also simulate the specific values of materials—whether industrial and smooth or handmade and textural—in our sensorimotor areas.

Two EEG follow-up studies bring the matter still closer to home for designers. In the first, participants looked at three paintings of Lucio Fontana, works in which the painter had slashed the canvas with a sharp object. Their responses were measured against a modified computer version of the same paintings, somewhat softened and without the violent force of the originals. The recordings clearly showed motor-system activity in viewing static abstract images without any explicit sign of movement, yet the intensity of the response was higher with the originals where the force of the knife was apparent, and this was true for those who were familiar with Fontana's paintings and for those who were not.[30] If we respond with sensorimotor activity to a slit in a two-dimensional canvas, is it not highly likely that we read the linear and material forces of our surrounding architectural environment—as Arnheim earlier surmised—in a similar way?

In the second EEG study participants viewed three black-and-white paintings of Franz Kline, again against a computer-modified control group. In his paintings, Kline used a broad brush and would apply a few lines or geometric forms to a canvas with quick strokes and a heavy use of paint. Again, the authors found premotor and motor activity in cortical areas, as well as reward-related activity in the orbitofrontal cortex, in addition to the cognitive areas of the prefrontal cortex related to categorization. The summary of their findings is interesting: "The cortical sensorimotor activation is a fundamental neurophysiological demonstration of the direct involvement of the cortical motor system in perception of static meaningless images belonging to abstract art," and the results "support the role of embodied simulation of artist's gestures in the perception of works of art."[31]

If architectural theory a few decades ago considered architecture largely as a visual art communicating its content through symbols, we now know that our perception of architecture is manifested as an embodied and emotional experience, likely set in motion by sensorimotor and mirror-circuit activity. The body and its reward circuits are directly affected by the architectural experience prior to any acts of reflection or symbolic interpretation. Much of postmodern architectural theory was too narrowly structured to allow such a possibility.

IV.

If the idea of form had any competitor within the architectural literature of the twentieth century, it was the complementary idea of space. The two, in fact, cannot be considered apart, in the sense that there can be no form without space, and the converse is obviously true. Again, this concept in modern architectural thought—in this case the notion of *Raumgefühl* or "feeling-for-space"—goes back to the late nineteenth century. Already in 1869 and 1878, respectively, Semper and Conrad Fiedler were highlighting the importance of space as a medium for architectural expression.[32] Two essays published in 1893, however, began to consider the spatial experience in a novel and compelling way, one now being reinforced by today's science.

The sculptor Adolf Hildebrand began the first essay, "The Problem of Form in the Fine Arts," almost two decades earlier, but consultations with prominent scientists such as Hermann Helmholtz and Wilhelm Wundt led him continually to recalibrate his ideas. Notable were Hildebrand's distinctions between the visual and kinesthetic factors of the spatial experience, paralleling his dual notions of "inherent form" and "effective form." In the latter, he noted, resides the artistic framework of design. He also embraced the idea of empathy and the "gestural expression" always present in our perception of form. Spatial qualities in many instances, in fact, are not distinguishable from formal properties. In perceiving the colonnade of a Greek temple, for instance, we do not read it as a closed spatial mass but as "a perforated, frontal layer of space. What we perceive is not a spatial body fronted by columns: the columns form part of the spatial body and our ideal movement into depth passes between them."[33]

What Hildebrand did not develop is the sensitivity of the human body to both movement and spatial depth. This distinction, as Mitchell Schwarzer has noted, goes to the art historian August Schmarsow, the first architectural theorist to have an "explicit understanding of the significance of kinetic perception."[34]

Schmarsow first outlined his thesis in his inaugural address at the University of Leipzig in 1893, under the intriguing title "The Essence of Architectural Creation." He opened his talk with the proposition that all buildings, in their most sublime and primal sense, are not simply forms but "spatial constructs," and "we call this art architecture; in plain words, it is the *creatress of space*."[35] Yet these spatial constructs are also not abstract artifacts, as he presciently noted; their spatial meaning is created only through "the residues of sensory experience to which the muscular sensations of our body, the sensitivity of our skin, and the structure of our body all contribute."[36]

Schmarsow also speaks of architectural space from what today might be called a phenomenological perspective. The meaning of space for him goes back to primeval times—to the traces of footprints in the sand, the line drawn in clay with a stick, or the boundaries by which humans define themselves. Space is not a given event but something that we animate with "the backbone of our intuition of space," and the axial system that projects from our vertical standing: "Every spatial creation is first and foremost the enclosing of a subject; and thus architecture as a human art differs fundamentally from all endeavors in the applied arts."[37] Spaces become too narrow when they lack "elbowroom," they are too confining when they are too rigid or when they fail to leave room for the "sentient human being." In short—and paralleling Wölfflin's focus on the visual, corporeal, and vestibular effects of architectural masses—Schmarsow makes the case that space has similar effects on the observer from inside an enclosure, with a particular emphasis on depth or the possibility of our movement within a particular space.

Schmarsow would go on to develop these themes in several of his later writings, but his analyses of 1893 already draws close to the later observations of Maurice Merleau-Ponty, who too was much concerned with the issues of motility, spatiality, and human perception. For the French philosopher, the perceptual world is but a field of potential human action or activity, one that exists by virtue of our body's motile relationship with things. To cite a few of his examples, a woman wearing a hat with a feather knows how to keep a safe distance from something that might break it off; the feather has already been assimilated into the space of her person. The same is true of a racket in the hands of a tennis player; the tactile range of one's command of a spatial field has been extended by the racket. "The points in space do not stand out as objective positions in relation to our objective position occupied by our body," Merleau-Ponty notes, "they mark, in our vicinity, the varying range of our aims and gestures."[38] Stated more simply, the space around our bodies "is not a sort of ether in which all things float," it is always coded for activity upfront and personal, an extension of possibilities for movement that are elicited by our body's primal sense of self.[39] Architectural space is perceived through the medium of our body's motor potentialities, and we can understand space only through our body and the action we intend. Yet even the limits of the body's boundary are being called into question by today's neuroscience.

Both the human body and space have in fact become malleable concepts. Traditionally we have thought of the body as something defined by or contained within our skin, but a number of studies over the past two decades have shown that the sense of "self" is not necessarily fixed to the body but something constructed at each instance of time from a complex of sensory and cultural interactions. One often cited example is the so-called rubber-hand illusion, first demonstrated by Matthew Botvinick and Jonathan Cohen in 1998. In the original experiment, participants were seated at a table with their left arm resting on the table. A screen was positioned to hide the hand from their view, while a life-sized rubber hand was placed on the table directly in front of them. Someone then stroked both the real and surrogate hand in the same areas synchronously. The subjects soon began to project the tactile sensations onto the rubber hand, and even "felt" the sensation when the rubber hand alone was stroked. Some of the participants pointed to the rubber hand when asked to touch their own hand with the other hand.[40] In a later variation on the study, researchers noted the same compliance of the body image without the rubber hand—by simply stroking or tapping the empty table top as the hand was being touched in a similar way. Moreover, when the rubber hand was threatened with injury, subjects displayed a strong skin-conductance response as if the real hand was about to be harmed.[41]

Various experiments employing three-dimensional virtual realities (VR) have taken body ownership and self-consciousness to another interesting level of investigation. In one series of studies, subjects wearing head-mounted VR displays were filmed from behind in a space without environmental cues and the image of another person (or their own) was projected in front of and/or alongside them in their virtual displays. The researchers again stroked them on their back while they were observing avatars or virtual bodies receiving the same stroking. When the stroking occurred synchronously, the participants again reported being touched even when only the mannequin or virtual body was being touched, and they even began to self-identify or shift their self-location toward the mannequin or virtual body—that is, where the touch was actually seen.[42]

The neuroscientist Olaf Blanke has interpreted these findings to mean that self-location (the first-person perspective) and self-identification are in effect two distinct neurological processes, with self-identification being dependent on the integration of bodily signals with vestibular cues, while self-location is dependent on bimodal somatosensory and visual signals.[43] The brain, it seems, perceives this field around us not with one but with several neuronal maps, not all of which are spatial.[44] A low-hanging apple in a tree, for instance, is not measured by its geometric coordinates in place, but by a motor understanding of whether we can reach it. Architectural spaces function in a similar way in terms of their affordance to our movement or sense of enclosure.

What we are describing is the idea of peripersonal space, which is another area of intensive study today. Peripersonal space is the space (and its objects) near our body and within the limits of our immediate action, and it is highly ductile in its envelope. It is an area first explored culturally and psychologically in the investigations of Edward T. Hall and Robert Sommer, respectively, but once again mirror mechanisms have transformed the issues in a fundamental way. Peripersonal space seems to be regulated by two neural networks located within different areas of the premotor cortex and parietal lobe: one relating to the priming of the limbs for such activities as reaching or grasping, a second for defending the body and defining a safe boundary around it.[45] Both circuits, as Hall had earlier suggested, are plastic in their spatial limits.

Walking, for instance, extends or continually reshapes our peripersonal space in a forward direction.[46] Our peripersonal space, however, may expand in every direction when we are walking a dangerous street at night. Tools or other implements, such as a hammer or a cane, also extend peripersonal space, although with other nuances coming into play. For instance, easily manipulated and familiar objects such as toothbrushes or teapots, when placed within peripersonal space, evoke strong cross-modal activity in the parietal and premotor networks, as do photographs of these objects.[47] Yet these responses tail off once the objects are moved into extrapersonal space—that is, beyond the peripersonal boundary. In another experiment objects with positive affective valence, when placed at a fixed distance, were judged to be reachable and therefore within our peripersonal space, but unreachable when they had a negative or neutral meaning for us.[48] Such findings not only demonstrate the idea of affordances but also sharpen the idea that the perceptual field is structured by skillful bodily activity.[49]

Emotional and social factors also affect our peripersonal space. It is self-evident that we will let someone with whom we are intimate into our peripersonal space, while keeping others outside of this sphere. Yet simple social interactions with others can also remap the boundaries of our peripersonal space. In one experiment in which two people previously unknown to each other played an economic game in a cooperative way, the peripersonal spaces between them merged together, but this was not the case when one person failed to cooperate.[50] In another study, researchers found that when we observe one individual touching another at a distance, our tactile network becomes active not only with the touch of another's hand but also when someone's hand approaches the vicinity of another's hand. Effectively, we are simulating an intrusion into our own peripersonal space.[51]

If painters and novelists have long exploited this distinction between peripersonal and extrapersonal space, the distinction also has major relevance to architectural design. The space we inhabit is not architecturally neutral or an entity mapped on some stable Euclidean grid, but a state of being that is both plastic and dynamic in its perception. It is plastic in the sense that our personal space can be modified through tools and cultural conditioning. It is dynamic in the sense it can be modified by the features of the built environment as well as by changes in the social and emotional demeanor of the perceiving individual. Space is always pregnant with meaning or the suggestion of meaning related to some action. Designers can exploit these possibilities.

The source of lighting in a designed environment, or how one is offered the possibility of movement within an interior of a building, similarly carries with it significance. We noted earlier the research regarding the perceived "permeability" of space, as well as the neuroimaging study in which people were more likely to judge curvilinear spaces (over rectilinear spaces) or rooms with higher ceilings as "beautiful" than others.[52] The neuroscientist Oshin Vartanian, the lead author in the study of curvilinearity, concluded with the following summation of his research:

> Given our increasing propensity to spend time indoors, our results suggest that a systematic evaluation of how the physical features of built environments affect human behavior, emotion, and brain function is both timely and within reach. Not only is there the prospect that this interdisciplinary enterprise could lead to the design of more pleasant work and life spaces, but these data could also shed light on perhaps a more fundamental question: why it is that we have come to prefer the places that we do.[53]

Vartanian could not be more correct, for it has now been amply demonstrated that the human body, or any living body for that matter, does not passively move within a spatial field. The body is a source of action and is conditioned both by the way we perceive the world and how we maintain our orientation within it. In this regard, Jon Goodbun has proffered the very suggestive idea that architecture can be thought of as a prosthetic impulse—that is, "We imagine the building and our spatial environment as a second skin, an extension or projection of our body and our psychology; we wear spaces and morphology like clothing or a membrane, an interface or prosthesis, physically and psychically, and indeed socially and collectively."[54]

One study involving the use of immersive environments underscores this point in a vivid way. In this study, researchers had participants with VR headpieces stand before a distant wall, between two side walls that, in different experiments, were placed far apart and close together. The headpieces projected in front of them the rear images of their own bodies being stroked with a stick (filmed from behind), synchronously and asynchronously. In both side wall locations, the participants experienced the same self-location drift toward their virtual body. In the condition of the narrow side walls, however, synchronous stroking led subjects to perceive the walls as closer to them, with some even reporting the sensation of being touched by the side walls. The asynchronous condition of stroking did not alter the spatial perception. A coauthor of this study, Isabella Pasqualini, offered this explanation of the results: "The present participants experienced differences in illusory touch and room retraction depending on *room-size*, suggestive of a mild self-identification not only with the virtual body, but also with the walls through an involvement of somatosensory mechanisms, compatible with suggestions by Wölfflin and Schmarsow."[55]

When we view architecture through the experiential media of form and space, the possibilities for research are unending. A room filled with natural light at a distance may entice us to move toward it. Aspects of the room may encourage us to move closer toward or away from an object of attraction. A material with a rough and coarse texture may work architecturally in extrapersonal space, but it may create a sense of unease in our peripersonal space; our bodies will naturally steer away from something perceived to be dangerous to the rub or bump of human contact. We remain ever sentient of our architectural spaces through the emotional tone or tenor of forms, colors, scales, textures, and rhythms. It seems likely, as philosophical models of empathy suggest, that environmental conditions alter both our sense of self and hold the key for intersubjective relationships.[56] Susanne Langer once noted that architectural space "contracts or expands under the tensions of form," and that in creating space the architect in a sense creates the "image" of a culture: "Therefore any building that can create the illusion of an ethnic world, a 'place' articulated by the imprint of human life, must seem organic, like a living form."[57] Richard Etlin has referred to the multiple dimensions of existential space as personifying the "spatial sense of self."[58] We can only add the rather obvious observation that *architectural space in itself has a profound influence on and connection with the body*—scarcely a novel notion for anyone who has ever walked into a Kyoto shrine or climbed the staircase of Brunelleschi's dome in Florence.

7

The Atmosphere of Place

To live in an environment which has to be endured or ignored rather than enjoyed is to be diminished as a human being.

SINCLAIR GAULDIE[1]

The philosopher Jeff Malpas has noted that the distinction between *space* and *place* remains poorly defined today, and he points out that place is often treated under the general rubric of space.[2] The same can also be said for the treatment of place within architectural literature, although a number of writers in the decades immediately following the Second World War—Dagobert Frey, Bruno Zevi, Rudolf Schwartz, Kevin Lynch, Robert Sommer, and Edward Hall, among others—made serious efforts to highlight its importance. They were also enjoined and inspired by a number of phenomenologically minded writers such as Martin Heidegger, Maurice Merleau-Ponty, Gaston Bachelard, Max Jammer, and Otto Friedrich Bollnow.

It was only in the 1970s that place became an expressed notion within architectural discussions. In 1971, in *Existence, Space & Architecture*, Christian Norberg-Schulz used the dual notions of "existential space" and "architectural space" to reflect upon the meaning of place. When his book *Genius Loci* appeared in 1979, however, place had become the centerpiece of his Heideggerian analysis, and here we also find a break from the analytical language and interests of his earlier years toward a more interpretative viewpoint.[3] Perhaps Kenneth Frampton's influential editorial of 1974, "On Reading Heidegger," provided the strongest arguments for preferring the architectural term place over the abstraction of space—not the least of which was its existential foothold.[4] Similar arguments were expressed by others around the same time, as we find in Yi-Fu Tuan's *Topophilia* (1974) and *Space and Place* (1977), Edward Relph's *Place and Placelessness* (1976), Kent Bloomer and Charles Moore's *Body, Memory, and Architecture* (1977), and David Seamon's *A Geography of the Lifeworld* (1979).

Relph's book perhaps best captured the topographic languor of this decade. Pitting "existential outsideness" (not belonging to a place) against the psychological richness of "empathetic insideness" (identifying with a place)—he pleaded to restore the deep emotional and cultural attachment we are inclined to share with the place in which we live. His plea was also framed as a protest against the "placeless geography, a labyrinth of endless similarities" that defines our modern cities, creating a situation in which placelessness has become the norm in the world of mass culture and global communication, a society that often revels in the commodification of kitsch.[5] One source cited in Relph's study is the Scottish architect Sinclair Gauldie, who had earlier made a similar point in an equally pressing tone: "To live in an environment which has to be endured or ignored rather than enjoyed is to be diminished as a human being. The society which ignores this fact is at risk, for it is presuming too far upon human adaptability: drabness, confusion, and mediocrity make an imponderable but real contribution to the frustration and depression which produce stultified, sick, or apathetic citizens."[6] The influence of Heidegger in the resurrection of the idea of place also should be noted. Malpas argues that Heidegger was the first to suggest that "the connection between place and experience is not, however, that place is properly something only encountered 'in' experience, but rather that place *is integral to the very structure and possibility of experience.*"[7] Place is the ontological medium through which everything appears, the compass by which we orient and collect ourselves with respect to the world, and memory "cannot be understood independently of the place in which memory is located."[8] Just as the location of the bridge, as Heidegger has famously noted, "*gathers* the earth and landscape around the stream" into a meaningful place, so is building "not merely a means toward dwelling—to build is already to dwell."[9] Heidegger also points out that the etymology of the German word for space (*Raum,* related to the English word "room") "means a place cleared or freed for settlement and lodging."[10] The fact that neuroscience today has demonstrated that the place-recognition areas of the brain are adjacent to and tightly connected with the memory-formation engine of the hippocampus only lends further support to Heidegger's contention.

Place is the humanization or enculturation of space. When we give a place a name, we endow it with meaning and acknowledge its existence, a point that has been frequently noted in ethnological literature. Christopher Tilley reminds us that in aboriginal cultures places or landscapes are not "natural," they are socialized or "sedimented in history and sentiment," and that the "holding of the land" requires both a knowledge of the physiographic features of the landscape and the connection of place to one's ancestral history: "Failure to protect songs, ceremonies and sacred objects is equivalent to giving the land away"[11] (Figure 7.1). In this way, places are nested within landscapes or cityscapes "as perceived and embodied sets of relationships between places, a structure of human feeling, emotion, dwelling, movement and practical

FIGURE 7.1 *Petroglyph from Dinosaur National Monument, near McKee Springs, Utah (c. 1100 AD). Photo courtesy of Bob Condia.*

activity within a geographical region which may or may not possess precise topographic boundaries or limits."[12]

Others have also written eloquently about the importance of place for architects. Karsten Harries devoted lengthy sections of *The Ethical Function of Architecture* to drawing out the connection of place with dwelling, and he too underscored Heidegger's distinction between dwelling and simply residing in a place or building: "To dwell is to feel at home. Building allows for dwelling by granting a sense of place."[13] Harries, similar to Relph, also stressed today's "homogeneity, the indifference of place," the loss of intimacy and rootlessness that by the 1980s and 1990s had become evident features of the modern urban environment. In the decades since, our path toward a global culture has tended to exacerbate this situation, and one might ask whether there is a price to be paid for our current ease with generic placelessness. Global positioning devices and the communication tools of social media further erode our attention from the physical features of a place. Our cultivated skills in wayfinding, as models of neural plasticity would predict, seem to be diminishing. Is this the downside to "niche construction"—just as we construct our placeless environments, so does our sense of placelessness alter the nature of who we are?

Nevertheless, the idea of place making in architecture, as the decade of the 1960s made abundantly clear, can be an elusive and futile pursuit without more secure moorings than sociological prescriptions generally allow. Past hypotheses regarding the relational connection of place and human behavior were more often than not too vague and generalized to inform the architect in any meaningful way. The architecture of place has to impress us more sensuously, deeply, and personally. Do not tourists flock to (and today vastly overtax) the alleyways of Venice in large part because its bridges and canals archetypically epitomize the ever more illusive notion of place? The whiff of a Parisian boulangerie, as Edward Hall once noted, is an unforgettable experience of place etched into olfactory consciousness.

If place has a tangible physiognomy, it would be its *atmosphere*—that is, its familiarity and appropriateness, defined by how its sensory appeal and emotional attunement perceptually enlist attention and are understood by those experiencing it. Atmosphere draws upon the embodied sensorimotor or mirror processes by which we engage every environmental situation, but it is also something more. It suggests that the atmosphere of the human habitat should have a "presence" or authenticity of feeling, one formed not only by the ingenious assembly or composition of materials but also by how we measure its emotional depth and richness—that is, how we read and internalize it.

Again, such cultural concerns are not especially new to architecture, as nearly every generation of designers have given some voice to them. In his *Cours d'architecture* (1771–77), Jacques-François Blondel's list of "nuances imperceptibles" available to the designer—with the capacity to "carry away, to move," "to lift the spirit of the spectator"—runs over thirty pages.[14] In *Le génie de l'architecture* (1780), Nicholas Le Camus de Mézières's insisted that not only should every room of a household be fitted with its unique character but also that the designer, like the skillful painter, must "learn to take advantage of light and shade, to control his tints, his shadings, his nuances, and to impart a true harmony to the whole."[15] The then-novel fashion of a lady's boudoir should be the "abode of delight," whereas a dining room should be a place of festivity, in which "gaiety, freshness, lively colors, and the character of youth and beauty set the tone of the decoration."[16] He goes on to add that "we must start from this principle whenever we intend to arouse emotion through Architecture, when we set out to address the mind and to simulate the soul, rather than to build by piling one stone on another, indiscriminately copying arrangements and ornaments that are imposed by convention or borrowed without reflection."[17] Such advice defines a starkly different perspective from the leveling design tendencies we often view in today's architectural culture.

II.

The meteorological term "atmosphere" was coined in the seventeenth century, and it is therefore a new word to describe a much older way of thinking about design. Ictinus, Callicrates, and Phidias certainly understood their task in constructing and detailing the Parthenon was to create an atmosphere in keeping with the gold-and-ivory statue of Athena and the city's panathenaic festivals. The designer of every synagogue, church, mosque, monastery, and Buddhist temple has since sought to provide the appropriate atmosphere for the prescribed rituals, yet designers rarely think of secular or utilitarian buildings in terms of atmosphere. Do community centers, surgery rooms, or work offices have atmosphere? They do, of course, although we rarely acknowledge it. It is perhaps for this reason that the term "atmosphere" has been so infrequently invoked in design circles.

To my knowledge, Gottfried Semper in 1860 was the first architect to use the term when proposing "the haze of carnival candles" as the "true atmosphere" (*wahre Atmosphäre*) for architecture, but the concept is broader in its dimensions.[18] Around the start of the twentieth century the word became relatively common in a few design circles. Frank Lloyd Wright, by Google's count, employed the word on fifty-seven occasions in his writings, yet this emotionally laden term all but disappeared in the second half of the century.

Only later did the idea make a comeback. In the 1980s and 1990s the German philosopher Gernot Böhme began to call for a "new aesthetics" to replace the "judgmental aesthetics" of the postmodern era, which he viewed as little concerned with the sensory aspects of design and more with making judgments, fostering discussions, and setting up standards for criticisms.[19] If the "old aesthetics" was dominated by language and the belief that the task of the artist was to communicate some idea or theory, the "new aesthetics"—taking its start in Walter Benjamin's idea of "aura"—presents an alternative way of seeing artistic production as "an indeterminate spatially extended quality of feeling," one that can be absorbed into "one's own bodily state of being."[20]

In applying the concept to design, Böhme argues that architecture is scarcely the visual or spatial art that it has conventionally been made out to be; rather, it is one accessible mainly through its "mood"—that is, we understand ourselves through our movement in space only because we "feel" our presence in a place and "sense its *atmosphere*."[21] Atmosphere is "the space of mindful physical presence" and the architect (through the use of form, light, sound, physical constellations, social and cultural entreaties) modulates space "by creating confines or expanse, direction, delimiting or transgressive atmospheres."[22] Böhme also surmises that this current "rediscovery of the human body" might eventually lead to a renaissance across the arts, and most especially in the field of architecture.

Böhme was not entirely alone in his thinking. His "space of mindful physical presence" recalls Thomas Thiis-Evensen's analyses of architectural archetypes through such atmospheric qualities as motion, weight, and substance. "Based on the study of a building task," the Danish architect suggests that the designer "creates for himself a spatial image which he feels responds to what the building 'wants to be,' both practically and expressively. Understanding of archetypes and their expressive potentialities is essential when this vision is to be turned into a realization."[23] Harries similarly approached the idea of atmosphere with his "natural language of space," a locution by which he means exploiting the sensory qualities of a place's materiality, color, light, ornament, temperature, and sociability.[24] The thoughtful architect, he points out, knows how to endow materials and design with a sense of place that fits with our behavior, expectations, and moods.

Peter Zumthor's book *Atmospheres* advanced the notion still further. Equating atmospheric "quality" in design with "how a building manages to move me," the architect goes on to enunciate the means through which the designer can create a mood and sense of expectation through materiality, the sound and temperature of a place, light, and levels of intimacy. Atmosphere also extends beyond the limits of built forms and encompasses the "things themselves, the people, the air, noises, sound, colours, material presences, textures, forms too—forms I can appreciate. Forms I can try to decipher. Forms I find beautiful."[25]

Around the same time Juhani Pallasmaa began to speak of atmosphere as "the overarching perceptual, sensory, and emotive impression of a setting or social situation," the "unifying coherence and character for a room, space, place, and landscape, or a human encounter."[26] He made the observation that vernacular settings composed of aesthetically uninteresting elements are often said to have atmosphere because they possess a specific materiality, scale, rhythm, color, and multiple variations. People untrained in architecture, he added, often experience atmosphere better than architects do.

"Atmosphere" is an elusive but at the same time a resilient term in design. There are, of course, a multitude of atmospheric effects within a room, a setting, a city, or a landscape. Tonino Griffero sees atmosphere as the "meeting of *aisthésis* and *pathos*," as "the spontaneous and circular intertwinement between the repertory of architectural gestures and the repertory of the felt-bodily and spatial experiences of the user."[27] The nebulous notion of atmosphere, in his view, allows us to return "aesthetics" to its original meaning—that is, to a nonjudgmental self-engagement with the dimensions of our own existence, the way in which we actually live our lives and thereby counter the "irritating levelling of places and a lack of specific value core."[28]

Böhme has extolled the "ecstatic" nature of atmosphere, in that it allows us the possibility of standing outside ourselves and transcending the ordinary and the everyday. Whereas the traditional designer is taught to focus almost singularly on form, function, and space, Böhme argues that contemporary design should begin to account for our "bodily feelings"—that is, the way in which something impresses, illuminates, and determines the space around us. In this way atmosphere is neither a quality of things nor of the people experiencing them but something in between, "a kind of spatially extended feeling" known to all but in a more intimate and non-representational manner.[29] Atmosphere offers us a richer and more profound understanding of ecology by exploiting that subtle relationship between our natural and built environments and how they affect our temper, moods, and well-being.

Others have approached the idea of atmosphere in more existential terms. Jean-Paul Thibaud, for instance, refers to atmosphere as the art of "impregnation" and "tonalization," the nuances gained by recognizing the "immersion and infusion, and *tiny connections*" through which we paint our existence.[30] Pérez-Gómez views atmosphere through the layered meaning of the German word *Stimmung*. Although generally translated as "mood" or "temperament," the word has many shades of meaning, such as harmony, proportion, and the tuning of a musical instrument. He defines architecture as the search for "appropriate moods and atmospheres for human actions," found not in the building itself but in "the meaningful event made present: life itself."[31] All such formulations, in their own way, recall Aldo van Eyck's frequently invoked response in the 1960s to the overly rationalist tenor of high modernism—that architects should concern themselves not with "space and time" but rather with "place and occasion."[32]

III.

Atmospheres are prereflective, sensorimotor, kinesthetic, polymodal, and emotional articulations of a more pervasive mood, which is enacted through our engagement with the natural and constructed environments. The play of atmospheric effects can be seen as a palpable medium leading to an experience of primal attraction, arousal, or simply the condition of biological restoration and rest.

The current interest in biophilic design documents this last capacity. It grew up around a body of research related to the well-known restorative effects of nature on human cognition and biological systems, whether it is a fifteen-minute walk in an urban park or an extended stay at the seashore or mountains.[33] Explanations for these benefits are sundry—ranging from the concordance of our sensory systems with the elements of the natural environment in which they have evolved to Jay Appleton's "habitat-selection" thesis of 1975, which posited that we "relate pleasurable sensations in the experience of landscapes to environmental conditions favourable to biological survival."[34] Based on his studies of landscape painting and British picturesque parks, he reasoned that our deeply seated preferences for specific natural

FIGURE 7.2 *An African savannah. Photo courtesy of Tim Graham, Getty images.*

environments (water, stands of trees with broad and low canopies, cropped grass in the foreground, topologies offering both prospect and refuge) were honed by evolution over millions of years in the savannahs of eastern Africa (Figure 7.2).

Appleton's thesis was tested in the 1980s by the psychologists Stephen and Rachel Kaplan, whose two studies *Cognition and Environment* (1982) and *The Nature of Experience* (1989) amassed extensive research to support what they would term "Attention Restoration Theory."[35] In essence, the Kaplans argue that the attention required in our everyday activities in hardened environments progressively drain our cognitive resources, whereas the pulse of contact with nature both relaxes our nervous systems and offers us a pleasurable and replenishing perceptual experience. Roger Ulrich, beginning in the late 1970s, added to this model with his studies of participants viewing slides of nature and architecture. Not only did his participants consistently favor viewing images of nature over images of buildings (with physiological monitors also showing significant restoration/stress recovery values) but the scenes of buildings consisting of "modern synthetic elements such as glass and concrete" had the opposite effect, in some cases inducing the emotions of sadness, anger, and aggression.[36] In 1993 Ulrich, in summarizing his and the work of the Kaplans, expressed his puzzlement over the fact that his subjects consistently preferred even "undistinguished natural scenes" over "comparatively attractive Scandinavian townscapes."[37] The number of research studies regarding the benefits of greener environments within urban areas—on overall health, levels of stress, attention, sociality, and even crime rates—is now quite extensive.[38] Numerous studies evaluating the health of large populations with access to green areas have also quantified similar health benefits.[39]

One area of recent study has been the Asian custom of "Forest-Bathing"—a two- or three-day hike into a forest. Such extended walks have been shown to spike the production of white blood cells in the human immune system, increasing intracellular proteins known to fight cancerous tumors, obesity, type 2 diabetes, and a variety of cardiovascular diseases.[40] At least part of this effect seems to be due to the inhalation of forest phytoncides, the essential oils emitted from trees.[41] In other words, the atmosphere that we literally breathe can improve our health and well-being.

Conceived as well within the framework of evolutionary psychology is the work of the architect Grant Hildebrand. In 1991 he applied Appleton's thesis of prospect and refuge to thirty-three houses of Frank Lloyd Wright in the effort to demonstrate that the American architect had consistently followed these principles in his domestic designs.[42] In *The Origins of Architectural Pleasure* (1999), Hildebrand broadened his reach and surveyed a number of ways buildings can excite us. The book is rich in observations, and he makes the case that not only is atmospheric "pleasure" a legitimate purpose of design but also that the pleasure that we take in certain environmental features—such as enticement, the thrill of peril, and complexity of order—are built into our biology.[43]

Both culture and the architectural environment play a significant role in our social response to the atmospherics of place. Jan Gehl and his team of architects in Copenhagen have done a number of studies of what makes a successful urban environment, all of which place a high importance on the importance of walkability and freedom of pedestrian movement, as well the details on the architectural environment itself. Long building facades with little scale, color, and permeability induce us to walk faster—likely because of their unpleasant monotony. By contrast, non-monolithic facades with human scale, color, and openings with features like cafes encourage people to slow down and engage with the street life.[44] Drawing in part upon Gehl's work, Colin Ellard physiologically monitored subjects walking two streets: one dominated by a blank façade of frosted glass, the other consisting of small restaurants and stores with open doors and windows. The latter produced lively states of arousal and strong positive emotion, whereas the former resulted in the negative response of unhappiness and boredom.[45] Ellard compares the lively street to the experiments done with rats in enriched environments, which we discussed earlier. He also cites the research of Colleen Merrifield and James Danckert to the effect that even a brief exposure to perceptual boredom can change the brain and body's chemistry, leading to a condition of stress.[46]

Only a few studies at this early date have approached the idea of atmosphere more directly. Several researchers over the past few decades, for instance, have used surveys and physiological monitors to assess the atmosphere of religious buildings—such as monasteries, meditation centers, and houses of worship—and found restorative, cognitive, and immunological benefits for those who experience them.[47] Obviously, the state of mind induced by prayer and meditation in itself would also play a major role in the reception of these environments, but what of the environment in itself?

One pioneering fMRI study of atmospheric character, however, had twelve architects examine two groups of "contemplative" and "ordinary" buildings. The latter group consisted of five office, housing, educational, and commercial buildings, while the five contemplation-inducing buildings were the Roman Pantheon, Chartres Cathedral, the Alhambra, Ronchamp, and the Salk Institute (Figure 7.3). Four images were presented for each building, allowing one mentally to approach the building and enter it or its plaza. The architects likely visiting familiar sites were asked not to judge what they saw, but to imagine themselves experiencing the buildings firsthand. The results showed two very different brain-activation patterns among the architects. Ordinary buildings recruited activity in the executive control and attention areas of the prefrontal

FIGURE 7.3 *Oculus of the Pantheon, Rome (27 BC–14 AD). Photograph by author.*

cortex related to goals and semiotic interpretation. The contemplative buildings, by contrast, virtually shut down the prefrontal cortex and instead activated areas involved with emotions, sensorimotor, and multisensory interactions—that is, the integration of premotor, motor, spatial, visual, auditory, and vestibular information. "The significant activation of these areas," the researchers go on to say, "underscores the central role that higher-order sensory-motor function and 'embodiment' may play in the experience of contemplative buildings and thus its aesthetic nature, as also articulated by the study participants in their exit questionnaire."[48] At the very least this study demonstrates that the atmospheric qualities of the built environment do indeed alter our neurological patterns, which is an area now ripe for further research.

In architectural terms, the atmosphere of Chartres or the Pantheon is notable for its "high-level" stylistic features of scale and drama, but it is a rare exception to the world in which we generally live and design. The vast majority of design efforts are centered on what cinematic critics might describe as "low-level" mood-inducing features—that is, the materials, gravity of structure, lighting, scale, proportions, textures, color, the temperature and sound of space, and the human vitality contained within.[49] How, then, does the consideration of atmosphere at this level lead us to "mindful physical presence" of which Böhme spoke?

IV.

One fMRI study of 2008 indirectly sheds some interesting light on this question. Several studies had previously shown that when we watch someone being touched, mirror circuits in our frontal and parietal areas become active as we simulate ourselves being touched in these areas. In this particular experiment, the subjects watched four instances of touch: someone touching a chair, someone touching another's arm, a palm branch touching an arm, and a palm branch touching a chair. The experiment yielded the expected results in the first three instances, but what was surprising was the fourth instance in which the image of an inanimate palm branch was touching an inanimate chair. The authors concluded their study with an intriguing statement:

> The same mirroring/simulation principles seem to apply to the observation of any touch. This mechanism might underpin the activation of an abstract notion of touch. It does not matter to which degree an observed touch is intentional or accidental, whether an observed touched object is animate or inanimate, or whether an observed person or object is touched on the right or left side; the sign of any touch evokes activation in a shared neural circuitry.[50]

Architecture, of course, is the art of composing materials and forms that touch one another, and this conclusion substantiates what Pallasmaa, writing in the same year as this study, referred to the "unconscious touch in artistic experience," or how this "hidden tactile experience determines the sensuous qualities of the perceived object."[51] The traditional architectural word for this haptic composing of materials touching one another is "detailing."

Such an understanding brings to mind Marco Frascari's observations on the tactile sensibility of his mentor Carlo Scarpa. Details, Frascari noted, are in fact minimal units of signification, but in Scarpa's case they were more (Figure 7.4). The palimpsest of Scarpa's drawings reveals the tense struggle involved with forming the appropriate detail, "the result of the memory effects of the organs of touch and sight in the making and using of architecture."[52] In such a way, Frascari concludes, Scarpa came to realize perfectly Alberti's notion of *concinnitas* (harmony), the ingenious placing of materials and the fact that "each detail tells the story of its making, of its placing, and of its dimensioning."[53] Frampton has referred to Scarpa's focused efforts as "the adoration of the joint," and it is interesting that this tectonic dimension of design—so strong at the peak of high modernism—reappeared in Frampton's analysis in the waning days of the postmodern era.[54]

FIGURE 7.4 *Carlo Scarpa, Bridge to the Fondazione Querini Stampalia, Venice (1961–63). Photograph by author.*

The coincidence is perhaps self-explanatory. Toward the beginning of Tim Ingold's book *Making* (2013), the anthropologist distinguishes the theorist from the craftsman: the former "makes through thinking," while the latter "thinks through making." The former, he observes, thinks and then applies the fruit of this labor to the production of form, whereas the "way of the craftsman, by contrast, is to allow knowledge to grow from the crucible of our practical and observational engagements with the beings and things around us."[55] There can be little doubt that the postmodern era suffered from a surfeit of theory, but the more pressing question remains: Is the architect a theorist or a craftsman?

Architects may want to respond that they are both, but are they really so magisterial? And where does theory really enter into the design process, except as a rationale? Designers are also taught that they, like every artist, "create" designs, but the poet Joseph Brodsky disagrees and prefers the humbler notion that creative people of every persuasion "make" designs—the end result necessarily acquiring a patina gleaned from the working process itself.[56] What, in any case, can one actually theorize about the detailing of materials or the pleasure contained within the act of making? Even the etymology of the term "architect," *arkhi* (chief) + *tektōn* (builder), defines the architect's classical status principally as artisanal. Ingold, like Frascari, defines the act of "making" as bringing "pieces into a sympathetic engagement with one another," and, in citing the writings of the archaeologist André Leroi-Gourhan, he points to the "rhythmicity and mnemonic character" of artistic production—a perspective now supported by our knowledge of sensorimotor mechanisms.[57] In this way, a sketch or a drawing is better seen not, as we generally say, as a "projection of thought" but rather as the "process of thinking" in itself.[58] It is a gathering and focusing of thought, because in design nothing is more basic than pondering, often with models, drawings, or on a computer screen, how one assembles the parts into a whole.

Designers work with materials, and materials have manufacturing properties such as techniques of production, molding, polishing, cutting, and joining. They have material qualities such as hardness and softness, weight, ductility elasticity, roughness and smoothness, textures, light reflection or opaqueness, transparency, and color, among other attributes. They have sensory qualities, such as visual, tactile, olfactory, thermal, and auditory values. They have as well, as several experiments have shown, gender and cultural properties. Females seem to think of "sexy" materials in different ways than males, and Turkish designers think of "elegant" materials in different ways than do Dutch designers.[59] Wool may display a sense of warmth not only by the visual intensity of its color but also by its touch.[60] The hard and thermally cool materials of high modernism, such as steel and glass, may appear to some designers as having a "professional" quality, but they may convey to non-designers a very different set of values. Several studies have shown that in simply viewing a material, the tactile areas of our sensory cortex become active, which supports Frampton's remark that "the unavoidable earthbound nature of building is as tectonic and tactile in character as it is scenographic and visual."[61] In an embodied way, we touch what we see, and what we feel is not simply the materials but how they are joined.

Richard Sennett emphasizes the relationship of the head and the hand, the fact that "technical understanding develops through the powers of imagination" and such skills are not inevitable but have to be cultivated through human effort and labor.[62] Sennett goes on to critique his former mentor Hannah Arendt and her somewhat gloomy distinction between *animal laborans* and *homo faber*, a distinction, he argues, that overlooks the fact that thinking and feeling are an essential part of the process of making. There is another dichotomy proposed by Arendt that is equally relevant to our theme, which is the devaluation of action (*vita activa*) through its subordination to the process of contemplation—modern society's priority of *theōria* over *praxis*.[63] One can certainly construct the case that architecture's infatuation with theory had brought us to this unsocial juncture today. One may think back fondly, as Colin Rowe did in the early 1970s, on the "impeccably good intentions of modern architecture, its genuine ideas of social service," but such theorizing when lacking a deeper ethos of authenticity or truthfulness, he pointed out, quite easily descends into "anachronism, nostalgia, and probably, frivolity."[64] The role of the architect, it needs to be highlighted, is not to theorize the "making" but to construct or give life to the places in which we dwell. *Vita activa* in this sense entails not only making things but also making experiences, which is the hallmark of our vital natures.

V.

In an architectural era in which many contemporary designers have openly scorned the "detail" in favor of the "concept," it is necessary to pursue the detail's relationship to atmosphere in greater depth. One of the more classic descriptions of the power and role of detailing can be found in Roger Scruton's *The Aesthetics of Architecture* (1979), in which the philosopher, over many pages, argues that the "sense of detail" resides not in its visual or theoretical values, but rather "in the organization of perception and feeling."[65] Detailing imparts grace and humanity to the design and the failing of modern architecture, in his view, is the lack of the designer's "flair" for detail. A Gothic nave, for instance, may strive for maximum height, but because of its articulated richness it is a world apart from "the downcasting inhumanity of the modern skyscraper," glazed yet without the saving grace of detail.[66]

A shell niche in Borromini's Church of San Carlo, Scruton offers, gains its vitality entirely from its "textural quality," the appropriate play of curved tactile-inspired forms within the larger undulating forms of the church as a whole. We enjoy these playful offerings because they also allow us to evaluate their fitting deployment. In once again invoking Alberti's notion of *concinnitas*, Scruton laments (even at this early very stage of postmodernism) that we may be losing "the rich tradition which made such an expression possible," because "the *search* for meaning in architecture, whether in the vernacular or in the highest art, will always require that sense of the appropriate, manifest, as we have seen, in the fitting correspondence of part with part."[67] From such a perspective, detailing provides the means through which we engage emotionally with the built environment.

The undisputed master of the architectural detail and its historical trajectory, Edward Ford, seems to agree. If architecture has its tools for "abstraction," such as its geometries, rhythms, and proportions, it also has its tools of "animation," not the least of which is the detail's "tactile, sculptural, animated intrusion into the rigid, abstract, and geometric building."[68] The point of the animated detail for Ford is nothing less than "to alter the perception of a building at an isolated point toward empathy and away from abstraction," to establish what Zumthor refers to as "levels of intimacy" between the occupant and the building.[69] Ford even goes so far as to describe the appreciation of the autonomous detail as the process of escaping the symbolic and associative qualities of building and finding an "understanding of its essence."[70] Such a statement would have been considered heresy in years past.

Our current understanding of mirror mechanisms and their empathetic underpinnings suggest that these connections are quite real. Borromini's shell niche with which Scruton was so enamored achieves its presence because its plastic surface and scale allow us to simulate tracing our fingers, hands, and mind along its surfaces. Its articulated curvatures fit the hand and at the same time speak to the more expansive curvatures of the church's walls. It succeeds because the surfaces project what Pallasmaa has described as "authoritative radiance and depth of feeling."[71] Jon Goodbun has recast our relationship with architectural forms and details in terms of Gibson's affordances.[72] We empathize with the clay tile of a vernacular Italian rooftop, he argues, because its curvature fits our hands. The handmade scale of Italian villages and small towns please because they accommodate the pedestrian in the way that the modern metropolis never can or at least has rarely attempted to do. By contrast, the unarticulated smooth surfaces of modern architecture are often uninteresting up close because they offer no such tactile or perceptual connection. They are seen at their best advantage at a distance, or, even better, when viewed in photographs, a medium that many architects generally prefer to stage uninhabited by humans. They thus become simply sculptural objects.

Affordance might be a good way to think of the relationship between detailing and atmosphere. A room or a building with atmosphere invites us to feel-into its many dimensions, to be at home, as it were, with a domestic sense of psychological and physiological comfort. The brick pattern of Doge's Palace in Venice pleases everyone because it expresses, in the words of Bruce Metcalf, a "bodily-kinesthetic intelligence," a kind of "felt experience and the body" inherently tactile and rooted in human biology[73] (Figure 7.5). Perception, as we have seen, is an active process. It is a form of thinking that we do with our bodies—with our hands, our movements, as well as with our heads. Not only has the near obsession with theory in the recent years seriously undermined the atmospheric and therefore experiential aspects of bringing forth a design, but I believe, somewhat counterintuitively, it has inhibited and diminished creativity. The problem is encapsulated by the struggling architecture student who spends three-quarters of the semester's studio time trying to come up with a "concept." Given the temporal demands of the final presentation, there is no time left for detailing.

FIGURE 7.5 *Doge's Palace, Venice (begun 1340). Photograph by author.*

We are therefore forced to reiterate our earlier question: Is the student being trained to be a theorist or a craftsman? Do we design symbols to be interpreted through far-flung analogies or a place in which humans dwell? Educational values today demand a closer scrutiny, and it is time to accept the fact that much of what paraded as architectural theory in the second half of the twentieth century has now become irrelevant in view of our present understanding of ourselves—at least with regard to the architectural experience.

8

The Hearth and the Storyteller

We ask, what are the minimally sufficient conditions for the appearance of the phenomenal self, that is, the fundamental conscious experience of being someone?

OLAF BLANKE AND THOMAS METZINGER[1]

Between 1969 and 2003 in Germany, near the village of Bilzingsleben, an archaeological team excavated a site that served as a base camp around 370,000 years ago.[2] The site, along the shores of a lake, was functionally divided into several work areas adjacent to the outlines of three oval structures presumed to have served as habitats, three to four meters in diameter. Hearths were placed inside and their doorways were oriented to the southeast, away from the predominant wind direction. A general activity zone, approximately six meters by thirty meters, was found a short distance away and there several stone implements were found containing carefully etched incisions, likely serving some marking function. Perhaps the most interesting aspect of the site was a large, nearly circular paved area, approximately nine meters in diameter. Remnants of a hearth were found in the center of the circle, and along the eastern edge there was a very large travertine boulder that served as an anvil. Another boulder was placed at the western edge, surrounded by the skulls and horns of large aurochs. The presence of smashed skulls in and around the forum suggests that it was a place of ritualistic events. The inhabitants of this settlement were cognitively and culturally sophisticated members of the *Homo* genus—*Homo erectus*—a species that had survived the end of the interglacial period and made the necessary adaptations to continue their lineage in the colder ecological conditions that followed.

Another example of an early Paleolithic settlement is Terra Amata, which today lies on an elevated plane beneath a museum housing its reconstruction, in the French city of Nice. The site, which was originally built on a beach along the Mediterranean (with a higher sea elevation than today), was unearthed during building activities in the 1960s. During a temporary halt to construction, the archaeologist Henry de Lumley excavated the area over a few short months. What he found were the remnants of a series of gabled huts formed with

FIGURE 8.1 *Reconstruction of a shelter from Terra Amata, France. Courtesy of Karen Carr Studio and the Smithsonian National Museum of Natural History.*

center post and longitudinal beam (Figure 8.1). Some of the huts exceeded twelve meters or forty feet in length and inside each was a hearth. The huts, which have been dated to 380,000–400,000 years ago, were populated by another now-extinct species *Homo heidelbergensis*.[3]

A third example of early architectural thinking can be found in the travertine cave of Abric Romani, which lies above the Spanish town of Capellades, forty-five kilometers west of Barcelona. A multitude of artifacts have been found there but perhaps the most interesting are the excavations carried out in level N, which revealed, in the area of the cave designated as a sleeping area, the imprint of a large timber post, presumed to be part of a lean-to structure built against the rear wall of the cave. Inside were five hearths, 1.3 meters apart, around which 4–6 family members likely gathered.[4] Vegetal deposits reveal what are believed to be the remnants of grass beds, suggesting a cozy cave community inhabited sometime around 55,000 years ago. The cave was settled by Neanderthals, our sister species who likely split off from our lineage—as DNA evidence suggests—more than 500,000 years ago.

Vitruvius informs us that the Phrygians, in his day, carved trenches in natural hillocks and topped them with cones composed of rods, straw, and stripped branches. The Massilians built their huts from swamp reeds, earth, and clay. He also noted that human society began only with the control of fire.[5] In the last observation (as likely with the others), the Roman architect was both perceptive and likely correct.

II.

One of the more frequently voiced platitudes regarding our species is that we are by nature "social animals." The phrase is generally attributed to Aristotle, although his specific locution— *zōon politikon*—suggests to some a different reading.[6] The ambiguity resides in the fact that the Greek language had no word for "social" and *politikon* refers to the city or *polis*. Nevertheless, the idea has been repeated endlessly, although it is only in the last few centuries that people have reflected on what it really means to be "social." Charles Darwin is often cited as an authority in this regard, but he, interestingly, prefaced his remarks by noting that almost all animals are social.[7] Bees and termites, for example, live in highly complex social organizations. Smaller fish often swim alongside others in schools. Prairie voles and many birds mate for life, at a much higher rate of success (one should add) than humans. What, then, does it really mean to say that humans are social? What does the appellation really mean?

Darwin struggled with this question. On the one hand, he was quite catholic in that he attributed selected social instincts to many animals, such as a sense of beauty or love toward one another, sympathy, friendship, and faithfulness. He even allowed dogs the possibility of having a conscience, a belief that many dog lovers would not dispute today. On the other hand, he noted that humans possess an attribute that other animals do not have, which is a "moral sense." Yet how and when did this come about? At what point in our evolution did humans come to cultivate the ethical skills to appraise our social behaviors? To what extent did our large brains contribute to these skills? Are our social consciences embedded in instincts, or what biologists today might call genetic adaptations? Or is our sociality rooted in our culture, environment, or history, and if so how?

Wrapping around these questions, for architects at least, is another and more intriguing enigma. When did the first human, in a Laugierian moment of inspiration, raise four columns and connect them with horizontal branches and a gable roof? By some accounts at least, Adam's house in paradise (as Joseph Rykwert has referred to it) has been seen as the moment when culture was born, the moment when "natural man"—to use an old locution— became a man of reason.[8] Did it come about through some internal biological factor, such as the growth of the prefrontal cortex, or was it just a moment of enlightenment that, like Athena, sprang from the head of Zeus? Such a quandary, as we suggested earlier, is really born in that false dichotomy between nature and nurture, biology and culture, a distinction that still today haunts many discussions. There was likely no such biological moment, just as there was no such cultural moment. The web of relationships that make us human and are manifested in our sociality lay deeper in our ancestral past, as were the architects of the first huts. As social animals, we, like our mammalian cousins the Prairie voles, have always been mutually implicated in each other's existence, but what lessons does this hold for the architect? How does the built environment modulate our sociality?

If one consults almost any archaeological textbook of a few decades ago, the pages describing our cultural development were inevitably skewed toward descriptions of hand axes and stone points. And if one considers the Acheulean period of hand axe manufacture in particular (1.76 million to 200,000 years ago), one would have to conclude that hominin cognitive powers barely budged over these 1.56 million years. Today we have devised better methods to measure the growth and development of human cognition, defined not by the narrow technological parameters but rather in social and cultural terms. Our understanding of the human genome, for instance, allows us to define evolutionary timelines with much greater precision. We are beginning to understand what parts of the brain were expanding at which points in time. We are also learning when the spacing of the certain vertebrae permitted nerves to control tongue and breath movements—giving one the capacity to vocalize sound articulation. Social anthropologists today, based on models of caloric intake and the reduction of "gut" size, can postulate how changes in the diet allowed the metabolic energy to be diverted from the digestive tract to what is now the most energy-consumptive organ of the human body—the brain. The uptake of all developments has been a revision of the old story that we used to refer to as the "human revolution." No longer do we compress our cultural development to the past 50,000 years.

The genetic lines of the great apes and humans parted ways sometime between sixteen and eight million years ago, and only in the last six million years did the human branch of the evolutionary line began to move out of the tropical forests of central Africa and become active in the surrounding, less wooded savannahs. Two early hominin lines, *Ardipithecus ramidus* (Ardi) and *Australopithecus afarensis* (Lucy), have been found in East Africa. Ardi lived around 4.4 million years ago, but Lucy, a species that appeared around 3.85 million years ago, is the more interesting.[9] Whereas Ardi moved through trees with all four limbs and walked semi-upright on the ground, Lucy—as footprints preserved in volcanic ash of Tanzania demonstrate—had taken an important evolutionary turn. Her facial features may have been apelike, but she knew how to move about on two legs and how to use bones to scrape flesh from prey. She was also small in stature, scarcely more than a meter in height, and likely slept in trees.

The appearance of *Homo erectus* around two million years ago, with a human facial structure and body proportions, is a good place to start a cultural timeline. The species, with a cranial capacity almost double that of the Australopithecus lineage, had sufficiently formidable social skills to cross bodies of water and mountain ranges and migrate out of Africa. Early fossils of African *Homo erectus* indicate that its members had a large muscular build and lived entirely on the ground. The male was tall, later in this species' development approaching male height today, and the structure of his legs and hips allowed him to run as well as or better than athletes today. He lived in larger social groups and hunted, had better weapons, and operated within a much-expanded spatial range. The fact that this species (in various permutations) migrated to many parts of the world (Europe and Southeast Asia) speaks volumes to its adaptability and evolutionary success. Skull capacity was still smaller than modern humans, but fossils display smaller teeth, indicating a shift in dietary habits. And when we take into account the much larger body mass, smaller gut size, and significantly larger brain capacity, we are left with another question. What factor or combination of factors fueled these anatomical changes?

In the mid-1990s Leslie Aiello and Peter Wheeler addressed the problem of larger brains and encephalization with their "Expensive-Tissue Hypothesis."[10] In order to grow a larger brain, which consumes about 20 percent of our energy production, they point out that the body had to shed the large intestinal tract it inherited from our primate ancestors to offset the energy consumption of the brain, and this reduction was only possible through the introduction of high protein, easy-to-digest foods such as tubers and meat. Richard Wrangham has made a strong case that these changes entailed combining these foods with the introduction of cooking. Meat and high nutritional vegetables, he notes, are good protein sources, but cooking allows a gelatinization and denaturation of starches and proteins, which eases digestion by making foods more accessible to the activity of enzymes. Cooking enhances the metabolic absorption rate of nutrition with greater intestinal efficiency, allowing the larger stomach and intestinal tract of vegetarian primates to decrease in size. Cooking also offers other survival advantages, among them a greater diversity of potential food sources, a longer period of preservation, defense against pathogens, and even enhanced bodily energy that would have allowed shorter birth intervals.[11]

Cooking, moreover, requires a controlled use of fire, for which there is little hard evidence before the last 500,000 years—although there is sporadic evidence of fire's use as early as 1.5 million years ago, suggesting that tribes of *Homo erectus* acquired at least a partial control of fire. Gathering around a fire, of course, has its architectural and social implications. Not only does some kind of shelter, natural or otherwise, assist in igniting and sustaining a fire, but the conjunction of cooking and eating is fundamentally a social activity. Humans, almost alone in the animal world, share their meals together.

The early use of cooking is also supported by the biological evidence that the human brain, among other primates, today seems particularly well adapted to appreciate the smells, tastes, temperature, and textures of foods, which points to a long evolutionary run. Morten Kringelbach has noted that most mammals cease eating when the necessary nutrition is obtained to maintain homeostasis, but this is not the case with humans. When humans eat, it activates the integrative powers of the orbitofrontal cortex, which is the processing station for the pleasure circuit. Here the sensory stimuli of gustatory and olfactory sensations interact with other sensory processing areas and release endorphins into the bloodstream. Eating in combination with social interaction (another human pastime that stirs opioid activity) only enhances this feeling of pleasure, sometimes to the point where we overeat.[12]

Meat eating also worked in unison with advancing bipedalism, through which we acquired the fluid gait and territorial expansion necessary to forage in African savannahs. Bipedalism no doubt came about as Lucy and other earlier species made the ecological transition from the shaded forests, but stepping out into the sun carries with it another biological issue. If early hominins had continued to walk on all fours, there would have been a buildup of heat stress from the greater exposure to sunlight. The upright carriage, which reduced bodily areas exposed to direct sunlight, neatly solved this problem.[13] Bipedalism also allowed hominins to run greater distances with much improved caloric efficiency, and running in turn demanded greater sensorimotor control, which in itself required an enlargement of motor areas of the brain. With bipedalism, the arms, and in particular the hands, lost their original locomotive function and adapted to grasping tools and weapons. Now we have the development of different coordinate systems, such as body centered, head/eye centered, and rotational arm/hand systems, which required a further expansion of the parietal lobe. As the neuroscientist Atsushi Iriki has noted, bipedalism, with its cognitive demand for an enlarged body schema, allowed not only the expansion of perceptual space into temporal space (coordinating the throwing of a spear, for instance, at a moving animal) but also, eventually, an objectification of the self.[14]

Still another implication of the upright carriage was that it permitted the dropping of the larynx and the lengthening of the vocal tract—both of which were facilitated by the greater need for communication among hominins. To what extent did they communicate with one another after the chase, when they sat around a fire and enjoyed their meal? Did they gesture to each other or engage in such activities as chanting, beating a drum, or simply laughing? Just how old are these social behaviors?

When *Homo erectus* acquired a protolanguage remains a much-debated issue today. The fact that this species hunted in groups and challenged large animals indicates that they had some kind of protolanguage (gestural or vocal), one that allowed the joint intentionality of action needed to coordinate these activities tactically and strategically. Michael Arbib, in drawing upon the discovery of mirror-neuron systems, has built a model of gradual linguistic development from imitation (*mimesis* or the body's metric movements) to gestural pantomime, protosigns, and protospeech. In his view, *Homo erectus* was capable of employing strings of syllables or "unitary utterances"—that is, patterns of sounds capable of encoding complex descriptions such as coordinating an attack or celebrating the fact that an animal has been slain for the evening meal.[15] Similarly, Alison Wray sees the development of language as a "holistic" event, and argues that *Homo erectus* likely had an expanded and "complex inventory of functional exchanges." The species thereby made the transition from noise and gesture to phonetic sequences with specific meanings.[16]

Whatever the eventual outcome of these debates, the growth of the brain of *Homo erectus* during its evolution endowed its members with considerable cognitive powers—as the settlement at Bilzingsleben indicates. Some anthropologists have credited the minds of later members of *Homo erectus* (brains larger than 900cc) with possessing the third order of intentionality, which means that individuals had the mental power to believe that someone else has a belief about another's belief, which is not their own belief. Researchers have also suggested that *Homo erectus* was the first species to acquire the human capacity to laugh, which prepares the way to speech because laughing requires the lung to sustain long uninterrupted exhalations. Apes laugh, but because of their skeletal frame they cannot do without intermediate inhalations. Group laughter in humans has been explained as a way for groups to bond together through the opioid mechanisms that respond to such behaviors—in effect, laughter is a form of social "grooming-at-a-distance."[17]

With the advent of *Homo heidelbergensis* or the *Heidelbergs* sometime after 700,000 years ago—likely ancestors to *Homo sapiens*—social relations became more complex (Figure 8.2). The brain size of the *Heidelbergs* grew within the range of modern humans, and owing to their name (fossils first found near Heidelberg) we know they migrated out of Africa into Europe and parts of Asia. Their communities, as Terra Amata demonstrates, were larger (by some estimates climbing to 125 people) and they were more complex in their social organization and division of labor. With this species, we likely have the start of trade among distant communities and therefore the formation of cultural interchange between tribes. Locally, and beginning around 500,000 years ago, we have widespread evidence of communal hearths, which indicates a complete mastery of fire.

Anatomical evidence is amassing that the *Heidelbergs* possessed an enhanced capacity for vocalization or speech. The hyoid bone, a horseshoe-shaped bone that sits atop the larynx and controls the movement of

Homo erectus	Homo heidelbergensis	Homo sapiens
Enlarged brain, joint intentionality, hunting skills, cooked meat, greater range of hunting, handaxes, empathy, protolanguage, laughter, use of ochre	Larger social groups, near-sapiens brain size, division of labor, communal hearths, mentalizing, likely music, dance, song, figurines, clothing	Collective intentionality, syntactical language, burials, writing, agriculture, mathematics, cumulative cultural evolution

Homo erectus
2 Million to 143,000 years ago

Homo heidelbergensis
700,000 to 200,000 years ago

Homo sapiens
300,000 years ago

FIGURE 8.2 *Cultural timeline.*

the tongue (a bone that was in a higher location with *Homo erectus*) falls dramatically between the appearance of *Heidelbergs* and the later evolution of Neanderthal and humans. Such a drop permitted a wider and more nuanced range of the vocal sounds necessary for speech. Also around this time, neural circuits within the thoracic regions were evolving to support vocal intonation. The hypoglossal canal at the base of the skull, allowing nerves to control the tongue, mouth, and facial expression, was approaching human size and positioning around 300,000 years ago.[18] Relatedly, the shells of the outer and middle ear, which endow humans with a high sensitivity to the pitch of speech sounds, have recently been shown to exist in early Neanderthals (possibly with *Heidelbergs* as well) some 350,000 years ago.[19]

If speech among the *Heidelbergs* was moving toward the range of human vocalization, so must have other aspects of their social behavior—such as song, dance, and making rhythmic music. Steven Mithen has argued that these behaviors began with later members of *Homo erectus* and advanced with the *Heidelbergs*. Music and rhythm would therefore seem to be deeply encoded in the human genome because the neural networks for processing the two are widely distributed throughout the brain. Moreover, music in a certain sense may have an evolutionary priority to language, in that babies are sensitive to the rhythms, tempos, and melodies of "baby-talk" long before they are able to understand the meaning of words. Mithen believes that the exaggerated prosody or higher pitch and hyperarticulated vowels and pauses—universally used by adults in their communications with infants—are, at heart, a melodic means to modulate social relationships and emotional states.[20]

The propensity for dance among the *Heidelbergs* is likely, if only because the skeletal and muscular athleticism of this species was comparable, if not superior, to our own. Walking upright in itself introduces rhythmic patterns, which can be translated to other aspects of behavior. Psychologists and ethologists have for many years stressed the primal nature of ceremonial and ritualistic behavior in humans, but what is changing today is that many people are locating the start of these behaviors not with modern humans but with our more distant ancestors.

Merlin Donald, for instance, has made the most sustained argument in this regard by noting that rhythmic dance and other forms of "kinematic imagination" (imitation, gesticulation, pantomime, and complex bodily skills) could have appeared as much as two million years ago with the beginning of the *Homo* genus. Kinematic imagination is the ability to see one's body as a medium for action or as a communication device expressing itself through the articulation of rhythms. Children, even today, eagerly learn the kinematic skills of skipping a rope or bouncing a ball, and these mimetic social games were also the basis for the early arts of song, music, dance, and other ritualistic behaviors. Donald refers to kinematic imagination as a "supramodal" skill, and one of the characteristics distinguishing hominins from other species is the ability to rehearse, refine, and invent new movements. He calls this phase of development "mimetic culture."[21]

With the *Heidelbergs* we also have the question of whether they possessed an aesthetic sensibility. Ovate hand axes and diamond spear points are common archaeological artifacts going back to the earliest *Homo* lines, but several examples—from Boxgrove (500,000 years ago) and elsewhere—are notable for their nearly perfect symmetry and the delicate way in which they are fashioned. Some artifacts, in fact, seemed to have been made simply as aesthetic objects and were never used. The quality of many of hand axes at the very least testifies to a high level of manual skill and a strong early-human instinct for craftsmanship. These efforts extend well beyond simple functionality.[22]

Another archaeological find of great importance are the eight wooden javelins and spears unearthed in Schöningen, Germany, which date from around 400,000 years ago. Once again, the quality of their manufacture is their outstanding feature. Most were carved from trunks of spruce trees, notched in places and carefully shaped, with the tips located in the hardest wood at the base of the trunks. The javelins are over seven feet in length and have a frontal center of gravity for maximum distance and accuracy. They were used for killing large animals but they also demonstrate a capacity for abstraction and a craft-like attention to design, detailing, and execution.

The Ice Age cave paintings of France and Spain that begin to appear around 35,000 years ago are spectacular in their artistry, but they do not define the beginning of art, which more than likely took root and developed with these earlier species. There are indications that nonutilitarian or aesthetic behaviors in Africa may go well into the middle Pleistocene era.[23] The Tan-Tan figurine found in Morocco, likely natural but incised with groves and painted red, is estimated to be around 300,000 years old.[24] The Berekhat Ram Figurine, taken from a site on the Golan Heights, is dated to between 250,000 and 280,000 years ago. It is engraved to demarcate the head and arms and is deemed by recent investigators to be "a purposely modified object, of possibly iconic or symbolic meaning, and not qualitatively different from more recent examples of symbolic expression."[25]

Thus, when Adam and Eve made their appearance in East Africa, much of the heavy lifting, in evolutionary terms, had already been done. For many years the date of this event was deemed to be around 200,000 years ago, but a recent discovery of *Homo sapiens* fossils in Jebel Irhoud, Morocco, dates to 300,000 years—once again upending earlier evolutionary models.[26] The Sahara site, during this geological era, was not a desert but supported some vegetation, and the shape of the skull defines it as an intermediate stage between more archaic shapes of other *Homo* species and the globular forms of modern *Homo sapiens*.[27] Obviously much remains to be uncovered of our evolutionary past, but it is clear that our roots and cultural development, even at its earlier stages, took place over large tracts of Africa and likely other continents.

The strong cultural development that begins around 130,000 years ago similarly took place in different locations. A major site of early human activity is the Blombos cave on the south coast of Africa (Figure 8.3). Its artifacts date between 70,000 and 100,000 years ago, and include over 8,000 pieces of ochre together with the remnants of an ochre processing workshop, engraved stone and bone implements, marine shell beads used in a necklace, 500 facial points (again executed with exquisite symmetry), and faunal remains of fish, birds, tortoise and ostrich egg shells. The ochre workshop is interesting because the way the ochre was processed suggests an elementary knowledge of chemistry. Ochre blocks were mined from a distant site (thirty-five kilometers away), transported to the cave, then crushed, liquefied, and stored in large abalone shells. The elements of the tool kit included bone instruments, charcoal, grindstones, and hammer stones.[28] Two of the ochre pieces, however, are perhaps the most important artifacts found in recent times, because they were engraved with geometric patterns suggesting a symbolic way of thinking.[29] Excavations are still ongoing and similar artifacts have also been found in other areas along the South African coastline.

If we return to the question of when hominin social behaviors and an aesthetic sense first became manifest, the answer will never be given with certainty. Yet an intriguing thesis has recently been advanced by the anthropologist Polly Wiessner, drawing upon her lengthy stay with the Ju/'hoan Bushmen of southern Africa and supplemented by sixty-eight translated texts. If the daytime conversations of these societies generally focus on gossip or the economic

FIGURE 8.3 *Blombos cave, ochre, and artifacts. Photo by Chris Henshilwood. Permission: CC-BY-2.5; Release under GNU free documentation license.*

issues of social relationships, nighttime activities around the fire inevitably tend toward singing, dancing, religious ceremonies, and above all storytelling. A bright fire reduces the production of melatonin and allows the release of pent-up energy. The night light dims the body language of others and reduces the awareness of the self. Telling stories around a fire, she concludes, tends to focus on the "big picture" of human culture and draws out human imagination. Such activities bond social groups and likely generated the first cultural institutions.[30] In view of the evidence that is amassing, we can conclude that our sociality, which extends back at least several million years, likely took birth not so much in the Aristotelian or rationalist notion of *polis* than in the human capacity for *poiēsis*—the narrational chirping around the embers of the first firelights.

III.

Our greater certainty with regard to our evolutionary timelines and early behavioral patterns nevertheless still leaves us with many outstanding questions. A few million years may seem like a long time for change to take place, but from the perspective of natural selection this time span does not account for the many social and cultural skills that humans have acquired. The first theories of gene-culture coevolution in the late 1970s sought to address this problem, but what was initially lacking was a plausible model of human cognitive development, one that could account for our unique modes of biological and cultural transmission.

The lack of such a model, in turn, raised a number of other issues beyond the human timeline. For instance, what specifically are the cognitive and cultural abilities that distinguish humans from other primates, who too have been evolving over the last several million years? How did our different cognitive-cultural conditioning work together with our biological development? If physical factors such as bipedalism facilitated anatomical, neural, and cognitive changes, how did social and cultural behaviors accelerate or take advantage of these changes? Why did the human brain, alone among all existing mammalian species, achieve to the level of complexity that it did? Many theorists of a generation ago, with their shorter human timeline, assumed that it was the development of language that led to these great spurts of brain growth, but it is now clear that significant cognitive and social alterations in the brain far preceded the development of language.

Designers build habitats in which people live, work, play, and think, and it is imperative that we understand in some depth the biological and cultural dimensions of the people for whom we design. A good place to begin is with the 1.36-kilogram or 3-pound organ of the brain itself, which at any given moment has 15 percent of the body's blood flowing through its veins. It is, as we have seen, "expensive tissue" for the body to support, and early explanations tended to view its size as a compensating factor in service to our survival. Because we were smaller animals lacking the teeth of a hyena, the speed of a big cat, or the bulk strength of a wooly mammoth—so the explanation went—we needed a big brain to outthink their competitors. But where did these larger brains come from in the first place?

For several years, explanations ranged from epiphenomenal ones (larger brains are secondary consequence of larger bodies), to developmental ones (longer maternal metabolic input leads to fetal brain growth), or ecological ones (dietary changes and extractive foraging), but none by itself offered a satisfactory explanation. In 1998 Robin Dunbar put forth the proposition that socialization played the major role in the growth and development of the brain—that is, the larger brain grew out of the need for hominins to deal with expanding social groups as well as the mental exigencies of managing these relationships.[31] What was different in his proposal, however, was a viable explanation of why this was the case. In plotting social variables across different primate species, Dunbar was able to come up with a correlation of brain size with the group size of their communities, and in working backward with the current size of the human brain, he came up with the number 150, now known as "Dunbar's number." It is the predicted social circle of most humans—that is, the number of people with which we can maintain extended contact, given the size of our brains. Effectively, Dunbar turned conventional evolutionary theory on its head with the argument that we are by nature first and foremost social animals, and the social complexity of dealing with our families, friends, enemies, clans, and larger social alliances is what compelled the brain to grow its cognitive powers. More recently archaeological, material, and ecological factors have been drawn into the social-brain hypothesis, as well as such factors as human emotion.[32]

To follow up on this last point, Dunbar, in his earlier work with other primates, had placed much emphasis on the social role of grooming in their societies. The great apes, for instance, spend a considerable portion of the day grooming one another, which has to be worked into the competitive demands of foraging, resting, and eating. Why do apes groom one another in the first place? One answer is that grooming, in addition to its sanitary benefits, plays an important role in fashioning group cohesion and maintaining the hierarchical community order. Grooming is also a pleasurable event that releases endorphins. As hominin communities expanded and moved into the savannahs, they were less able to sustain this practice. Foraging and hunting expeditions could extend for days or even weeks, and there would have been little time or occasion for individual grooming. Changes in the social structure, such as pair-bonding, parental relationships, friendships, and tribal associations may have partially offset this emotional loss, but other social activities such as laughter, song, and dance allowed a kind of grooming at a distance. Simply sitting around a fire and enjoying a meal together increases group cohesion and feelings of concern toward one another. Dunbar refers to these behaviors as "amplifying" activities because they evoke strong emotional responses, release endorphins, create memories, and reinforce the sense of belonging to the group.[33] Language, religion, and storytelling were but later manifestations of these emotional expressions.

Although Michael Tomasello shares the socialization thesis in common with Dunbar, he came to the issue from a different perspective. The focus of his research has been the cognitive development of both children and primates—importantly, the distinctions between the two. And if Desmond Morris had viewed us as hairless apes in many of our behaviors, Tomasello adds a few disconcerting brush strokes to this portrait. Humans indeed may share many of the behavioral patterns of other primates, but they also have one cognitive adaptation that did not evolve elsewhere within the primate world, which is our ability to see other members of our species as intentional beings with mental lives similar to our own. How did this cognitive adaptation come about? Tomasello argues that it arose early, likely with the appearance of *Homo erectus* around two million years ago. It may have been competition with other primate species or the ecological changes of moving into the savannahs and hunting big game in large parties. This small step in collaborative efforts nevertheless had huge ramifications, because we began to engage in various forms of imitative, instructive, and collaborative learning.

One example is the gesture of pointing. Children acquire the skill around one year of age, but primates in the wild never acquire it.[34] Chimpanzees have never developed the motivation to collaborate beyond such basic self-directed instincts as grooming or begging for food. With the *Heidelbergs* came the more sophisticated communicative tools of pantomime or iconic signs, which required a new type of social thinking invoking representation, inference, and self-monitoring. They constituted in effect the middle communicative stage between pointing and language.

And with the beginning of our species around 300,000 years ago, we have the shift to collective intentionality, whereby skills are transmitted diachronically. Language was certainly a major step in this process, but Tomasello stresses that cognitive changes were driven with by a greater need for social cooperation, such as the establishment of cultural norms, group or tribal identifications, conformity, teaching, and the founding of collective institutions. These changes allowed the development of what he terms the "ratchet effect" of social-cultural transmission, the fact that humans alone can take the creative inventions and modifications of each generation and pass them down to the next for use and improvement.[35] In this way individual efforts are continuously enhanced by the processes of sociogenesis, or collaborative cultural invention. As Tomasello describes the matter, "Cumulative cultural evolution led to a plethora of culturally specific cognitive skills and types of thinking," but these ways of thinking were at the same time "built upon universal cognitive processes" that are then manifested in individual cultures.[36]

Others have weighed in on the issue. Kim Sterelny's "apprentice" model of cross-generational cultural learning, for instance, parallels the work of Tomasello by placing the idea of "trust" within the context of niche construction. "We have long been niche constructors, acting on our environment," he notes, "and as a consequence altering the costs and benefits of different actions at and across generations. Investments in relationships is a form of niche construction, one available to ancient hominins and one that can help explain trust."[37] His model also emphasizes how humans structure and modify their environments, enacting as it were coevolutionary positive feedback loops of information sharing.

Donald has also proposed a model of cognitive cultural staging. The phase of mimetic culture, which we saw earlier, was succeeded by "mythic" culture around 500,000 years ago, as hominins and early humans began to acquire the rudiments of language, build crude shelters with hearths, adorn themselves, and bury the dead. This phase was in turn succeeded by "theoretic" culture beginning around 50,000 years ago, where we have the "externalization of memory" through art and the introduction of writing. Today the prodigious growth of external memory devices, such as computers, has pushed our neurological or cognitive development into a phase of what he terms "superplasticity." Just as the symbolizing cultures of the past altered the wiring of the human brain, so will today's "deep enculturation" have a profound effect on human attention and emotions.[38]

What is undisputed today, however, is that our social cognition resides at the very core of our being, as it has evolved over millions of years. More pertinent to designers—if one were asked to single out the most obvious failing of architectural theory in the late twentieth century, one might respond that it was the lack of appreciation for the depth of our social natures and the role that the built and cultural environments play in shaping it.

IV.

The new developmental models that we discussed in Chapter 3 bring another dimension to our social evolution with their emphasis on the behavior and growth of the developing brain. The human organism more generally, rather than being specified by genetic programs, is continuously being reconstructed over the course of a life and therefore across generations. Influences within these processes are genes interacting on other genes, the agency of hormones, epigenetic factors such as maternal and later social contact, and a host of cultural and environmental factors. In essence, the human organism is continually being modified by the factors of inheritance, learning, aging, and changing states of health. The timing of these interactions is paramount. Much of the research regarding social cognition has today shifted the focus from the cultural imperatives of the past to the earliest stages of brain development in the womb and early childhood. These are the stages at which environmental and behavioral effects on the brain and our later social relations are most pronounced.

From the moment of conception to a full-term delivery, the human embryo and fetus is highly sensitive to its surroundings, and normal development depends on a tight sequence of events or windows of development. In the earliest stages of embryogenesis, for example, cells are created and divide, and the rudiments of organs are formed. Exposure to toxic chemicals and pollutants, as we have long known, can disrupt this process with severe long-term consequences. At three months, the fetus begins to share hormonal (prolactin and oxytocin), physiological (touch, smell, heart rhythms), and emotional bonds with its mother—a process that is generally referred to as synchrony. Four-dimensional ultrasonography demonstrates that twins within the womb reach out to each other with motoric intention beginning in the fourteenth week of gestation—a social relationship that continues to develop in subsequent months.[39] During this period, the types of food the mother eats, the chemicals she ingests, the stress hormones that infiltrate the amniotic fluid—all affect the course of growth. Around the eighteenth week of gestation, the fetus begins to hear sounds, and by the seventh month the fetus responds to voices outside of the womb. Around this time, the olfactory receptors and taste buds also become functional. During the stress of labor large amounts of the hormone oxytocin are released into the mother's and child's blood stream, priming each to seek contact with one other.

Neonates, only hours out of the womb, preferentially look at faces over other stimuli, and quite naturally prefer to look at their mother's face over the faces of strangers. Infants are sensitive to other babies crying, to the pitch, intensity, and temporal structure of speech, and prefer human voices to nonsocial stimuli. The basis of their socialization, however, is conditioned in large part by the mother. Already at birth, the mother continues the process of synchronization with the infant through eye-to-eye contact, high-pitched vocalization, and a tactile give-and-take between mother and child.[40] Ruth Feldman defines synchrony as the capacity to engage in temporally matched interactions, "based on physiological mechanisms, in particular oscillator systems, such as biological clock and cardiac pacemakers, and attachment-related hormones, such as oxytocin."[41] Effectively, the newborn is learning the rhythmic structure of another person and modifying behavior to fit this intensely personal relationship. The pace, physiological rhythms, and arousal contours of these social exchanges not only facilitate the infant's self-regulation (autonomic reactivity) but also lay the foundation for the child's eventual capacity for intimacy, sense of self, and empathy toward others.[42]

Colwyn Trevarthen reports that in the infant's first few weeks there is already a "rhythmic purposeful consciousness" manifested in expressive acts of imitation, an up-and-running "inner autopoetic, self-making process."[43] An important part of social development is touch and song. Touch, in the first six months, conveys warmth and tactile stimulation, draws the infant's attention, improves maternal adaptation, and bonds the infant with the mother's smiles and vocalization. It also predicts neurobehavioral development, and even shapes the "electrical activity" of each individual's brain.[44]

Songs or lullabies contribute to synchrony in a similar way, only now by cultivating networks receptive to sound and the voice modulations of songs. Mothers and adults generally speak to infants with a high-pitched voice modulated in wide ranges and the use of hyperarticulated vowels, short phrases, pauses, and liberal repetition. Sometimes referred to as prosody, this is entirely a cross-cultural phenomenon and is multimodal in the sense that these interactions between mother and child are not just vocal but performed with facial and tactile give-and-takes. Stephen Malloch refers to these interactions as "communicative musicality" and regards them as the social foundation on which coordinated companionship arise.[45] Anne Fernald notes that this bonding process with a newborn child goes through four distinctive stages. Initially, with neonates, music serves as an auditory stimulus and orientational focus bonding the mother and child, and within a few weeks it becomes an attentional, arousal, and emotional modulator. In the third phase, prosody begins to communicate the intentions and feelings of the mother, and lastly, around fourteen months, its serves as an acoustic highlighting of words, as the child begins to acquire the skill of language.[46]

Trevarthen emphasizes how the "amphoteronomic" or the rhythmic co-regulation of the vital states of the fetus in the mother's womb allows the child to be "born for art."[47] Ellen Dissanayake has made the case that the vocal and rhythmic exaggerations of "baby talk" ingrain within the infant the essential "rhythms" and "modes" that later manifest themselves in both human love and the arts.[48] More recently, she has made the case that "in interactions between ancestral mothers and infants—simplification or formalization, repetition, exaggeration, elaboration (and, for older infants, manipulation of their expectation, or surprise) of simultaneous vocal, visual, and kinesic expressions—are the origins of the capacities later used by humans in making and responding to music."[49]

A more overtly musical expression of this behavior, of course, is the lullaby and play song, whose universal use is finely tuned to the infant's ability and mood and has important attentional and affective consequences.[50] Lullabies before bedtime, for instance, are sung with a slow tempo, low pitch, falling pitch contours, and with a soothing tone of voice. Other types of maternal songs, however, can be sung to entertain, make the infant smile, gurgle, and laugh, or facilitate feeding and learning. They have been shown in many ways to have a highly beneficial effort on overall brain growth and development; in fact some have argued that these social interactions are vital because they begin the process of growing and sculpting the cortical and subcortical regions of the brain. At birth, the brain is the least developed organ and is only about 25 percent of its eventual size. Its neurological circuits are minimally formed and mainly limited to sensory areas, although the primal default social network is up and running with infants as early as two weeks after birth.[51]

The period beginning with the last trimester and continuing to twenty-four months of age is one of prodigious neuronal growth, myelination, and synaptic development. This growth is particularly strong in the right hemisphere where, according to Allan Schore, "the cortical and subcortical systems of the infant's right brain become tuned to dynamic self-organization upon perceiving certain patterns of exteroceptive social information, namely, the visual, auditory, and tactile stimuli emanating from the smiling, joyful, soothing, and calming face as well as the expressive body of a loving mother."[52] Limbic structures come online early. The amygdala is active at birth but only eight weeks later does the anterior cingulate cortex begin to mature; it coordinates play and separation behaviors, stimulates affective vocalizations, and aligns these activities with the autonomic systems. The orbitofrontal cortex, which is central to the development of the pleasure circuit, control of behavior, and affect-related meanings, undergoes a critical period of maturation around nine months of age, one that is largely conditioned by earlier social attachment.[53]

The social brain, of course, continues to develop throughout childhood and major changes also take place during the teenage years. The human brain is not fully formed until the mid-twenties, and circuits continue to be rewired (neural plasticity) throughout one's life in the unfolding of social relationships—all of which raises two important questions for designers. What can architects learn from this better understanding of our social natures? What role does the physical environment play within this socialization process?

From a developmental perspective, social and environmental relationships in fact are very much interconnected. If today's developmental models suggest that culture is not a fixed body of transmitted knowledge imported into the mind of the newborn, but a set of social skills generated anew by each generation and continually being modified over the course of a life—then sociality is not an activity imparted to the organism from without but something conditioned by the totality of environmental conditions within. Social relationships cannot be divorced from environmental relations, and environmental factors necessarily affect social development.

We earlier cited research on environmental and social deprivation in early life, and their aberrant consequences for both brain growth and social development were remarkably similar. One of the more shocking demonstrations of this fact is the case of 170,000 Romanian orphans reared during the communist regime of Nicolae Ceaucescu in deplorable architectural surroundings with severe overcrowding, lack of nutrition, inadequate toilet and wash facilities, little or no human contact or schooling. Many of the orphans released after the fall of the government displayed severe physical, mental, and social retardation.[54] By contrast, enriched environments, as numerous studies have also shown, increase cellular development in the brain, stimulate sensory, cognitive, and motor functions, reduce levels of anxiety, enhance memory, and cultivate social relationships.[55]

Such studies would suggest that we should give special attention to environmental factors in early childhood development and later to the physical design of school environments. Of course, social development (its growth or deterioration) does not stop with adulthood. Environmentally degraded urban areas have long shown to be correlated with poor health, drug and alcohol abuse, crime, violence, and other destructive social behaviors. It is time to recognize the fact that the blight and excessive hardscapes found in so many of our dilapidated urban centers, as well as in isolated rural areas, border on inhumane environments, and are in need of major interventions. What are the environmental standards fit for human occupation?

Another thing that we can learn from our sociality and its development is the need to shift design attention away from the abstractions of the anonymous "occupant" and toward a better understanding of our fragile humanity and social interconnectedness. The human organism is not a passive respondent to the characteristics of the environment, but an active agent who seeks information and constructs social relationships in a meaningful way. Such a recognition would entail a deeper probing of social aspects our human natures, such as the reach or extent of our artistic impulse, the human penchant for ritualization, gestures, and play, the cultivation of beauty and sense of community, and above all a shared cultural ethos under which we all can prosper.

9

Ritualization and the Ethos of Design

Restoring the practical nature of situations as a primary vehicle of design enables us to move away from inconclusive play with abstract forms and functions.

DALIBOR VEZELY[1]

Several years ago, I spent an academic year in Paris working by day in Henri Labrouste's reading room at the old Bibliothéque Nationale. Once a week, along my walk home, I made a stop at the abbey church of Saint Germain des Prés to listen to an early-evening performance of a classical trio or quartet. The recitals were free and open to the public, the musicians young and talented. The acoustics were superb and the audience small. One could sit only a few feet away from the performers and this proximity transformed the event into something special. Perhaps the most compelling part of the recital was the interplay among the musicians, the give-and-take between the instruments, the fingers pressing down tightly on the strings or keyboard, the pauses of instruments between passages, the furtive eye-contact with one another, the occasional glance at a spectator, and, of course, the parts of the performance working perfectly in unison. Music was the bond that cemented this small community of two dozen or so listeners, but it was social nature of the playful event that stood out. Theories of embodied simulation suggest that as I was watching the performance, my mirror circuits were simulating the movements of the arms, hands, and feet, the rhythmic swaying of the bodies, and the pauses that gave relief to the straining muscles of the fingers. In this sense, I myself was bodily partaking in the musical ritual, as were the others present. Music was almost secondary to the social, aural, and kinesthetic sharing of the performance.

Aspects of ritual were readily apparent in other ways. The violins, cellos, and pianos were not objects of ordinary use but works of art beautifully crafted and shaped by centuries of European culture, universally pleasing to the eye. The postures of the musicians assumed were highly stylized in the way one held a violin bow or sat erect at a keyboard. Clothing was muted and simple. The weekly performances took place in a medieval church rebuilt in the eleventh century, a place designed specifically to house rituals and still emitting that "aura of incense" of which Émile Durkheim spoke. A magic circle was demarcated within an open area of the nave by the chairs surrounding the musicians. This rite of the multisensory performance similarly defined a community and allowed each member to surrender the sense of "self" to the whole. For the audience and musicians, it brought something into existence that was not there previously: delight, vitality effects, and sensory seduction. Emotion, rhythm, special objects, styles, demarcated places, performance, and sense of community—they are the hallmarks of rituals, art, and architecture.

Ritual, the re-enactment of a social bond, has long been a focus of cultural theorists. Ritualized behavior takes us far back into hominin culture, back to the time when the first primate employed a stick to strike a beat on a hollow log or a mother hummed a few sounds to her newborn. Jean Molino sees music, language, dance, chanting, and pretend play as having a common origin in primeval times, growing out of the muscular and neural control of bodily rhythmic movements.[2] Jerome Lewis—in noting that some cultures employ the same word to refer to music making, singing, dancing, and rituals—regards music, or rituals more generally, as central to a group's self-identification. They are "foundational cultural schemas," which, like an architectural style, provide a framework for the collective cultivation of "our aesthetic sense, enjoyment of harmony, desire to cooperate, curiosity, and pleasure-seeking propensities."[3] Ritualization or ritualized behaviors, when seen in this light, are more than learned or occasional behaviors. Socialization is active at the start; it is the foundation upon which rituals and their artistic offspring are constructed, or rather, the means through which socialization manifests itself. The making of music and dance is a bodily expression of the self, but only within the context of existing social body.

Suzanne Langer has characterized dance as "the art of the Stone Age, the act of primitive life par excellence."[4] Dance holds a hegemony over the other arts, she argues, because it is in essence a social gesture. A dancer's body is a "ready for rhythm," a seeking to liberate oneself "from the usual bonds of gravity and muscular inertia."[5] All dance in this way is "ecstatic," a standing outside of oneself, whether it is the tribal dance defining the "magic circle" separating the sacred from the profane or the erotic and magnetizing dance of two partners performing a tango. Dance is more than a spatial relationship between two people, Langer notes: "the forces they exercise, that seem to be as physical as those which orient the compass needle toward its pole, really do not exist physically at all. They are dance forces, virtual power."[6] Dance is the human impulse to translate kinesthetic energy into visible and audible elements of this virtual social relationship.

Music and its rituals also demand a certain primacy among the arts. The psychologist Carol Krumhansl has demonstrated the close connection of musical emotion and the listeners' expectations or anticipation of the musical structure—such as tension and relaxation—and notes that in this way music shares a similar emotional resonance with dance.[7] The structure of classical music, in addition to its keys, has its tempos (*larghetto, andante*, or *allegro*), its qualifiers (*molto* or *non troppo*), and such mood markings as *dolce* or *appassionato*. These figures expand and contract, hasten and retard the time and intensity of the playing, and thereby alter its emotional reception.

Today many psychologists and neuroscientists view music and its rhythms as biological expressions of deeper-lying social and emotional mannerisms extending far back into evolutionary time. Jaak Panksepp and Cowlyn Trevarthen, for instance, speak of musical forms as not only "'embedded' in intersubjective and cultural dynamics" but also something that "evolved as an evolutionary exaptation of social-emotional systems."[8] Ritualized expressions more generally, including the "rhythmic rituals" of gesture and dance, are not unique to humans; they are at least vaguely related to "the instinctive affiliative calls, vocal expressions of passion and displays of intentions in body movement of other highly social animals."[9] Nevertheless, they are part and parcel of our humanity. "Being emotionally controlled," Panksepp and Trevarthen elaborate, "these *other*-within-*self* intersubjective representations establish sympathetic resonances, and intersubjective contagions, probably by intrinsic affective systems situated much lower than the neocortex, making complementary adjustments to the intelligence and feelings expressed in gestures of other bodies and sensed by sight, sound and touch through neocortical processes that are epigenetically programmed by experience."[10]

The classic neuroimaging study of musical rhythms recording the phenomenon of "chills-down-the-spine" was undertaken around the turn of this century. In a scanner, ten participants selected their favorite piece of classical music as their vital signs were monitored. When the chills appeared, researchers found activity in the areas of the brain involved with the pleasure circuit—areas that since have been shown to be active with other euphoric experiences such as romantic love, sex, foods, and social events.[11] The physiological monitors similarly displayed spikes during these rhythmic moments of intense emotional arousal. The body, in effect, responds to these ritualized events by producing a blend of hormones and endorphins. Intensely pleasurable music, within the confines of music hall or rock concert, composes its own symphony of neurochemical changes within the body.

Making or enjoying the arts is in many ways a form of play, an area to which the human or social sciences are again beginning to explore in depth.

Interest in play is not entirely new. Nineteenth-century writers from Herbert Spencer to Ernst Grosse were fascinated with it. William James similarly identified the "play instinct" as the social and aesthetic underpinning of all ritualistic behaviors: "I refer to that love of festivities, ceremonies, ordeals, etc., which seems to be universal in our species."[12] Play, in these social and aesthetic forms, manifests itself in many ways—in tribal dances, religious ceremonies, operas, and masquerades. It was, however, the social dimension of the "organized crowd" of ritualized events that James found particularly intriguing: "The perception of them is the stimulus; and our reaction upon it is our tendency to join them and do what they are doing, and our unwillingness to be the first to leave off and go home alone."[13]

Ellen Dissanayake, in drawing on her anthropological fieldwork in non-Western cultures, makes the case that ritualistic play satisfies our social and emotional natures on multiple levels—that is, by appealing to our inherent sensory and cognitive dispositions, by evoking innate and culturally acquired associations, by using entertaining, tuning, driving, and "build-up" synchronization, and by manipulating our expectations.[14] All of these strategies, it should be noted, are also elements with which the creative designer can modulate. Architecture can exploit our sensory and cognitive dispositions with its striking use of spaces, forms, textures, materials, light, and color—their energetic and complementary relationships. Its dynamic rhythms of form can be fitted with cultural dressings instantly recognized by all. Good design can entertain by tuning, driving, and building up emotional intensity as one moves though a room or an urban square; similarly, good design can be a play on expectation and surprise. Max Weber famously bemoaned the "disenchantment of the world" in the face of modernism's overbearing rationalism. Is it perhaps not time to reconsider investing design with some small measure of enchantment by setting the stage for ritualization?

II.

Historically, the practice of architecture has been steeped in rituals. Joseph Rykwert, for instance, has written in depth on the many rites surrounding the building of a temple or a town in ancient times.[15] The town, for instance, was never haphazard or grown by accretion, but always a designed entity made possible through the intercession of the gods. The Messenians, according to Pausanias, first sent prophets to consult the oracle at Delphi for where the town would be located, and only when omens were favorable did the king order the stone and masons to be assembled. When all was ready, the Messenians made sacrifices to Zeus and other divinities and called upon their divine heroes to return and live with them. Only after these protocols and prayers were enacted did the workers begin to erect the encircling wall, temples, and houses, all the while having their labors regulated by the musical rhythms of Boiotian and Argive flutes.[16]

Festivals directed to cultural or religious themes were also commonplace in the ancient world. Perhaps the most notable were the lesser and greater Panathenaea held every mid-summer in Athens. The festival began as a way to honor the birth of Athena by presenting her statue on the Acropolis with a new robe, one designed and woven by priestesses over the previous nine months. As the event evolved over time, the preparations grew more elaborate. The greater Panathenaea, which was held every four years, was preceded on its eve with dancing. The next morning at sunrise a torch-race opened the festival, followed by a crosstown procession of citizens to the Acropolis, where the robe was presented and sacrifices were made—events depicted on the frieze of the Parthenon. The festival continued for as many as twelve days and featured musical and rhapsodic contests, athletic and equestrian contests, sea races, and, of course, general feasting and revelry. The festival brought together all residents, even freed slaves, and no doubt fostered community bonding and social healing.

Roman architecture was also not without its many rituals. Mythology tells us that Romulus's first act in founding Rome was to have augurs discern the location of the city from the flight of birds, which was followed by the requisite sacrifices and prayers. He then ordered a fire to be built around the perimeter, through which the future townspeople had to jump in order to purify themselves of all moral and physical stain. Then Romulus dug a circular trench into which the residents threw clumps of soil from their native lands. Finally, an altar was built to house the sacred flame, which was required by law to burn without cessation. Only at this point did construction of the city commence.[17]

Augury was the major axis of communication between the gods and humanity, and the *augurium* in Rome, as Indra Kagins McEwen informs us, was the Temple of Jupiter at the highest point on the Capitol.[18] Cicero, who himself was an auger, calls these men "the highest and most important authority in the commonwealth," with the power to adjourn assemblies and force consuls to resign their office.[19] Vitruvius, as we might expect, was steeped in ritualistic thinking. In the fourth chapter of book one, he "emphatically" states his opinion that the "old principles" of augury should be restored before selecting the site of city and he goes on to give instructions of how to read a sacrificial victim's liver. The entire fourth book is devoted to the design of temples, and how the styles of each should reflect the characteristics of the god or goddess. Even seemingly casual remarks carry the status of ritualistic precepts. The steps of temples, he notes, should be of an odd number, so that if one begins to mount the steps with the right foot one will also enter the temple with the same foot.[20] Because every house of the Roman and Greek city contained a shrine and was therefore a temple, ritual prescribed that one must enter and leave the Roman house with the right foot.[21]

One can trace the course of rituals in religious rites, civic festivals, and architectural affairs down through the Middle Ages and into modern times, but it is true that we think very differently today. Yet if our systems of belief have changed, it does not mean that our predilection for collective rituals (today transformed most visibly into displays such as major sporting events) has in itself declined. We must admit, however, that such affairs have also lost much of their larger social meaning. The emotional result has been the cool and isolating cultural demeanor of modern global society—our team against their team. One must ask whether the idea of a cultural ritual can today be redeemed.

Maclom Quantrill, for one, has bemoaned the waning power of rituals in architecture (Figure 9.1). In writing parts of *The Environmental Memory* from a Venetian hotel room overlooking the west porch of San Marco, he reports that the church "is an urban work of art that radiates its splendor as much at dawn and dusk as at high noon. San Marco resonates in the space of the piazza as a cornerstone of civilization; it has both a cosmic and personal scale. And inside, it is certainly a house of memories that encompasses many moments, places, and occasions in the Byzantine world."[22] There are an abundance of large buildings populating our cities today, but it is unlikely that many of them, like San Marco, will acquire such value. In fact, one can argue that most of the exercises in architectural "bigness" of the past half-century are now more often seen as colossal failures, collective symbols in which the voice of the individual person has been muted. At the very least, one does not think of them as houses of memory or cornerstones of civilization. Humans still enjoy particular types of environments, locally colored with memories, with optimal levels of sensory richness or complexity.

Yet ritualization in architecture need not really be thought of in this way, or at least not always at this scale. Few will ever receive a commission to build a cornerstone of civilization, and ritualization can also be, and perhaps should be, an idea that is most at home with its modesty. A candle-lit dinner, a morning walk, and a weekly social outing with a friend are rituals for many people, important rituals by which a human life unfolds in all its magnanimity. Many of the major architects of the twentieth century extensively studied their clients' smallest habits of behavior. Design decisions enacted at this scale can be seen as the judicious framing of human forms and social interactions—that is, providing room or the medium for everyday ritualistic experiences to take place.

FIGURE 9.1 *Portio of the west porch of San Marco Basilica, Venice. Photograph by author.*

Hans-Georg Gadamer sees the idea of ritual in this sense when he reports that every work of art "signifies an increase in being," a "sensuous abundance" that is both enriching and irreplaceable.[23] Just as the rituals and festivals of many cultures bring people together and allow us to tarry in the moment of conciliation, free of everyday tensions and pressures, so does the good work of art allow us to tarry, linger, and dwell in the present. Art's purpose, for Gadamer—and the same could be said for architecture when it aspires to art—is to transform "our fleeting experience into a stable and lasting form of an independent and internally coherent creation."[24] Architecture can also impress us when it is unobtrusive, or when it simply provides a framework for us to act with regard to our singular and collective needs. Good community design, as Gadamer points out, allows that festive moment when there is no separation between one person and another, and this in itself is its measure of success.

Building upon Ludwig Wittgenstein's notion of ceremony, the anthropologist Wendy James has, through the "lived-in ceremonial forms in which we pass our days," referred to humanity as the "ceremonial animal," and cautions us from drawing a hard and fast line between our daily activities and so-called ritualistic behaviors. "Ritual, symbol, and ceremony are not simply present or absent in the things we do," she goes on to say, they are built into everything we do: "Examples of human action free of them are impossible to find, because all human action relates in some way to areas of culturally specified significance we participate in with others."[25] Alberto Peréz-Goméz, who has long been concerned with the decline of the binding power of *mythos* under the instrumental forces of *logos*, makes a similar point when he argues that the rituals of our everyday lives might be better approached through the Greek notion of *poiēsis*—that is, bringing into being something that did not previously exist, yet something particularly resonant and "empathic" to the participant, and something that impresses a particular moment with the memory of time.[26]

Friedrich Schiller famously described the object of the "play instinct" to be "*living shape*, a concept which serves to denote all aesthetic qualities of phenomena and—in a word—what we call *Beauty* in the widest sense of the term."[27] Rykwert, in his essay "The Necessity of Artifice," has suggested a more nuanced understanding of play for architecture, when he warns designers not to succumb to "the techniques of advertising and the nightjoys of neon," but rather attend to the physical form itself, "the stage on which the action occurs," the demarcation of the place for "social situation." "The task of designers," he goes on to say, "is to clarify, to reconcile, to fortify," and "the 'savant' exercise of their skill is the real contribution which they can make to the creation of a valid human environment."[28]

"Artifice" is a term rife with its own ambiguity. On one level, it signifies an ingenuity or artful skill exercised by the hand of the designer; on another, it takes on the meaning of an artful stratagem or clever cultural retort, a rhetorical trope. This ambiguity, in turn, allows us to see the empathy of "play" from two perspectives. The architect plays during the act of shaping or demarcating social form—to the extent that it is often said that one "loses oneself" in the play of design. The finished design, however, is itself a drama or social "gesture," a performance that the designer offers the resident to take occupation of and find self-realization within. Residents, however, must recognize the hospitable and skillful nature of the proffered gesture, one they should find neither imposing nor unpleasing. Just as importantly, the play must be appropriate and conducive to their social and personal lives.

Gadamer also had much to say about the idea of play, and particularly the need to strip it of the subjectivity of earlier aesthetic theory. He points out that the German word for "play" (*Spiel*) originally meant dance, and that play is not the exercise of aesthetic consciousness but rather "experience"—that is, "an experience that changes the person who experiences it."[29] The importance of play lies in not something that a person does, but in the "play itself," and the "primacy of play over the consciousness of the player," as he phrases it, arises when play presents its own structure or set of rules, rules that liberate the player "from the burden of taking the initiative."[30] In this way, play—everything from a childhood game to the high cultivation of design skills—is a form of self-presentation within a recognizable structure. He underscores this point by referring to the meaning of the Greek term *mimesis*, which—although usually translated as imitation—is actually a creative representation of something more profound, in the same way that classical Greek drama represents life by exploring the deeper meaning of life. Mimesis is not real but something presented within the rules of play "as show, as appearance," which, if done well, "enables us to see more than so-called reality."[31] Semper, in the passage we cited earlier on the "haze of carnival candles," went on to make a similar point in noting that "the destruction of reality, of the material, is necessary if form is to emerge as a meaningful symbol, as an autonomous human creation."[32] The great artistic masters of the past did not simply "blurt out" what they wanted to say; artistic pleasure, from the ritualistic perspective of the occupant, at times calls for a certain "carnival spirit" or the joy of the carnival mask.

Designers may or may not bemoan the loss of ritualized thinking in our highly secularized and narrowly defined cultures, but the occupants of the abodes for whom we design more often than not have the expectation that architecture should make a connection with the values of importance to them. Problems arise when ritual is neglected. On the one hand, we have the sterile material environments that confront and frankly bore the occupants of so many of our larger building complexes and urban centers; on the other hand, we have the arty statement of feigned "resistance" to the expectations of the status quo. Resistance, however, generally offers little presence or weight of substance. Ritualistic thinking suggests finding a deeper understanding or accord with the more vital components of aesthetic culture, the "foundational cultural schemas" of which Lewis spoke. Ignoring these cultural schemas diminishes, when it does not occlude entirely, the social dimensions of the dwelling perspective.

Many designers are still taught today that design is the process of finding a rational "solution" to a problem, yet a better understanding of the depth of our ritualized behavior should persuade us to think otherwise. Design requires competence and a strong measure of elaboration, but also, as Rykwert suggests, taking our primeval social impulses more seriously. Ritualization seeks out more than simple meanings or functional relationships. From a designer's perspective, ritualization suggests what David Leatherbarrow has referred to as "architecture oriented otherwise," or what Jan Gehl has called "the human dimension" of design.[33] Good design at the same time opens a dialogue between the designer and the shared experience of the constructed environment.

If the contemporary human and natural sciences have arrived at one profound revelation, it would be that we are, through our empathetic bearings, deeply connected with one another at the innermost level of our being. Such a connection is no longer a commonplace slogan or speculative aphorism of sociology textbooks. It is now a well-documented fact.

III.

Earlier I severed artistic judgment of beauty from the concept of aesthetics in order to focus on the immediacy of the perceptual or embodied act without this complication. In doing so, I turned my back on much of the tradition of Western aesthetics and such questions as to whether beauty and its normative standards are inherent in the object or something that resides in our subjective appraisal of it. Twentieth-century aesthetic theory was generally quite hostile to the idea of beauty, and in retrospect one can view the debasement of beauty as the very hallmark of the theoretic or rationally grounded culture conditioned by rapid technological innovations and a fascination with the novelties of form. Even today, if one reaches across the spectrum of the humanities, one rarely comes across a psychologist or philosopher willing to approach the issue of beauty.

Yet, at a social level, the idea of "beauty" in itself cannot be dismissed so easily. Every day we make aesthetic judgments about people and things. We find one fountain pen, the shape of a wine glass, or an automobile more appealing or better designed than another. We are emotionally moved or disappointed with a book or concert performance. We speak fervently of a glowing sunrise or sunset. We find comeliness in the faces and minds of those we love. An understanding of beauty and its related concepts seem to be woven into our human natures and it would be foolish to deny the reality of an experience that transcends all cultural boundaries. In viewing architecture as experience, we cannot ignore the fact that people prefer certain environments over others and sometimes use the word "beauty."

In the 1990s, evolutionary psychologists brought the idea of "beauty" to the fore with the claim that its appreciation may indeed have a biological basis. It is, as several writers have argued, an evolutionary adaptation tied to our reproductive success and is therefore hardly reversible, even to the efforts of twentieth-century warriors of resistance. Some have taken issue with the assertion that an appreciation of beauty is a biological adaptation, but even if it is true it does really tell us anything about the experience of beauty. Why is it, for instance, that some aesthetic experiences move us profoundly, while others do not?

Coming at the matter from a very different perspective, neuroscience in the first years of this century set out to find the neural correlates or operations of aesthetic judgments, and there is today, as we have seen, a gathering concurrence in the identification of the specific hormones, neurotransmitters, and brain regions involved with a pleasing aesthetic experience.[34] When such efforts are focused on the brain's response to specific objects, forms, or proportions, however, they are removed from our present efforts, which concern the personal and social dimensions of the architectural experience. Perhaps a better way to approach the matter is through the experience of beauty itself, and in this regard we can pose two questions. Is the experience of beauty more deeply implicated in our being than any reasoned judgment of form might presume? And if so, wherein resides the experience?

In an earlier essay, we discussed the idea of "naturalizing" aesthetics, which, as Steven Brown pointed out, is a system that "evolved first for the appraisal of appetitive objects of biological importance, including food sources and suitable mates, and was later co-opted for artworks such as songs and paintings."[35] Admittedly, it was a long evolutionary road from these appetitive objects to a cultural appreciation of a sculptural work such as Laocoön (Figure 9.2). It was a route that human biology and enculturation constructed on multiple layers, but certain aspects nevertheless remain discernible. Yet of what does its base layer consist?

Dissanayake, who supports the idea of a naturalistic aesthetics, argues that aesthetic experience satisfies us biologically and culturally when the event itself is both accessible and striking perceptually, has "tangible relevance" to the lived world of the experiencer, has an "evocative resonance" or a complexity of meaning, and offers up a "satisfying fullness" or richness of experience. The artistic experience succeeds when "life interests are touched, experiential depths are sounded, greater possibilities are evoked, and the works that embody these have been constructed and composed with care and commitment."[36] Such perceptual and emotional responses, once again, are easily transposed into architectural design.

The idea of naturalizing aesthetics also has another benefit in that it, when pursued, can extend the boundary of aesthetic evaluation beyond the human timeline. Do not many insects and animals, for instance, experience aspects of beauty in a similar way? Charles Darwin's theory of sexual selection, for instance, argued that an "aesthetic faculty" was also a major component of evolution within many realms of the animal world, and support for his view has recently been advanced by the research of the ornithologist Robert Prum, who has proposed a "coevolutionary aesthetic theory" for both human and nonhuman organisms, one that, in his view, "provides a heuristic, non-reductive account of the nature of art, the origin of aesthetic properties, and the process of aesthetic change."[37] Art, for him, is a biological coding or communication, as it were, a sensory and cognitive experience of nature that coevolves with its evaluation and therefore sets in motion its own evolutionary consequences. Just as flowers and the sensory systems of bees coevolved with one another,

FIGURE 9.2 *Laocoön, Copy after Hellenistic original. Museo Pio-Clementino, Vatican. Photograph by Marie-Land Nguyen. Creative Commons.*

just as the songs of birds coevolved with mating preferences—so have human aesthetic preferences coevolved with our standards of judgment. "Art and aesthetics," Prum goes on to say, "are emergent consequences of advertisement communication, evaluation, choice, and evolutionary feedback: they cannot be reduced to more fundamental processes."[38]

This joining of genetic and cultural components has a certain allure, but once again does it really speak to the social and emotional depth of human aesthetic experience? In *Truth and Method* (1960), Gadamer focused his deliberations not on aesthetic consciousness or judgments of beauty but rather on the sensory experience itself. The work of art acquires its truth or its meaning "in the fact that it becomes an experience that changes the person who experiences it."[39] In his essay written fifteen years later "The Relevance of the Beautiful," he drew upon Baumgarten's idea of sensuous cognition and reports that "there is something in our experience of the beautiful that arrests us and compels us to dwell upon the individual appearance itself."[40] It is in this moment of lingering, as it were, that the beautiful work of art "transforms our fleeting experience into the stable and lasting form of an independent and internally coherent creation. It does so in such a way that we go beyond ourselves by penetrating deeper into the work."[41] Great works of art certainly demonstrate this process, but within the everyday world a comely face or a satisfying conversation allow us to tarry or dwell, even momentarily, within the experience. And if the essence of the beautiful is to have a "certain standing in the public eye," as Gadamer argues, this standing also "implies a whole form of life that embraces all those artistic forms with which we embellish our environment, including decoration and architecture."[42]

There is an echo of Gadamer's analysis in the "new aesthetics" of Gernot Böhme, who, in explicating his idea of atmosphere, argues that one today cannot speak of beauty in any conventional aesthetic sense because beauty is not an act of judgment but something born of the experience itself. Citing the atmospheric paintings of J. M. W. Turner, he makes the case that the "only thing that counts is the quality of the impression emanating from a person, a scene, an object, a piece of architecture."[43] The great works of art, such as the Venus of Milo or the Alhambra, he goes on to say, will always be deemed beautiful, yet our range of experiences has expanded and we may characterize a building as beautiful, for instance, because it intensifies our existence, it "is that which mediates to us the joy of being there."[44]

There is another aspect to Gadamer's idea of beauty that is instructive, which is the social ethos that it presumes. Preeminent in this regard is the idea of the *festival*—that social event that allows no separation between people, that day or occasion that brings everyone together. The festival is "an experience of community and represents community in its most perfect form."[45] Its beauty—apart from the "sensuous abundance" that so fascinated James—resides in the celebratory act, in the fact that "we are gathered for something" and thereby relinquish our subjectivity. All artistic performances may achieve the same end, but architecture for Gadamer stands apart in one important respect. The designer only achieves a "happy solution" when the building both fulfills its practical purpose and when it adds "something new to the spatial dimensions of a town or landscape."[46] In this way Gadamer suggests that a building should fit into a community's way of life "by providing ornament, a background of mood, or a framework," but it also "should have an enlivening effect and must, to some extent, draw attention to itself."[47]

Gadamer's binding of beauty with an ethos—the association of beauty with the social good—is an exception within the literature of the twentieth century, which by and large shied away from such connections. Yet with the loss of these social values we must ask whether there was there anything gained. Countercultural movements are effective in challenging the status quo and commanding the media's ephemeral focus of attention, but such movements are often characterized by a frivolity of form that cannot be overcome by its self-set limitations. Countercultural success is, more often than not, short lived.

In response to the dominant twentieth-century perspective, a few voices have revisited the issue of beauty in recent years. Elaine Scarry's *On Beauty* makes the case that not only does beauty prompt a copy of itself (open a path for further exploration) but also in this way revives our search for truth and justice.[48] Pérez-Gómez argues that the task of the architect is to "*lovingly* transform the *prima materia* of the world" through "harmonic, rhythmic action," and to produce such wonder that the designer "must both love his work and care profoundly for the Other to whom it is addressed."[49] He also views beauty as a kind of biological or homeostatic operation, in the sense that it "is life-affirming, a gift of meaning central to our psychosomatic health, to a sense of attunement with our environment."[50]

Such arguments recall Roger Scruton's belief that aesthetic values cannot be separated from ethical values, and together they are the means through which "we shape our surroundings as a home by farming, by building, by arranging the world."[51] Environmental degradation or bad design, he goes on to argue, is a form of moral degradation, treating people as impersonal objects instead as living organisms to be respected. The trees, flowers, orchards, and buildings portrayed by Van Gogh open up the painterly charm of nature, and are therefore as pleasing to us as when a face of a friend opens into a smile. Great art is moral in that it reveals something to us about ourselves: "What is revealed to me in the experience of beauty is a fundamental truth about being—that being is a gift."[52]

The question of beauty's relationship with the good has recently been explored from still another direction. In *Neurobiology and the Development of Human Morality*, the psychologist Darcia Narvaez, in drawing upon the current research related to the developing brain, sets out to demonstrate that human cultures are ever malleable (social trust and values can increase or lessen over generations), and that human morality and the appreciation of beauty similarly emerge both from biological factors and from our early and later cultural development. Once again, the timing and extent of our neurobiological development are crucial to this process. In a few brief remarks regarding the idea of beauty, which she frames under the heading "Paths to Moral Wisdom," she underscores the importance of beauty, harmony, and congruence in one's life, and their relation to the cultivation of truth, goodness, and personal integrity.[53] She concludes with the observation that creativity is not simply "play," but an activity in which the designer should assume a measure of moral responsibility. We might infer from her discussion that designers should be driven by a shared ethos for "beauty" in their creative acts of making—that is, the search for a proper aesthetic attitude is nothing less than a moral and professional obligation. As awkward as it may sound today, we nevertheless raise the question of whether it is possible for designers again to unite around such a common ethos.

IV.

Few architects in recent years have considered such a question, but two philosophers very much involved with architecture have raised the issue. Karsten Harries, in attempting to draw out the lessons that Heidegger might hold for design, was willing to confront the problem. Writing in the 1990s, before the last embers of the postmodern movement flickered, he set out in *The Ethical Function of Architecture* "to help articulate a common ethos," one more communitarian and generous in its spirit and scope.[54] Yet by the end of his study, his optimism seems to have waned.

In citing a talk given by Rudolf Schwarz in 1951 (at the conference, incidentally, in which Heidegger read his essay "Building, Dwelling, Thinking"), Harries recounts the architect's comments that no one today can understand a baroque church by simply viewing it with a "clever" or aesthetic eye. The true understanding of the church requires that one participate in the entire spiritual and communal score that gave rise to it in the first place: the festal celebration of the mass, the prayers, the songs, and the community's ethos to which one pledges one's allegiance. Architecture today, Harries concedes, cannot by itself reconstruct such a "transcendent order," which seemingly can only emanate from the evident forces of a more encompassing cultural compass. "Why is the road to what is here called 'real architecture' so bitter?" he asks at one point.

> It is bitter, first of all, because it goes against our desire to place ourselves at the center, bitter also because we have to recognize how difficult it is, no matter what our intentions, to read the contours of the order in which we are to stand, which is to grant us a sense of place and which architecture is to help reveal.[55]

Hence, the architect, it seems, is left with few options, other than providing a "suitable framework" from which such a cultural ethos might be glimpsed. This framework, however, is little more than "a groping representation, if you wish, of an ideal of essential humanity."[56]

Harries's pessimism toward the reemergence of another transcendent order in the last decades of the twentieth century is well-taken, but is the "ideal of our essential humanity" simply a concept that we can only gropingly approach? Can it not be found, as he suggested elsewhere in his study, within the contours profession itself—that is, within the cultural values and insights that we can today bring to the task of design? One neuroimaging study that we cited earlier, for instance, concluded that an architect's neurological patterns when experiencing contemplative buildings are not too dissimilar to those of someone engaged in meditation, prayer, or state of awe.[57] It is not that these neurological patterns in themselves are so telling, but the fact that good design seems to inspire a mental change of reference, a different way of thinking—for both the designer and user experiencing the building.

And can we not experience a baroque church in other ways than through the "clever eye" of an aesthetic formalist? The psychiatrist Iain McGilchrist, for instance, writes about his experience in visiting Balthasar Neumann's baroque church of Vierzehnheiligen (Figure 9.3). He notes that before he entered the pilgrimage church he expected to be enraptured or overwhelmed by the ornate detailing, but that upon entering he found that "the most surprising thing about it is the calm sense of unified space within it, which exerts a magnetic attraction. I tried unsuccessfully three times to leave the church before finally tearing myself away."[58] McGilchrist, it seems, entered the same frame of mind as the architects in the neuroimaging scanner. Does this not reveal a vivid aspect of our essential humanity: the satiation or pleasure of beauty (or however else one wishes to describe it) that literally takes hold of our very being?

Dalibor Vesely has also considered the problem of a collective social ethos. He built his model with the aid of such classical terms as *prepon, poiēsis, mythos, mimesis*, and *praxis*. He defined the first of these terms as "a harmonious participation in the order of reality," and it implies "that order is represented in such a way that it becomes conspicuous and actually present in sensuous abundance."[59] *Poiēsis*, the making of something new, encompasses every field of artistic creation and, particularly with architecture, can be cultivated or imbued with a social ethos. Vesely also interprets the Greek term *mimesis* in its pre-Platonic sense of creative representation, the representation of something animate and concrete, such as the fulfillment of a human life. Architecture in this way is a representation (*mimesis*) not of nature or abstract ideas, but of concrete human situations.[60]

On this basis Vesely sought to construct a contemporary *mythos* for design, "a poetic mythos as the soul of all the creative arts, including architecture"—the last art of which, he further argued, today suffers from an acute displacement of its social and cultural meanings. This displacement is due to the complexity of modern life but also to the subjugation of aesthetic representation to the forces of technological determinism and instrumental reasoning. The key term that might alter this course is the idea of *praxis* or action, which Vesely defined as "living and acting in accordance with ethical principles."[61]

FIGURE 9.3 *Balthasar Neumann, Basilica of Vierzehnheiligen, Staffelstein, Germany (1743–72). Photograph by Bbb. Creative Commons.*

This ethical grounding for *praxis*—the cure for today's excess of *theōria* as Arendt once characterized it—is central to his argument on two fronts. One lies in the formation and interpretation of a poetic *mythos*, the symbolic dimension of culture that opens up and connects with human existence. The second and no less important dimension resides in the archetypical nature of spatial "situations"—that is, the role that significant gestures, rituals, settings, and conversations play in our social relationships. "That practical nature," he notes, "is revealed not only in how people act or in what they do in a particular setting but also in the nature of the setting itself."[62] Situations also involve our relationships with things, but not in the sense of ephemeral design fashions or other technical innovations. Rather, they are the things most familiar to us and are related to our places of dwelling in a Heideggerian sense. What is ultimately lacking, in the view of Vesely, is the failure of architecture simply to attend to the richness of human existence:

> The tendency to express the richness of life through transparent, clearly defined functions grows out of the replacement of the traditional understanding of creativity, based on the creative imitation of praxis and poetic knowledge (*technē poiētikē*), by the imitation of rationally formulated standards of theoretical knowledge (*technē theōrētikē*). This replacement has led to the degeneration of practice to technique and to a serious impoverishment of culture.[63]

From such a perspective, architecture might be thought of as representation (*mimesis*), but a representation of concrete human situations rather than of functions or abstract ideas. Yet for so much of the twentieth-century theory, architecture was intellectualized to the point where our bodies (our essential organismic condition), our living habits, and our affective ways of viewing the world were pushed from view. The meaning of a designed artifact lies not in its semiotic interpretation but deeper within our organic condition, the way in which (as phenomenologically minded architects of the past articulated) we emotionally couple with the environment, assert our social and encultured natures, and thereby win back a sense of mutuality and belonging. Only in this way can architecture become a social art unified by a practical ethos.

Vesely's perspective, I am suggesting, has been strengthened and enhanced by current cultural models. It is not so much that we lack the idea of a collective ethos, but that we have yet to turn away from the technological, functionalist, and judgmental aesthetics of the past and recognize, in the words of Harries, our "essential humanity." The influence of the cultural and biological sciences, which in the past have been viewed as reductionist in their behavioral or sociobiological impulses, are today actually tracking in the opposite direction by highlighting the depth and breadth of our complexity.

In this way, they are offering new support for reclaiming a common ethos for design.

V.

For better or worse, we are beginning to understand many of the internal workings of the human organism—the neurological and psychological nuances of our embodied condition, how we perceive, feel, and find a social resonance with the world. The basic principle of niche construction, with which we opened this book, states that just as we design our built environments, so do our built environments in part design who we are and what we will become. Buildings, together with our cultural environments, alter our behaviors and condition how we grow, behave, think, and relate to one another. Such an understanding implies that we—in lieu of pursuing self-serving formalist pursuits—can no longer deny our biological and social inheritance or resign ourselves to the material hardness and impersonal values so often found in today's global architectural culture. What we are now learning about ourselves was not only unfathomable just a few decades ago but this understanding also sets out a common path on which we might walk. By shifting the focus of our efforts to how we experience design, we at the same time bring to design a measure of dignity and respect. Yet how do we make the transition from old to new ways of thinking about design?

One can certainly make the case that architectural theory, as it has been taught and promulgated in recent decades, has failed contemporary practice. And it is equally clear that theory has in many ways remained wedded to the thinking of the past and failed to keep pace with the times. Because theory very much remains fundamentally speculative in its underpinnings, it has become removed from the practicalities of everyday life. Theory has become consumed by the abstruse tactics of its borrowings and failed to develop a grander strategy for appealing to and sheltering more basic human wants and needs. The movements of the bishop and queen on the chessboard have been stymied by the impetuous actions of their own pawns.

Alongside this failing of theory has been the difficult transition the profession has made in recent years into digital design. Especially in design education, students are today often taught to "think" architecture on their small laptops, and the one or two courses introducing hand drawing or working with materials are scarcely able to overcome the abstraction of the medium or the tedium of deliberating at such a small scale. It is not uncommon today to see students each year flittering away hundreds of hours of studio training in search of the elusive design "concept"—fearful all the while that any small change to their first stab at a building will lead to dozens of hours of corrective keyboard work. Such a medium necessarily precludes them from harvesting knowledge or cultivating an approach to design more attuned to the future occupants, who, of course, must endure the failings of their creations.

At the level of architectural practice, we have to ask, in a practical way, how do we make the transition from focusing exclusively on the formal characteristics of design (the built object as symbol or statement) to how someone actually experiences it? In what corner of the curriculum does one turn to learn the nuances of our modes of perception, the intensity of our emotional grounding, or our innate proclivity toward social relationships and personal expression?

Adding another course of theory or a few teams of consultants to architectural projects will not really attend to the core of the problem. Such approaches inevitably fail because they—in addition to eroding further the designer's flexibility and control—delimit the role that imagination and the creative personality have to play in genuine artistic production. Someone had to teach Pablo Casals how to hold a bow, but only through his many hours of practice was he able to perfect the musical shape of movements. Similarly, it is the designer alone who ultimately bears the responsibility for being well practiced in his or her craft, and it is only by having a credible base of knowledge—both through personal experience and humanist studies—that the designer will be able to think about built work in truly creative ways. This base of knowledge, it must be stressed, will not in itself distill a "solution"; it will only define a more nuanced set of variables that have to be considered and interpreted by the designer.

Ultimately, I believe the problem goes back to a reform of the design studio itself, the place where one historically has been initiated into the rites of practice. It is the structure and pedagogical approach of the studio that will have to change, and this will entail a substantial focus on self-directed or group research in the early stages of every design challenge. The goal is not to turn the design studio into a research project, but to allow the young designer, little by little and over the course of years, to acquire a sufficient knowledge of the new human and biological sciences necessary to allow one to think about design from a more informed perspective. The good news is that the next generation of students will naturally be attracted to this ever-expanding field of knowledge—information that, as architectural programs begin to employ the new research tools of neuroimaging or immersive environments, will become ever more focused on matters of interest to designers. Such efforts may even lead architectural faculties to securing significant research funding specifically directed to how we experience the built environment, in the same way that their colleagues in the humanities and science departments have long been doing.

I believe we are on the verge of a revolution in the way that we approach design. We can no longer plead ignorance of the great strides in knowledge that have shaken the humanities and natural sciences. We can no longer pretend that such interdisciplinary efforts are inherently reductive or deterministic, an anathema to creative thinking. When taken seriously, they are in fact the opposite in that they open the design experience to a host of new variables, many of which have been ill-considered and overlooked in recent years. The field of design must have its own revolution, and only in this way will we expand, in a critical way, the parameters of design to reveal better the people for whom we design. Architects, it must be emphasized, will retain their creative mandate and design will become a thoughtful and open-ended process of interpretative or hermeneutic deliberation. The difference is that it will no longer be guided by the speculative constructs of borrowed theory but rather by a more basic understanding of the human organism and its existential engagement with the built environment. This is the epiphany that needs to take place—if indeed architectural design is to move beyond its present models and become a truly humanistic endeavor.

Notes

Architects Make Culture

1 Richard Neutra, *Survival through Design* (Oxford: Oxford University Press, 1954), p. 18.
2 Maxine Sheets-Johnstone, *The Primacy of Movement*, 2nd edn. (Philadelphia: John Benjamin Publishing Company, 2011), pp. 310–311.
3 Tim Ingold, "Complementarity to Obviation: On Dissolving the Boundaries between Social and Biological Anthropology, Archeology and Psychology," in Russell Gray & Paul Griffiths (eds.) *Cycles of Contingency: Developmental Systems and Evolution* (Cambridge, MA: MIT Press, 2003), p. 259.
4 Juhani Pallasmaa, "Body, Mind and Imagination: The Mental Essence of Architecture," in Sarah Robinson & Juhani Pallasmaa (eds.) *Mind in Architecture* (Cambridge, MA: MIT Press, 2015), p. 55.

Introduction

1 Eileen Gray & Jean Badovici, "Description," *L'Architecture Vivante* (Winter 1929), p. 3. Cited from Caroline Constant, "E.1027, Eileen Gray," in David Leatherbarrow & Alexander Eisenschmidt (eds.) *The Companions to the History of Architecture, Volume IV, Twentieth-Century Architecture* (New York: John Wiley & Sons, 2017), p. 235.
2 See Wolfgang Hermann, *The Theory of Claude Perrault* (London: Zwimmer, 1973).
3 See Barry Bergdoll, "Romantic Historiography and the Paradoxes of Historicist Architecture," in Martin Bressani & Christina Contandriopoulos (eds.) *The Companions to the History of Architecture, Volume III, Nineteenth-Century Architecture* (New York: John Wiley & Sons, 2017), pp. 91–94.
4 A point precociously made by Hannah Arendt in *The Human Condition* (Chicago: University of Chicago Press, 1958).
5 Martin Heidegger, *Being and Time*, trans. by John Macquarrie & Edward Robinson (New York: Harper & Row, 1962), p. 28.
6 The appraisal of Maxime Sheets-Johnstone, in "Emotion and Movement: A Beginning Empirical-Phenomenological Analysis of Their Relationship,"

Journal of Consciousness Studies 6:11–12 (1999), pp. 264–265. See also Chapter 4.

7 See Evan Thompson, *Mind in Life: Biology, Phenomenology, and the Sciences of the Mind* (Cambridge, MA: Harvard University Press, 2007), p. 363. See also Chapter 4.

8 A concept introduced in Sigfried Giedion's *Space, Time and Architecture: The Growth of a New Tradition* (Cambridge, MA: Harvard University Press, 1941).

9 Dalibor Vesely, *Architecture in the Age of Divided Representation: The Question of Creativity in the Shadow of Production* (Cambridge, MA: MIT Press, 2004), p. 373. See Chapter 9.

Chapter 1

1 Louis Sullivan, *Kindergarten Chats and Other Writings* (New York: Wittenborn Art Books, 1976), p. 133 (author's emphasis).

2 Johann Gottfried Herder, *Outlines of a Philosophy of the History of Man*, trans. T. Churchill, 2nd ed. in two volumes (London: J. Johnson, 1803), p. 410.

3 See Vesely, *Architecture in the Age of Divided Representation*, p. 373.

4 Walt Whitman, *Complete Poetry and Collected Prose* (New York: The Library of America, 1982), p. 930.

5 Richard Etlin, "Louis Sullivan: The Life-Enhancing Symbiosis of Music, Language, Architecture, and Ornament," in Marles Kronegger (ed.) *The Orchestration of the Arts—A Creative Symbiosis of Existential Powers* (Dordrecht: Kluywer Academic Publishers, 2000).

6 Ibid., pp. 175–176.

7 Sherman Paul, *Louis Sullivan: An Architect in American Thought* (Englewood Cliffs, NJ: Prentice-Hall, 1962), pp. 98–99.

8 Ibid., p. 98.

9 John Dewey, "The New Psychology," *Andover Review* 2, pp. 278–289. Posted online December 2001, p. 5.

10 Ibid., p. 6.

11 Sullivan, *Kindergarten Chats* (Note 1), p. 97, 99.

12 Louis Sullivan, "Essay on Inspiration," in Robert Twombly (ed.) *Public Papers* (Chicago: University of Chicago Press, 1988), p. 26.

13 Ibid., "The Artistic Use of the Imagination," p. 65.

14 Ibid., "Ornament in Architecture," p. 81.

15 Sullivan, *Kindergarten Chats* (note 1), p. 24.

16 Ibid., pp. 50–52.

17 Ibid., p. 133.

18 Sullivan to Carl Bennett, cited from Robert Warn's "Bennett, Client and Creator," *Prairie School Review* 10:3 (1973), p. 7.

19. Louis Sullivan, "Artistic Brick," *Public Papers* (note 12), p. 202.
20. Ibid., p. 203. Lauren Weingarden has observed that he drew upon the most recent theories of color perception. See her "The Colors of Nature: Louis Sullivan's Architectural Polychromy and Nineteenth-Century Color Theory," *Winterthur Portfolio* 20:4 (Winter 1985), pp. 243–260.
21. Gustav Klemm, *Allgemeine Cultur-Geschichte der Menschheit* (Leipzig: Teubner, 1843), I:22.
22. William Whewell, "On the General Bearing of the Great Exhibition," *Lectures on the Progress of Arts and Science* (New York: A. S. Barnes & Co., 1856), p. 12.
23. See Robert Latham & Edward Forbes, *The Natural History Department of the Crystal Palace Described* (London: Crystal Palace Library, 1854).
24. Gottfried Semper, *Style in the Technical and Tectonic Arts; or, Practical Aesthetics*, trans. H. F. Mallgrave & Michael Robinson. (Los Angeles: Getty Publication Programs, 1860/2004), pp. 237–247. See also *Gottfried Semper: The Four Elements of Architecture and Other Writings*, trans. H. F. Mallgrave & Wolfgang Herrmann (New York: Cambridge University Press, 1989).
25. Max Weber, *The Protestant Ethic and the Spirit of Capitalism*, trans. Talcott Parsons (London: Routledge, 1992), p. 182.
26. See Kurt Junghanns, *Der Deutsche Werkbund: Sein erstes Jahrzehnt* (Berlin: Henschelverlage Kunst und Gesellschaft, 1982), pp. 140–142.
27. See in particular Francesco Dal Co, *Figures of Architecture and Thought: German Architecture Culture 1880–1920* (New York: Rizzoli, 1990), pp. 170–261.
28. See Frederic Schwartz, *The Werkbund: Design Theory and Mass Culture before the First World War* (New Haven: Yale University Press, 1996).
29. On Hellerau, see Didem Erici "The Laboratory of a New Humanity: The Concept of Type, Life Reform, and Modern Architecture in Hellerau Garden City, 1900–1914" (Ph.D. diss. University of Michigan, 2008); Marco De Michelis & Vicki Bilenker, "Modernity and Reform: Heinrich Tessenow and the Institut Dalcroze at Hellerau," *Perspecta* 26 (1990), pp. 143–170.
30. Cited in Lawrence Scaff, "Social theory, Rationalism and the Architecture of the City: Fin-de-siècle Thematics," in *Theory, Culture & Society* #12 (London: Sage, 1995), p. 82.
31. Ibid., and see also Jürgen Habermas, "Modern and Postmodern Architecture," in trans. Shierry Weber Nicholsen *The New Conservatism: Cultural Criticism and the Historians' Debate* (Cambridge, MA: MIT Press, 1989).
32. Max Weber, "Science as a Vocation," in trans. H. Gerth & C.W. Mills *From Max Weber: Essays in Sociology* (New York: Oxford University Press, 1946), p. 155.
33. Max Horkheimer & Theodor Adorno, *Dialectic of Enlightenment*, trans. John Cumming (New York: Continuum, 1989).
34. Eric Mumford, *The CIAM Discourse on Urbanism, 1928–1960* (Cambridge, MA: MIT Press, 2000), pp. 16–27.

35 See Michelangelo Sabatino, *Pride in Modesty: Modernist Architecture and the Vernacular Tradition in Italy* (Toronto: University of Toronto Press, 2010).
36 See Bruno Zevi, "A Message to the International Congress of Modern Architecture," in Andrea, Oppenheimer Dean, *Bruno Zevi on Modern Architecture* (New York: Rizzoli, 1958).
37 Ernesto Nathan Rogers, "Continuità," *Casabella-Continuità* 199:2 (December, 1953). Editorial.
38 Ernesto Nathan Rogers, "Continuità o crisi," *Casabella-Continuità* 215 (April–May, 1957). Editorial.
39 Manfredo Tafuri, *History of Italian Architecture, 1944–1985*, trans. Jessica Levine (Cambridge, MA: MIT Press, 1989), p. 53.
40 Paolo Portoghesi, "Dal Neorealismo al Neoliberty," *Communità* 65 (December 1958), pp. 69–79.
41 See Reyner Banham, "Neoliberty: The Italian Retreat from Modern Architecture," *Architectural Review* 125 (April 1959), p. 235.
42 Peter Eisenman, Preface to Aldo Rossi, *The Architecture of the City*, trans. Diane Ghirado & Joan Ockman (Cambridge, MA: MIT Press, 1982), p. 3.
43 Aldo Rossi, *The Architecture of the City*, p. 166.
44 Ibid., p. 166.
45 Martinbo Stierli, "In the Academy's Garden: Robert Venturi, the Grand tour of the Revision of Modern Architecture," *AA Files* 56 (2007), pp. 42–55.
46 Daniel Bell, *The Cultural Contradictions of Capitalism* (New York: Basic Books, 1973).
47 See Herbert Gans, *The Urban Villagers: Group and Class in the Life of Italian Americans* (New York: The Free Press, 1962).
48 Robert Venturi, *Complexity and Contradiction in Architecture* (New York: Museum of Modern Art, 1966), p. 22.
49 See Heinrich Wölfflin, *Renaissance and Baroque*, trans. Kathrin Simon (Ithaca: Cornell University Press, 1966).
50 Venturi, *Complexity and Contradiction* (note 48), p. 25.
51 Ibid., pp. 46–52.
52 Ibid., pp. 102–103.

Chapter 2

1 Edward T. Hall, *The Hidden Dimension* (Garden City, NY: Doubleday & Company, 1966), *Caption to plate 23 & 24*.
2 Ashley Montagu, *Culture and the Evolution of Man* (New York: Oxford University Press, 1972), p. 154.
3 Ashley Montagu, *The Humanization of Man: Our Changing Conception of Human Nature* (New York: Grove Press, 1964), p. 16.

4   See B. F. Skinner, *Walden Two* (Indianapolis: Hackett Publishing Company, 1948).; B. F. Skinner, *Science and Human Behavior* (New York: Macmillan, 1953).
5   Clifford Geertz, *The Interpretation of Cultures: Selected Essays* (New York: Basic Books, 1973), p. 5.
6   Ibid., p. 449.
7   See H. F. Mallgrave & David Goodman, *An Introduction to Architectural Theory: 1968 to the Present* (Chichester: Wiley-Blackwell, 2011), pp. 37–43.
8   Geertz, *The Interpretation of Cultures*, p. 44.
9   Ibid., p. 48.
10 Ibid., p. 69.
11 Robert Ardrey, *African Genesis* (Madison: University of Wisconsin, 1961), pp. 145–176.
12 Robert Ardrey, *The Territorial Imperative: A Personal Inquiry into the Animal Origins of Property and Nations* (New York: Antheum, 1966), p. 78.
13 Irenäus Eibl-Eibesfeldt, *Love and Hate: The Natural History of Behavior Patterns*, trans. Geoffrey Strachan (New York: Holt, Rinehart & Winston, 1971), p. 4.
14 Ibid., p. 236.
15 Desmond Morris, *The Naked Ape: A Zoologist's Study of the Human Animal* (New York: McGraw-Hill, 1967), p. 84.
16 Ibid., p. 241.
17 For a nuanced study of the debate, see Ullica Segerstråle, *Defenders of the Truth: The Battle for Science in the Sociobiology Debate and Beyond* (Oxford: Oxford University Press, 2000).
18 Edward O. Wilson, *Sociobiology: The New Synthesis* (Cambridge, MA: Belknap Press, 2000), p. 575.
19 Ibid., p. 547.
20 Wilson, *Sociobiology*, p. 575.
21 Edward O. Wilson, "What Is Sociobiology," in Michael S. Gregory et al. (eds.) *Sociology and Human Nature: An Interdisciplinary Critique and Defense* (San Francisco: Jossey-Bass, 1978), p. 11.
22 Eugene Ruyle, "Genetic and Cultural Pools: Some Suggestions for a Unified Theory of Biocultural Evolution," *Human Ecology* 1:3 (1973), pp. 201–215.
23 F. T. Cloak, "Is a Cultural Ethology Possible?" *Human Ecology* 3:3 (1975), pp. 161–182.
24 Richard Dawkins, *The Selfish Gene* (Oxford: Oxford University Press, 2009), p. 2.
25 Ibid., p. 192.
26 See A. Hunter Dupree & Talcott Parsons, "The Relations between Biological and Socio-Cultural Theory," *Bulletin of the American Academy of Arts and Sciences* 29:8 (May 1976), pp. 14–18.
27 William H. Durham, "The Adaptive Significance of Cultural Behavior," *Human Ecology* 4:2 (1976), p. 89.

28 William H. Durham, "Toward a Coevolutionary Theory of Human Biology and Culture," in Arthur L. Caplan (ed.) *The Sociobiology Debate: Readings on the Ethical and Scientific Issues Concerning Sociobiology* (New York: Harper & Row, 1978).

29 L. L. C. Cavalli-Sforza & Marcus Feldman, *Cultural Transmission and Evolution: A Quantitative Approach* (Princeton, NJ: Princeton University Press, 1981).

30 Charles Lumsden & Edward O. Wilson, *Genes, Mind, and Culture: The Coevolutionary Process* (Hackensack, NJ: World Scientific, 1981), pp. 1–2.

31 Peter Richerson & Robert Boyd, *Not by Genes Alone: How Culture Transformed Human Evolution* (Chicago: University of Chicago Press, 2005), p. 5.

32 Richard Neutra, *Survival through Design* (New York: Oxford University Press, 1954), p. 5.

33 Ibid., p. 244.

34 Ibid., p. 83.

35 Ibid., pp. 245 & 352.

36 Ibid., pp. 91 & 199–200.

37 Ibid., p. 202. Author's emphasis.

38 Kevin Lynch, *The Image of the City* (Cambridge, MA: MIT Press, 1960). On work related to Lynch today, see the work of Eve Edelstein and Eduardo Macagno on the website of the Academy of Neuroscience for Architecture. http://www.anfarch.org/research-projects/calit2-wayfinding-project/.

39 Lloyd Rodwin (ed.), *The Future Metropolis* (New York: George Braziller, 1961).

40 Melvin Webber, "The Urban Place and the Nonplace Urban Realm," in Melvin Weber et al. (eds.) *Explorations into Urban Structure* (Philadelphia: University of Pennsylvania Press, 1964).

41 Robert Gutman, "The Questions Architects Ask," *Transactions of the Bartlett Society* 4 (1966), p. 81; and "What Architectural Schools Expect from Sociology," *Journal of Architectural Education* 22:2/3 (1968), pp. 13–20.

42 Hall, *The Hidden Dimension*, p. 59.

43 Harold Proshansky et al., *Environmental Psychology: Man and His Physical Setting* (New York: Holt, Rinehart & Winston, 1970).

44 Roger Ulrich, "View Through a Window May Influence Recovery from Surgery," *Science* 224 (April 27, 1984), pp. 420–421. See John Zeisel, *Inquiry by Design: Environment/Behavior/Neuroscience in Architecture, Interiors, Landscape, and Planning* (New York: W. W. Norton & Company, 2006, revised edition). The first edition appeared in 1981.

45 Serge Chermayeff & Christopher Alexander, *Community and Privacy: Toward a New Architecture of Humanism* (Garden City, NY: Anchor Books, 1963), p. 20.

46 Christopher Alexander, *Notes on the Synthesis of Form* (Cambridge, MA: Harvard University Press, 1964).

47 Christopher Alexander et al., *A Pattern Language: Towns, Buildings, Construction* (New York: Oxford University Press, 1977).

48 Christopher Alexander, *The Nature of Order: An Essay on the Art of Building and the Nature of the* Universe, 4 vols. (Berkeley, CA: The Center for Environmental Structure, 2002–05), I:8.

49 Bill Hillier & Adrian Leaman, "A New Approach to Architectural Research," *Environment and Planning B: Planning and Design* 3 (1972), pp. 147–185.

50 Bill Hillier, "In Defense of Space," *RIBA Journal* 80:11 (1973), pp. 540–544.

51 Bill Hillier et al., "Space Syntax," *Environment and Planning B: Planning and Design* 3 (1976), p. 150.

52 Zeisel, *Inquiry by Design*, p. 16.

53 The literature is already immense. A good starting point might be Marica Cassario & Annalise Setti, "Environment as 'Brain Training': A Review of Geographical and Physical Environment Influences on Cognitive Ageing," *Ageing Research Reviews* 23 (2015), pp. 167–182; see also Saif Haq et al., "Movement and Orientation in Built Environments: Evaluating Design Rationale and User Cognition," in *SFB/TR 8: Spatial Cognition* (University of Bremen/Freiburg, 2008), www.sfbtr8.uni-bremen.de.

Chapter 3

1 Daniel Lord Smail, *On Deep History and the Brain* (Berkeley: University of California Press, 2008), p. 113.

2 Ibid., pp. 8–9.

3 John Dewey, *Art as Experience* (New York: A Perrigee Book, 2005), pp. 15–19.

4 Ibid., p. 44.

5 Jakob Von Uexküll, *A Foray into the Worlds of Animals and Humans*, trans. Joseph D. O'Neil (Minneapolis, MN: University of Minnesota Press, 2010), pp. 139–146.

6 Kurt Goldstein, *The Organism: A Holistic Approach to Biology Derived from Pathological Data in Man* (New York: Zone Books, 2000), p. 210.

7 Ibid., p. 214.

8 Maurice Merleau-Ponty, *The Phenomenology of Perception*, trans. Colin Smith (London: Routledge & Kegan Paul, 1962), p. 229.

9 Maurice Merleau-Ponty, *The Visible and the Invisible*, ed. Claude Lefort, trans. Alphonso Lingis (Evanston: Northwestern University Press, 1968), pp. 248 & 138.

10 See my *Architecture and Embodiment: The Implications of the New Sciences and Humanities for Design* (New York: Routledge, 2013), pp. 128–130. See also Mina Kalkatechi, "A Forgotten Chapter of the Bauhaus: Psycho-Physiological Aesthetics and the Inception of Modern Design Theory" (Ph.D. diss. Illinois Institute of Technology, 2016).

11 See, for instance, Vittorio Gallese, "The Manifold Nature of Interpersonal Relations: The Quest for a Common Mechanism," *Philosophical Transactions of the Royal Society London B* 358 (2003), pp. 517–528; "Embodied

Simulation: From Neurons to Phenomenal Experience," *Phenomenology of Cognitive Science* 4 (2005), pp. 23–48; "Mirror Neurons, Embodied Simulation, and the Neural Basis of Social Identification," *Psychoanalytic Dialogues* 19 (2009), pp. 519–536; Vittorio Gallese et al., "A Unifying View of the Basis of Social Cognition," *Trends in Cognitive Sciences* 8:9 (September 2004), pp. 396–403; Vittorio Gallese & C. Sinigaglia, "What Is So Special about Embodied Simulation?" *Trends in Cognitive Sciences* 15:11 (November 2011), pp. 512–519; Massimo Ammaniti & Vittorio Gallese, *The Birth of Intersubjectivity: Psychodynamics, Neurobiology, and the Self* (New York: W. W. Norton & Company, 2014).

12 See, for instance, Ulrich Neisser, *Cognition and Reality: Principles and Implications of Cognitive Psychology* (San Francisco: W. H. Freeman and Company, 1976).

13 Michael Arbib, *The Metaphorical Brain 2: Neural Networks and Beyond* (New York: Wiley & Sons, 1989), p. 39.

14 Michael Arbib, "(Why) Should Architects Care about Neuroscience," in Philip Tidwell (ed.) *Architecture and Neuroscience* (Helsinki: Tapio Wirkkala-Rut Bryk Foundation, 2013), p. 52.

15 Kevin Laland et al., "How Culture Shaped the Human Genome: Bringing Genetics and the Human Sciences Together," *Genetics* 11 (February 2010), p. 137.

16 Scott Williamson et al., "Localizing Recent Adaptive Evolution in the Human Genome," *PLoS Genetics* 3:6 (2007), e90.

17 F. John Odling-Smee et al., *Niche Construction: The Neglected Process in Evolution* (Princeton, NJ: Princeton University Press, 2003), p. 241.

18 Atsushi Ikiki & Miki Taoka, "Triadic (ecological, neural, cognitive) Niche Construction: A Scenario of Human Brain Evolution Extrapolating Tool use and Language from the Control of Reaching Actions," *Philosophical Transactions of the Royal Society B: Biological Sciences* 367 (2011), pp. 10–23.

19 Ajit Varki et al., "Explaining Human Uniqueness: Genome Interactions with Environment, Behaviour and Culture," *Genetics* 9 (October 2008), p. 758.

20 Qing Li, "Effect of Forest Bathing Trips on Human Immune Function," *Environmental Health and Preventative Medicine* 15 (2010), pp. 9–17.

21 Louis Carroll, *Alices's Adventures in Wonderland*. Ch. 5, "Advice from a Caterpillar."

22 Susan Oyama, *Evolution's Eye: A Systems View of the Biology-Culture Divide* (Durham: Duke University Press, 2000), p. 29.

23 Ibid., p. 48.

24 Ibid., p. 95.

25 Ibid.

26 Kevin Laland et al., "Niche Construction, Ecological Inheritance, and Cycles of Contingency in Evolution," in Susan Oyama et al. (eds.) *Cycles of Contingency: Development Systems and Evolution* (Cambridge, MA: MIT Press, 2001), p. 117.

27 Tim Ingold, "Building, Dwelling, Living: How Animals and People Make Themselves at Home in the World," in M. Strathern (ed.) *Shifting Contexts* (London: Routledge), pp. 57–80. Cited from Tim Ingold, *The Perception of the Environment: Essays on Livelihood, Dwelling and Skill* (London: Routledge, 2000), p. 180.

28 Tim Ingold, "From Complementarity to Obviation: On Dissolving the Boundaries between Social and Biological Anthropology, Archaeology, and Psychology," in Oyama et al. (eds.) *Cycles of Contingency*, p. 263.

29 Ingold, *The Perception of the Environment*, p. 186.

30 See Alvar Aalto, "The Humanizing of Architecture," (1940), in Göran Schildt (ed.) *Aalto in His Own Words* (New York: Rizzoli, 1998); Aldo Van Eyck, "Kaleidoscope of the Mind," in *Miracles of Moderation* (Zürich: Eidgenössische Technische Hochschule, 1976); Alexander et al., *A Pattern Language*.

31 Ingold, *The Perception of the Environment*, p. 186.

32 Francisco Varela et al., *The Embodied Mind: Cognitive Science and Human Experience* (Cambridge, MA: MIT Press, 1991), p. 174.

33 Ibid., p. 173.

34 See, for instance, Andy Clark, *Being There: Putting Brain, Body, and World Together Again* (Cambridge, MA: MIT Press, 1997); George Lakoff & Mark Johnson's *Philosophy in the Flesh: The Embodied Mind and Its Challenge to Western Thought* (New York: Basic Books, 1999); Alva Noë's *Action in Perception* (Cambridge, MA: MIT Press, 2004); Shaun Gallagher's *How the Body Shapes the Mind* (Oxford: Clarendon Press, 2005); Mark Johnson's *The Meaning of the Body: Aesthetics of Human Understanding* (Chicago: University of Chicago Press, 2007); Thompson's *Mind in Life: Biology, Phenomenology, and the Sciences of Mind* (2007); and Alva Noë's *Out of Our Heads: Why You Are Not Your Brain, and Other Lessons from the Biology of Consciousness* (New York: Hill and Wang, 2009).

35 See, in particular, Hanne De Jaegher & Ezequiel Di Paolo, "Participatory Sense-Making: An Enactive Approach to Social Cognition," *Phenomenology and the Cognitive Sciences* 6:4 (2007), pp. 485–507; Ezequiel Di Paolo, "Extended Life," *Topoi* 28 (2009), pp. 9–21; Ezequiel Di Paolo & Hanne De Jaegher, "The Interactive Brain Hypothesis," *Frontiers in Human Neuroscience* (June 7, 2012). Doi: 10.3389/fnhum.2012.00163; Tom Froese & Tom Ziemke, "Enactive Artificial Intelligence: Investigating the Systemic Organization of Life and Mind," *Artificial Intelligence* 173:3–4 (2009), pp. 466–500.

36 Francisco Varela, "Neurophenomenology: A Methodological Remedy for the Hard Problem," *Journal of Consciousness Studies* 3:4 (1996), pp. 330–349 (author's emphasis).

37 Evan Thompson, *The Mind in Life: Biology, Phenomenology, and the Sciences of the Mind* (Cambridge, MA: MIT Press, 2007), p. 363.

38 Ibid., p. 370.

39 Ibid., p. 371.

40 Ibid., pp. 382–383.

NOTES

41 Ibid., p. 386.

42 Ibid., p. 403.

43 See Merlin Donald, "The Definition of Human Nature," in Dai Rees & Steven Rose (eds.) *The New Brain Sciences: Perils and Prospects* (New York: Cambridge University Press, 2004), pp. 53–56. See also *A Mind So Rare: The Evolution of Human Consciousness* (New York: W. W. Norton & Company, 2001).

44 Thompson, *Mind in Life*, p. 404.

45 These three dimensions owe much to the three "cycles of operation" Thompson and Varela proposed for studying the human organism, in their paper "Radical Embodiment: Neural Dynamics and Consciousness," *Trends in Cognitive Sciences* 5:10 (October 2001), p. 424.

46 See, for instance, Antonio Damasio's, "somatic-marker hypothesis," first articulated in *Descartes' Error: Emotion, Reason, and the Human Brain* (New York, 1994).

Chapter 4

1 Johann Wolfgang Von Goethe, "Palladio: Architecture," in *Goethe on Art*, trans. John Gage (London: Scolar Press, 1980), pp. 196–197.

2 Bryan Kolb et al., "Brain Plasticity and Behavior," *Current Directions in Psychological Science* 12:1 (2003), pp. 1–4.

3 Thomas Ebert & Christo Pantev, "Increased Cortical Representation of the Fingers of the Left Hand in String Players," *Science* 270:5234 (1995), pp. 305–307.

4 See Gottfried Schlaug, "Increased Corpus Callosum Size in Musicians," *Neuropsychologia* 33:8 (1995), pp. 1047–1055; Christian Gaser & Gottfried Schlaud, "Brain Structures Differ between Musicians and Non-Musicians," *The Journal of Neuroscience* 23:27 (October 8, 2003), pp. 9240–9245.

5 Glenn Schellenberg, "Music Lessons Enhance IQ," *Psychological Science* 15:8 (2004), pp. 511–514.

6 Maria Forgeard et al., "Practicing a Musical Instrument in Childhood Is Associated with Enhanced Verbal Ability and Nonverbal Reasoning," *PloS One* 3:10 (2008), e3566; see also Sylvain Moreno, "Can Music Influence Language and Cognition?" *Contemporary Music Review* 28:3 (2009), pp. 329–345; Sylvain Moreno et al., "Short-Term Second Language and Music Training Induces Lasting Functional Brain Changes in Early Childhood," *Child Development* 86:2 (2015), pp. 394–406.

7 Aisling Mulligan et al., "Home Environment: Association with Hyperactivity/impulsivity in Children with ADHD and their Non-ADHD Siblings," *Child Care Health Development* 39:2 (March 2013), pp. 202–212. See also Harkaitz Bengoetxea et al., "Enriched and Deprived Sensory Experience Induces Structural Changes and Rewired Connectivity during the Postnatal Development of the Brain," *Neural Plasticity* (2012). Doi:10:1155/2012/305693.

8 Mulligan et al., "Home Environment"; Bengoetxea et al., "Enriched and Deprived Sensory Experience Induces Structural Changes and Rewired Connectivity during the Postnatal Development of the Brain."

9 Stanislas Dehaene & Laurent Cohen, "Cultural Recycling of Cortical Maps," *Neuron* 56 (October 25, 2007), pp. 384–398; Stanislas Dehaene et al., "How Learning to Read Changes the Cortical Networks for Vision and Language," *Science* 330 (December 3, 2010), pp. 1359–1364.

10 D. H. Hubel & T. N. Wiesel, "The Period of Susceptibility to the Physiological Effects of Unilateral Eye Closure in Kittens," *Journal of Physiology* 206:2 (1970), pp. 419–436.

11 Colin Blakemore & Grahame Cooper, "Development of the Brain depends on the Visual Environment," *Nature* 228 (October 31, 1970), pp. 477–478.

12 See Richard Tees, "Effects of Early Auditory Restriction in the Rat on Adult Pattern Discrimination," *Journal of Comparative and Physiological Psychology* 67:3 (1967), pp. 389–393; Richard Tees & Glenda Midgley, "Extent of Recovery of Function after Early Sensory Deprivation in the Rat," *Journal of Comparative and Physiological Psychology* 92:4 (1978), pp. 768–777; Glenda Midgley & Richard Tees, "Effect of Visual Experience on the Habituation of Orienting Behavior," *Behavioral Neuroscience* 97:4 (1983), pp. 624–638.

13 Saul Schanberg & Tiffany Field, "Sensory Deprivation Stress and Supplemental Stimulation in the Rat Pup and Preterm Human," *Child Development* 58 (1987), pp. 1431–1447.

14 Mayumi Nishi et al., "Effects of Early Life Adverse Experiences on the Brain: Implications from Maternal Separation Models in Rodents," *Frontiers in Neuroscience* 8:166 (June 2014); Belinda Garner et al., "Early Maternal Deprivation Reduces Prepulse Inhibition and Impairs Spatial Learning Ability in Adulthood: No Further Effect in Post-Pubertal Chronic Corticosterone Treatment," *Behavioral Brain Research* 176 (2007), pp. 323–332; Bart Ellenbroek et al., "The Effects of Early Maternal Deprivation on Auditory Information Processing in Adult Wistar Rats," *Biological Psychiatry* 55 (2004), pp. 701–707.

15 Thomas Insel & Larry Young, "The Neurobiology of Attachment," *Nature Reviews Neuroscience* 2 (February 2001), pp. 129–136; Jennifer Ferguson et al., "The Neuroendocrine Basis for Social Recognition," *Frontiers in Neuroendocrinology* 23 (2002), pp. 200–224. See also Darcia Narvaez, *Neurobiology and the Development of Human Morality: Evolution, Culture, and Wisdom* (New York: W. W. Norton & Company, 2014).

16 Mark Rosenzweig et al., "Effects of Environmental Complexity and Training on Brain Chemistry and Anatomy: A Replication and Extension," *Journal of Comparative and Physiological Psychology* 55:4 (1962), pp. 429–437.

17 Henriette Van Praag et al., "Neural Consequences of Environmental Enrichment," *Nature Neuroscience* 1 (December 2000), pp. 191–198.

18 P. Sampedro-Piquero et al., "Effects of Environmental Enrichment on Anxiety Responses, Spatial Memory and Cytochrome C Oxidase Activity in Adult Rats," *Brain Research Bulletin* 98 (2013), pp. 1–9; Tiago Costa-Goes et al., "Environmental Enrichment for Adult Rats: Effects on Train and State

Anxiety," *Neuroscience Letters* 584 (2013), pp. 93–96; Frederic Mármol et al., "Anti-Oxidative Effects Produced by Environmental Enrichment in the Hippocampus and Cerebral Cortex of Male and Female Rats," *Brain Research* 1613 (2015), pp. 120–129; A. J. Hannel, "Review: Environmental Enrichment and Brain Repair: Harnessing the Therapeutic Effects of Cognitive Stimulation and Physical Activity to Enhance Experience-Dependent Plasticity," *Neuropathology and Applied Neurobiology* 40 (2014), pp. 13–25.

19 Michael Eckert & Weckliffe Abraham, "Effects of Environmental Enrichment Exposure on Synaptic Transmission and Plasticity in the Hippocampus," *Current Topics in Behavioral Neuroscience* 15 (2012), pp. 165–187.

20 Yevgenia Kozorovitskiy et al., "Experience Induces Structural and Biochemical Changes in the Adult Primate Brain," *Proceedings of the National Academy of Sciences* 102:48 (November 29, 2005), pp. 17478–17482.

21 Gilbert Gottlieb, "Probabilistic Epigenesis," *Developmental Science* 10:1 (2007), pp. 1–11.

22 Erwin W. Straus, "The Upright Posture," *The Psychiatric Quarterly* 26:1 (1952), pp. 529–561.

23 Maxime Sheets-Johnstone, *The Primacy of Movement*, 2nd ed. (Amsterdam: John Benjamins Publishing Company, 2011), p. 477.

24 Tim Ingold, "CULTURE ON THE GROUND: The World Perceived Through the Feet," *Journal of Material Culture* 9:3 (2004), p. 331.

25 Walter Freeman, "Emotion Is Essential to All Intentional Behaviors," UC Berkeley Previously Published Works (2000), p. 9.

26 Cited from Jonathan Cole, *Pride and the Daily Marathon* (Cambridge, MA: MIT Press, 2007), p. x.

27 Alexandra Reichenbach et al., "Reaching with the Sixth Sense: Vestibular Contributions to Voluntary Motor Control in the Human Right Parietal Cortex," *NeuroImage* 124 (2016), pp. 869–875.

28 Roger Sperry, "Action Current Study in Movement Coordination," *The Journal of General Psychology* 20 (1939), pp. 295–313.

29 Lutz Jäncke et al., "The Architecture of the Golfer's Brain," *PLoS ONE* 4:3 (2009), 34785. Doi:10:1371/journal.pone0004785.

30 Anne Kavoundoudias et al., "The plantar sole is a 'dynamometric map' for human balance control," *NeuroReport* 9 (1998), pp. 3247–3252.

31 Anne Kavoundoudias et al., "From Balance Regulation to Body Orientation: Two Goals for Muscle Proprioceptive Information Processing?" *Experimental Brain Research* 124 (1999), pp. 80–88.

32 Caroline Blanchard et al., "Differential Contributions of Vision, Touch and Muscle Proprioception to the Coding of Hand Movements," *PLoS ONE* 8:4, e62475–e62475.

33 Juhani Pallasmaa, "An Architecture of the Seven Senses," in Steven Holl et al., *Questions of Perception: Phenomenology of Architecture* (San Francisco: William Stout, 2006), p. 33.

34 Bernard Berenson, *The Florentine Painters of the Renaissance* (New York: G. P. Putnam's Sons, 1902), p. 50.

35 Fuzhong Li et al., "Improving Physical Function and Blood Pressure in Older Adults through Cobblestone Mat Walking: A Randomized Trial," *Journal of the American Geriatrics Society* 53:8 (2005), pp. 1305–1312.
36 Sarah Robinson, *Nesting: Body, Dwelling, Mind* (Richmond, CA: William Stout Publishers, 2011), p. 49.
37 Ingold, "Culture on the Ground," pp. 315–340.
38 Friedemann Pulvermüller, "Brain Mechanisms Linking Language and Action," *Nature Reviews Neuroscience* 6 (July 2005), pp. 576–582.
39 Simon Lacey et al., "Metaphorically Feeling: Comprehending Textural Metaphors Activates Somatosensory Cortex," *Brain Language* 120:3 (March 2012), pp. 416–421.
40 Vittorio Gallese & Sjoerd Ebisch, "Embodied Simulation and Touch: The *Sense* of Touch in Social Cognition," *Phenomenology and Mind* 4 (2013), pp. 269–291.
41 Christian Keysers, et al., "A Touching Sight: SII/PV Activation during the Observation and Experience of Touch," *Neuron* 42 (April 22, 2004), pp. 335–346.
42 Christian Keysers, *The Empathic Brain: How the Discovery of Mirror Neurons Changes our Understanding of Human Nature* (Social Brain Press, 2011), p. 122.
43 See Giacomo Rizzolatti & Corrado Sinigaglia, *Mirrors in the Brain: How Our Minds Share Actions and Emotions*, trans. Frances Anderson (Oxford: Oxford University Press, 2008).
44 Robert Vischer, "On the Optical Sense of Form," in H. F. Mallgrave & I. Ikonomou (eds.) *Empathy, Form, and Space: Problems in German Aesthetics, 1873–1893* (Santa Monica: Getty Publications, 1994), p. 98.
45 Gallagher, *How the Body Shapes the Mind*, p. 238.
46 See Giacomo Rizzolaii & Michael Arbib, "Language within Our Grasp," *Trends in Neuroscience* 21:188 (1998), pp. 169–192.
47 See Gallese, "Embodied simulation: From neurons to phenomenal experience," 23–48; Gallese and Sinigaglia, "What is so special about embodied simulation?" pp. 512–19.
48 Marc Bangert et al., "Shared Networks for Auditory and Motor Processing in Professional Pianists: Evidence from fMRI Conjunction," *NeuroImage* 30 (2006), pp. 917–926. On mirror neurons being recorded elsewhere, see also Roy Mukamel et al., "Single-Neuron Responses in Humans during Execution and Observation of Actions," *Current Biology* 20 (April 27, 2010), pp. 750–756.
49 Beatriz Calvo-Merino et al., "Towards a Sensorimotor Aesthetics of Performing Art," *Consciousness and Cognition* 17 (2008), p. 919.
50 Bruno Wicker et al., "Both of Us Disgusted in *My* Insula: The Common Neural Basis of Seeing and Feeling Disgust," *Neuron* 40 (2003), pp. 655–664.
51 Christopher Tilley, *The Materiality of Stone: Explorations in Landscape Phenomenology* (Oxford: Berg, 2004), p. 21.
52 Sigfried Giedion, *Space, Time and Architecture: The Growth of a New Tradition* (Cambridge MA: Harvard University Press, 1949), p. 13.

53 Heinrich Wölfflin, "Prolegomena to a Psychology of Architecture," in *Empathy, Form, and Space: Problems in German Aesthetics, 1873–1893*, Mallgrave & Ikonomou (trans.) (Santa Monica: Getty Publications, 1994), p. 49.

54 Fechner was particularly interested in the golden triangle. See Gustav Fechner, *Vorschule der Aesthetik* (Leipzig: Breitkoph & Härtel, 1876). Part of this text was translated for the journal *Empirical Studies of the Arts* 15:2 (1997), pp. 115–130.

55 Jaak Panksepp, "The Periconscious Substrates of Consciousness: Affective States and the Evolutionary Origins of the Self," *Journal of Consciousness Studies* 5:5–6 (1998), p. 566.

56 Thompson, *Mind in Life: Biology, Phenomenology, and the Sciences of the Mind*.

57 Sheets-Johnstone, "Emotion and Movement: A Beginning Empirical-Phenomenological Analysis of Their Relationship."

58 Giovanna Colombetti, *The Feeling Body: Affective Science Meets the Enactive Mind* (Cambridge, MA: MIT Press, 2014), p. 63.

59 Ibid.

60 Lisa Feldman Barret, "The Experience of Emotion," *Annual Review of Psychology* 58 (2008), pp. 373–403.

61 Barbara Montero, "Proprioception as an Aesthetic Sense," *Journal of Aesthetics and Art Criticism* 64:2 (2006), p. 236.

62 Jonathan Cole & Barbara Montero, "Affective Proprioception," *Janus Head* 9:2 (2007), pp. 302–304.

63 A point stressed by John Templar, *The Staircase: History and Theories* (Cambridge, MA: MIT Press, 1992).

64 Calvo-Merino et al., "Towards a Sensorimotor Aesthetics of Performing Art," p. 920. See also C. Urgesi et al., "Representation of Body Identity and Body Actions in Extrastriate Body Area and Ventral Premotor Cortex," *Nature Neuroscience* 10 (2007), pp. 30–31.

65 Robinson, *Nesting*.

66 Pallasmaa, "The Architecture of the Seven Senses," p. 35.

67 See Morten Kringelbach, "The Hedonic Brain: A Functional Neuroanatomy of Human Pleasure," in Morten Kringelbach & Kent C. Berridge (eds.) *Pleasures of the Brain* (Oxford: Oxford University Press, 2010), pp. 202–217. See also Martin Skov, "The Pleasure of Art," same volume, pp. 270–281.

68 Semir Zeki, *Inner Vision: An Exploration of Art and the Brain* (Oxford: Oxford University Press, 1999), pp. 99–103.

69 See Christoph Redies, "A Universal Model of Esthetic Perception Based on the Sensory Coding of Natural Stimuli," *Spatial Vision* 27 (2007), p. 97. See also Daniel Graham & Christoph Redies, "Statistical Regularities in Art: Relations with Visual Coding and Perception," *Vision Research* 50 (2010), pp. 1503–1509.

70 Thomas Albright, "Neuroscience for Architecture," in Sarah Robinson & Juhani Pallasmaa (eds.) *Mind in Architecture: Neuroscience, Embodiment, and the Future of Design* (Cambridge, MA: MIT Press, 2015), p. 207.

71 See Moshe Bar & Maital Neta, "Humans Prefer Curved Visual Objects," *Psychological Science* 17:8 (2006), pp. 645–648; "Visual Elements of Subjective Preference Modulate Amygdala Activation," *Neuropsychologia* 45 (2007), pp. 2191–2200.

72 Juhani Pallasmaa, "Hapticity and Time: Notes on Fragile Architecture," in Juhani Pallasmaa & Peter MacKeith (eds.) *Encounters 1: Architectural Essays* (Helsinki: Rakennustieto Publishing, 2012), p. 331.

73 See Kevin Rooney, "Vision and the Experience of Built Environments: Two Visual Pathways of Awareness and Embodiment in Architecture" (Ph.D. diss., Kansan State University, 2015).

74 Aude Oliva & Antonio Torralba, "Building the Gist of a Scene: The Role of Global Image Features in Recognition," *Progress in Brain Research* 155 (2006), pp. 23–36.

75 J. Keven O'Regan & Alva Noë, "A Sensorimotor Account of Visions and Visual Consciousness," *Behavioral and Brain Sciences* 24 (2000), pp. 940 & 1021.

76 There is evidence that at least some neurons, V1 & V2, respond to other contextual influences such as movements, contours, and color. See Thomas Albright & Gene Stoner, "Contextual Influence on Visual Processing," *Annual Review of Neuroscience* 25 (2002), pp. 339–379.

77 Thomas Albright, "An Excellent Lightness," *Science* 273 (August 23, 1996), pp. 1055–1056.

78 See A. D. Milner & M. A. Goodale, "Separate Visual Pathways for Perception and Action," *Trends in Neuroscience* 15:1 (1992), pp. 20–25.

79 See Giocomo Rizzolatti & Massimo Matelli, "Two different streams form the dorsal visual system: anatomy and functions," *Experimental Brain Research* 153 (2003), pp. 146–157.

80 Vittorio Gallese, "The Multimodal Nature of Visual Perception: Facts and Speculations," *Gestalt Theory* 38:2/3 (2016), p. 128.

81 Nancy Kanwisher et al., "A Locus in Human Extrastriate Cortex for Visual Shape Analysis," *Journal of Cognitive Neuroscience* 9:1 (1997), pp. 133–142; Zoe Kourtzi & Nancy Kanwisher, "Cortical Regions Involved in Perceiving Object Shape," *Journal of Neuroscience* 20:9 (May 1, 2000), pp. 3310–3318.

82 Nancy Kanwisher et al., "The Fusiform Face Area: A Module in Human Extrastriate Cortex Specialized for Face Perception," *Journal of Neuroscience* 17:11 (1997), pp. 4302–4311.

83 Paul Downing et al., "A Cortical Area Selective for Visual Processing of the Human Body," *Science* 293:5539 (September 28, 2001), pp. 2470–2473.

84 Isabel Gauthier et al., "Expertise for Cars and Birds Recruits Brain Areas Involved in Face Recognition," *Nature Neuroscience* 3:2 (2000), pp. 191–197; James Tanaka & Tim Curran, "A Neural Basis for Expert Object Recognition," *Psychological Science* 12:1 (2001), pp. 43–47.

85 Jonathan Cant & Melvyn Goodale, "Scratching Beneath the Surface: New Insights into the Functional Properties of the Lateral Occipital Area and

Parahippocampal Place Areas," *Journal of Neuroscience* 31:22 (June 1, 2011), pp. 8248–8258. There is also flexibility in these areas. See Zoe Kourtzi, "Visual Learning for Perceptual and Categorical Decisions in the Human Brain," *Vision Research* 50 (2010), p. 433.

86 Geoffrey Aguirre et al., "An Area within Human Ventral Cortex Sensitive to 'Building' Stimuli: Evidence and Implications," *Neuron* 21 (August 1998), pp. 373–383.

87 Russell Epstein & Nancy Kanwisher, "A Cortical Representation of the Local Visual Environment," *Nature* 392 (April 9, 1998), pp. 598–601.

88 Godehard Weniger et al., "The Human Parahippocampal Cortex Subserves Egocentric Spatial Learning during Navigation in a Virtual Maze," *Neurobiology of Learning and Memory* 93 (2010), pp. 46–55.

89 Russell Epstein et al., "Parahippocampal and Retrosplenial Contributions to Human Spatial Navigation," *Trends in Cognitive Sciences* 12:10, pp. 388–396.

90 Gaspare Galati et al., "Multiple Reference Frames Used by the Human Brain for Spatial Perception and Memory," *Experimental Brain Research* 206 (2010), p. 119.

91 Michael Arbib & James Bonaiuto, "Multiple Levels of Spatial Organization: World Graphs and Spatial Difference Learning," *Adaptive Behavior* 20:4 (2012), pp. 287–303.

92 Gerd Kempermann & Fred Gage, "New Nerve Cells for the Adult Brain," *Scientific American* 280:5 (1999), pp. 48–53.

93 Zoe Kourtzi & James DiCarlo, "Learning and Neural Plasticity in Visual Object Recognition," *Current Opinion in Neurobiology* 16 (2006), pp. 152–158; Hans Op De Beeck et al., "Discrimination Training Alters Object Representations in Human Extrastriate Cortex," *Journal of Neuroscience* 26:50 (December 13, 2006), pp. 13025–13036.

94 Charlette Alme et al., "Place Cells in the Hippocampus: Eleven Maps for Eleven Rooms," *Proceedings of the National Academy of Sciences* 111:52 (2014), pp. 18428–18435.

95 James B. Ranck, "Head-Direction Cells in the Deep Cell Layers of Dorsal Presubiculum in Freely Moving Rats," *Society of Neuroscience* 10 (1984), p. 599.

96 Michaël Zugaro et al., "Rapid Spatial Reorientation and Head Direction Cells," *Journal of Neuroscience* 23:8 (April 15, 2013), pp. 3478–3482.

97 Torkel Hafting et al., "Microstructure of a Spatial Map in the Entorhinal Cortex," *Nature* 436:11 (August 11, 2005), pp. 801–806.

98 Ibid., p. 801.

99 Joshua Jacobs et al., "Direct Recordings of Grid-Like Neuronal Activity in Human Spatial Cognition," *Nature Neuroscience* 16:9 (2013), pp. 1188–1191; Francesco Savelli et al., "Influence of boundary removal on the spatial representations of the medial entorhinal cortex," *Hippocampus* 18 (2008), pp. 1270–1282; T. Solstad et al., "Representation of Geometric Borders in the Entorhinal Cortex," *Science* 322 (2008), pp. 1865–1868.

100 Eleanor Maguire et al., "Recalling Routes around London: Activation of the Right Hippocampus in Taxi Drivers," *Journal of Neuroscience* 17:18 (September 15, 1997), pp. 7103–7110. Another fMRI study has since shown that the right hippocampus predicts the use of allocentric spatial representation, while the left hippocampus predicts the use of sequential egocentric representation, see Kinga Iglói et al., "Lateralized Human Hippocampal Activity Predicts Navigation Based on Sequence or Place Memory," *Proceedings of the National Academy of Sciences* 107:32 (August 10, 2010), pp. 14466–14471.

101 Arne Ekstrom et al., "Cellular Networks Underlying Human Spatial Navigation," *Nature* 425 (September 11, 2003), p. 187.

102 Jennifer Groh, *Making Space: How the Brain Knows Where Things Are* (Cambridge, MA: Harvard University Press, 2014), p. 200.

103 See Cicero, *De oratore* (London: Routledge & Kegan Paul, 1966), II:351–354. See also the first chapter of Frances Yates, *The Art of Memory* (London: Routledge & Kegan Paul, 1966).

104 See Daniel L Schacter et al., "The Future of Memory: Remembering, Imagining, and the Brain," *Neuron* 76 (November 21, 2012), pp. 677–694.

105 Eleanor Maguire & Sinéad Mullally, "The Hippocampus: A Manifesto for Change," *Journal of Experimental Psychology* 142:4 (2013), p. 1181.

106 Instrumental in this regard are the numerous writings of Juhani Pallasmaa and such recent studies as Joyce Malnar & Frank Vodvarka, *Sensory Design* (Minneapolis: University of Minnesota Press, 2004).

107 Hall, *The Hidden Dimension*, p. 47.

108 Richard Neutra, *Survival through Design* (London: Oxford University Press, 1954), p. 200.

109 Ibid., p. 147.

110 Yi-Fu Tuan, *Space and Place: The Perspective of Experience* (Minneapolis: University of Minnesota Press, 1977), p. 11.

111 J. Douglas Porteous, *Landscapes of the Mind: Worlds of Sense and Metaphor* (Toronto: University of Toronto Press, 1990), pp. 48–52.

112 Daniel Levitin, "The Illusion of Music," *New Scientist* 197:2644 (February 23, 2008), p. 34.

113 Daniel Levitin & Anna Tirovalas, "Current Advances in the Cognitive Neuroscience of Music," *Annals of the New York Academy of Science* 1156:211–231 (2009), pp. 211–231.

114 Lutz Jäncke et al., "Attention Modulates Activity in the Primary and Secondary Auditory Cortex: A Functional Magnetic Resonance Imaging Study in Human Subjects," *Neuroscience Letters* 266:2 (May 7, 1999), pp. 125–128.

115 Don Ihde, *Listening and Voice, Phenomenologies of Sound*, 2nd edn. (Albany: State University of New York Press, 2007), pp. 50–51.

116 R. Murray Schafer, "Acoustic Space," in David Seamon & Robert Mugerauer (eds.) *Dwelling, Place & Environment* (New York: Columbia University Press, 1985), p. 93.

117 R. Murray Schafer, *Our Sonic Environment and The Soundscape: The Tuning of the World* (Rochester, VT: Destiny Books, 1977/1994), p. 219.

118 Neutra, *Survival through Design*, p. 142.

119 Peter Zumthor, *Atmospheres: Architectural Environments: Surrounding Objects* (Basel: Birkhäuser, 2006), p. 29.

120 Schafer, *Our Sonic Environment and the Soundscape*, p. 222.

121 Ibid., p. 223.

Chapter 5

1 Neutra, *Survival through Design*, p. 118.

2 Otto Wagner, *Modern Architecture: A Guidebook for His Students to This Field of Art*, trans. H. F. Mallgrave (Santa Monica: Getty Publications, 1988), p. 77.

3 Adolf Loos, "Architektur" (1909), in *Trotzdem 1900–1930* (Vienna: Prachner Verlag, 1931/1982), pp. 90–104 (trans. mine).

4 Hermann Muthesius, *Style-Architecture and Building-Art*, trans. Stanford Anderson (Santa Monica: Getty Publications, 1994), p. 98.

5 Walter Curt Behrendt, *The Victory of the New Building Style*, trans. Harry F. Mallgrave (Los Angeles: Getty Publications, 2000), p. 89; J. J. P. Oud, "Architecture and the Future," *The Studio* 98 (1928), p. 405.

6 Sigfried Giedion, *Building in France, Building in Iron, Building in Ferro-Concrete*, trans. J. Duncan Berry (Santa Monica: Getty Publications, 1995), p. 94.

7 Henry-Russel Hitchcock & Philip Johnson, *The International Style* (New York: W. W. Norton & Company, 1966).

8 Hans-Georg Gadamer, *The Relevance of the Beautiful and Other Essays*, trans. by Nicholas Walker (New York: Cambridge University Press, 1986); Elaine Scarry, *On Beauty and Being Just* (Princeton: Princeton University Press, 1999).

9 Roger Scruton, "Why Beauty Matters," (2009). Https://vimeo.com/112655231.

10 Joseph Brodsky, "An Immodest Proposal," in *On Grief and Reason* (New York: Farrar, Straus and Giroux, 1997), p. 207.

11 Dennis Dutton, *The Art Instinct: Beauty, Pleasure, and Human Evolution* (New York: Bloomsbury Press, 2009); V. S. Ramachandran & William Hirstein, "The Science of Art: A Neurological Theory of Aesthetic Experience," *Journal of Consciousness Studies* 6:6–7 (1999), pp. 15–51; Anjan Chatterjee, *The Aesthetic Brain: How We Evolved to Desire Beauty and Enjoy Art* (Oxford: Oxford University Press, 2014).

12 Alexander Baumgarten, *Aesthetica/Ästhetik*, 2 vols. ed. Dagmar Mirback (Hamburg: Felix Meiner Verlag, 2007), §1.

13 Hume first published his essay "On the Delicacy of Taste and Passion" in 1754, and he followed in 1757 with "Of the Standard of Taste," one of his *Four Dissertations*. Burke's book first appeared in 1757, but he held back the introductory essay until the second edition of 1759.

14 Ernst Cassirer, *Kant's Life and Thought*, trans. James Haden (New Haven: Yale University Press, 1981), p. 287.

15 Immanuel Kant, *Kritik der Urteilskraft, Werke in zwölf Bänden*, vol. 10 (1977), §1:113. Frankfurt. www.wissensnavigator.com/documents/**kritikderurteilskraft**.pdf (trans. mine).

16 Ibid., §54:270.

17 Ibid., §54:276.

18 Steven Brown et al., "Naturalizing Aesthetics: Brain Areas for Aesthetic Appraisal Across Sensory Modalities," *NeuroImage* 58 (2011), p. 257.

19 Vittorio Gallese, "Visions of the Body: Embodied Simulation and Aesthetic Experience" (Franklin Humanities Institute, Duke University, 2017), p. 5.

20 Noë, *Action in Perception*, p. 1.

21 Thompson, *Mind in Life*, p. 383.

22 Andrea Jelić et al., "The Enactive Approach to Architectural Experience: A Neurophysiological Perspective on Embodiment, Motivation, and Affordances," *Frontiers in Psychology* 7:481 (March 2016), Doi: 10:3389/fpsyg.2016.00481.

23 Camilo Cela-Conde et al., "Activation of the Prefrontal Cortex in the Human Visual Aesthetic Perception," *Proceedings of the National Academy of Sciences* 101:16 (April 20, 2004), pp. 6321–6325.

24 Dewey, *Art as Experience*, p. 44.

25 Ibid., p. 16.

26 Mark Johnson, *The Meaning of the Body: Aesthetics of Human Understanding* (Chicago: University of Chicago Press, 1999), p. 212.

27 Mark Johnson, "The Embodied Meaning of Architecture," in S. Robinson & J. Pallasmaa (eds.) *Mind in Architecture: Neruroscience, Embodiment, and the Future of Design* (Cambridge, MA: MIT Press, 2015), p. 38.

28 Gadamer, *The Relevance of the Beautiful*, p. 53.

29 Hans-Georg Gadamer, *Truth and Method*, trans. Joel Weinsheimer & Donald Marshall (New York: Continuum, 1999), p. 61.

30 Ibid., p. 70.

31 Colombetti, *The Feeling Body*, pp. 1–2.

32 Giovanna Colombetti & Evan Thompson, "The Feeling Body: Towards an Enactive Approach to Emotion," in W. F. Overton et al. (eds.) *Developmental Perspectives on Embodiment and Consciousness* (New York: Erlbaum, 2008), p. 59.

33 Ioannis Xenakis & Argyris Arnellos, "Aesthetic perception and its minimal content: a naturalistic perspective," *Frontiers in Psychology* 5:1038 (September 2014), Abstract. Doi: 10.3389/fpsyg.2014.01038.

34 Richard Payne Knight, *An Analytical Inquiry into the Principles of Taste* (London: Mews-Gate & J. White, 1805), p. 196.
35 Alberto Pérez-Gómez, *Attunement: Architectural Meaning after the Crisis of Modern Science* (Cambridge, MA: MIT Press, 2016), p. 157.
36 Robert Lamb Hart, *A New Look at Humanism: In Architecture, Landscapes and Urban Design* (California: Meadowlark Publishing, 2015), p. 99.
37 Jaak Panksepp, *Affective Neuroscience: The Foundations of Human and Animal Emotions* (Oxford: Oxford University Press, 1998), p. 144.
38 Mariann Weierich et al., "Novelty as a Dimension in the Affective Brain," *NeuroImage* 49 (2010), pp. 2871–2878.
39 Dost Öngur et al., "Hippocampal Activation During Processing of Previously seen Visual Stimulus Pairs," *Psychiatry Research: Neuroimaging* 139 (2005), pp.191–198.
40 See Upali Nanda & Ben Jansen, "Image and Emotion: From Outcomes to Brain Behavior," *HERD* 5:4 (2012), pp. 40–59.
41 Bar & Neta, "Humans Prefer Curved Visual Objects," pp. 645–648; Bar & Neta, "Visual Elements of Subjective Preference Modulate Amygdala Activation," pp. 2191–2200.
42 Oshin Vartanian et al., "Impact of Contour on Aesthetic Judgments and Approach-Avoidance Decisions in Architecture," *Proceedings of the National Academy of Sciences* 110:2 (2015), pp. 10446–10453.
43 Oshin Vartinian et al., "Architectural Design and the Brain: Effects of Ceiling Height and Perceived Enclosure on Beauty Judgments and Approach-Avoidance Decisions," *Journal of Environment Psychology* 41 (2015), Abstract.
44 Arthur Stamps, "Visual Permeability, Locomotive Permeability, Safety, and Enclosure," *Environment and Behavior* 37:5 (2005), pp. 587–619; Arthur Stamps, "Effects of Permeability on Perceived Enclosure and Spaciousness," *Environment and Behavior* 42:6 (2010), pp. 864–886. See also David Techau, "Buildings, Brains and Behaviour: Towards an Affective Neuroscience of Architecture," *World Health Design* (January 2016), pp. 24–37. He looked at the eudaimonia (psychological and social engagement) and *hedonia* (well-being of occupants)—of open floor plans in green office buildings and found a number of affirmative responses from workers, among them fresher air and lots of natural lighting, more comfort with better seasonal control of temperature, and greater worker activity and vitality.
45 See Ellard's chapter on "Boredom" in his book *Places of the Heart: The Psychogeography of Everyday Life* (New York: Bellevue Literary Press, 2015).
46 Paul Hekkert et al., "'Most Advanced, Yet Acceptable': Typicality and Novelty as Joint Predictors of Aesthetic Preference in Industrial Design," *British Journal of Psychology* 94 (2003), pp. 111–124.
47 Paul Hekkert et al., "Design Aesthetics: Principles of Pleasure in Design," *Psychology Science* 48:2 (2006), p. 162.
48 Ibid., pp. 163–164.
49 See, for instance, Schacter et al., "The Future of Memory," pp. 677–694; Maguire & Mullally, "The Hippocampus."

50 Robert Zatorre et al., "Hearing in the Mind's Ear: PET Investigation of Musical Imagery and Perception," *Journal of Cognitive Neuroscience* 8 (1998), pp. 29–46; Robert Zatorre, "Brain Imaging Studies of Musical Perception and Musical Imagery," *Journal of New Music Research* 28:3 (1999), pp. 229–236.

51 Stephen Kosslyn, "Neural Foundations of Imagery," *Nature Reviews: Neuroscience* 2 (September 2001), p. 641.

52 William James, *The Principles of Psychology* (New York: Dover, 1950), II. 72 (author's emphasis).

53 Anton Ehrenzweig, *The Hidden Order of Art* (Berkeley: University of California Press, 1971), p. xii. See also Arthur Koestler, *The Act of Creation* (New York: The Macmillan Company, 1969). Juhani Pallasmaa has also made this point in "In Praise of Vagueness," in Peter MacKeith (ed.) *Encounters 2: Architectural Essays* (Helsinki: Rakennustieto Publishing, 2012), pp. 224–236.

54 For example, Iain McGilchrist, *The Master and His Emissary: The Divided Brain and the Making of the Western World*, p. 198, sees creativity as a struggle between the two hemispheres that compete with each other but at the same time must find some accommodation. Vinod Goel, in his paper "Creative brains: designing in the real world," proposes a "frontal lobe lateralization hypothesis." In attempting to map the creative processes of Jørn Utzon in his design for the Sydney Opera, Goel argues that creativity demands an array of imaginative streams: some vague and ambiguous, others precise and concrete. Vagueness (housed in the right prefrontal cortex) supports the associative processes that broaden the space of imagination, whereas precision (housed in the left prefrontal cortex) supports the inference processes that deepen the creative problem.

55 Hans Ulrich Gumbrecht, *Production of Presence: What Meaning Cannot Convey* (Stanford: Stanford University Press, 2004).

56 See Julie V. Lovine, "Ancient Lessons in Modern Forms," *The Wall Street Journal* (Monday, March 27, 2017), p. A12.

57 Esther Sperber, "The Wings of Daedalus: Toward a Relational Architecture," *Psychoanalytic Review* 103:5 (October 2016), p. 594.

58 See Irving Biederman & Edward Vessel, "Perceptual Pleasure and the Brain: A Novel Theory Explains Why the Brain Craves Information and Seeks It Through the Senses," *American Scientist* (May–June 2006), p. 250.

Chapter 6

1 Manfred Clynes, *Sentics: The Touch of Emotions* (Garden City, NY: Anchor Press, 1977), p. 53.

2 Johann Gottfried Herder, *Another Philosophy of History*, trans. by Ionnis Evrigenis and Daniel Pellerin (Indianapolis: Hackett Publishing Company, 2004), p. 63.

3 Vischer, "On the Optical Sense of Form," p. 92.

4 Wölfflin, "Prolegomena to a Psychology of Architecture."

NOTES

5   Ibid., p. 183.
6   Wölfflin, *Renaissance and Baroque*.
7   Adolf Göller, "What Is the Cause of Perpetual Style Change in Architecture?" in *Empathy, Form, and Space*, p. 195.
8   Cornelius Gurlitt, "Göller's ästhetische Lehre," *Deutsche Bauzeitung* 21 (December, 1887), pp. 602–607.
9   Bernard Berenson, *The Florentine Painters of the Renaissance* (New York: G. P. Putnam's Sons, 1896).
10 R. G. Collingwood, *The Principles of Art* (London: Oxford University Press, 1974), p. 147.
11 Vernon Lee & Clementina Anstruther-Thomson, "Anthropomorphic Aesthetics," in *Beauty and Ugliness and Other Studies in Psychological Aesthetics* (London: John Lane, The Bodley Head, 1912), pp. 28–29.
12 Clive Bell, *Art* (New York: Capricorn Books, 1954), pp. 17–18.
13 Rudolf Arnheim, *Art and Visual Perception: A Psychology of the Creative Eye* (Berkeley and Los Angeles: University of California Press, 1974), p. 47.
14 Rudolf Arnheim, *The Dynamics of Architectural Form* (Berkeley: University of California Press, 1977), p. 42.
15 Ernst Gombrich, *The Sense of Order: A Study in the Psychology of Decorative Art* (Ithaca: Cornell University Press, 1979), p. 4.
16 Ernst Gombrich, "'The Sense of Order': An Exchange," *New York Review of Books* (September 27, 1979).
17 Ernst Gombrich, "The Mask and the Face: The Perception of Physiognomic Likeness in Life and in Art," in *The Image and the Eye: Further Studies in the Psychology of Pictorial Representation* (Ithaca: Cornell University Press, 1982), p. 128. Gombrich's observations on innate musical structures have also been borne out more recent research on musical universals. See Andrea Ravignani et al., "Musical Evolution the Lab Exhibits Rhythmic Universals," *Nature Human Behaviour* 1:007 (December 19, 2016), and Steven Brown & Joseph Jordania, "Universals in the World's Musics," *Psychology of Music* (December 15, 2011). DOI: 10.1177/0305735611425896.
18 Christa Sütterlin, "From Sign and Schema to Iconic Representation: Evolutionary Aesthetics of Pictorial Art," in Eckart Voland & Karl Grammer (eds.) *Evolutionary Aesthetics* (Berlin: Springer 2013), p. 136.
19 Semir Zeki, "Clive Bell's 'Significant Form' and the Neurobiology of Aesthetics," *Frontiers in Human Neuroscience* (November 12, 2013). Doi: 10.3389/fnhum.2013.00730.
20 Tomohiro Ishizu & Semir Zeki, "Toward a Brain-Based Theory of Beauty," *PLoS One* 6:7 (2011), e21852.
21 Zeki, "Clive Bell's 'Significant Form' and the Neurobiology of Aesthetics," p. 9.
22 Clynes, *Sentics*, pp. 59–74.
23 Rizzolatti & Singaglia, *Mirrors in the Brain*, p. 35.
24 Thomas Van Rompay et al., "Grounding Abstract Object Characteristics in Embodied Interactions," *Acta Psychologica* 119 (2005), pp. 315–351.

25 Nina Gaissert et al., "Similarity and Categorization: From Vision to Touch," *Acta Psychologica* 138 (2011), pp. 219 & 229.

26 Cinzia Di Dio et al., "The Golden Beauty: Brain Response to Classical and Renaissance Sculptures," *PLoS One* 2:11 (2007), e1201. Doi:10:1371/journal.pone0001201.

27 Gerald Cupchik et al., "Viewing Artworks: Contributions of Cognitive Control and Perceptual Facilitation to Aesthetic Experience," *Brain and Cognition* 70 (2009), pp. 84–91.

28 David Freedberg & Vittorio Gallese, "Motion, Emotion and Empathy in Esthetic Experience," *Trends in Cognitive Sciences* 11:5 (2007), p. 197.

29 Semper, *Style in the Technical and Tectonic Arts; or, Practical Aesthetics*, pp. 731–732. Semper was describing the energetic forces of the rusticated blocks he used in the Dresden Art Gallery.

30 Allesandra Umilta, "Abstract art and cortical motor activation: an EEG study," *Frontiers in Human Neuroscience* (November 16, 2012). Doi: 10.3389/fnhum.2012.00311.

31 Beatrice Sbriscia-Fioretti et al., "ERP Modulation during Observation of Abstract Paintings by Franz Kline," *PlosOne* 8:10 (2013), e75241.

32 Semper considered the idea of space as the "future of architecture" most explicitly in his lecture of 1869, "On Architectural Styles." See Semper, *The Four Elements of Architecture and Other Writings*, p. 281. See Conrad Fiedler, "Observations on the Nature and History of Architecture," in *Empathy, Form, and Space: Problems in German Aesthetics*, pp. 125–146.

33 Adolf Hildebrand, "The Problem of Form in the Fine Arts," in *Empathy, Form, and Space: Problems in German Aesthetics*, p. 259.

34 Mitchell Schwarzer, "The Emergence of Architectural Space: August Schmarsow's Theory of *Raumgestaltung*," *Assemblage* 15 (August 1991), pp. 53–54.

35 August Schmarsow, "The Essence of Architectural Creation," in *Empathy, Form, and Space: Problems in German Aesthetics*, pp. 286–287 (italics in original).

36 Ibid., p. 286.

37 Ibid., p. 288.

38 Merleau-Ponty, *The Phenomenology of Perception*, p. 143.

39 Ibid., p. 243.

40 Matthew Botvinick & Jonathan Cohen, "Rubber hands 'feel' touch that eyes see," *Nature* 391 (February 19, 1998), p. 756.

41 Carrie K. Armel & V. S. Ramachandran, "Projecting Sensations to External Objects: Evidence from Skin Conductance Response," *Proceedings of the Royal Society of London B* 270 (2007), pp. 1499–1506. See also H. Henrik Ehrsson et al., "That's My Hand! Activity in Premotor Cortex Reflects Feeling of Ownership of a Limb," *Science* 305 (August 6, 2004), pp. 875–877.

42 Bigna Lenggenhager et al., "Spatial Aspects of Bodily Self-Consciousness," *Consciousness and Cognition* 18 (2009), pp. 110–117; Binga Lenggenhager et al., "Video Ergo Sum: Manipulating Bodily Self-Consciousness," *Science* 317 (2007), pp. 1096–1099.

NOTES

43 Olaf Blanke, "Multisensory Brain Mechanisms of Bodily Self-Consciousness," *Nature Reviews: Neuroscience* 13 (August 2012), pp. 556–571.

44 Giocomo Rizzolatti et al., "The Space Around Us," *Science* 277 (July 11, 1997), pp. 190–191.

45 Justine Cléry et al., "Neuronal bases of peripersonal and extrapersonal spaces, their plasticity and their dynamics: Knows and unknowns," *Neuropsychologia* 20 (2015), pp. 313–326.

46 Jean-Paul Noel et al., "Full Body Action Remapping of Peripersonal Space: The Case of Walking," *Neuropsychologia* 70 (2015), pp. 375–384.

47 Michiel Van Elk & Olaf Blanke, "Manipulable Objects Facilitate Cross-Modal Integration in Peripersonal Space," *PLoS ONE* 6:9 (2011), e24641.

48 Marcella Costantini et al., "When Objects Are Close to Me: Affordances in the Peripersonal Space," *Psychonic Bulletin & Review* 18 (2011), pp. 302–308.

49 Gabrielle Benette Jackson, "Skillful Action in Peripersonal Space," *Phenomenological Cognitive Science* (March 13, 2013). DOI: 1007/s11097-013-9301-7.

50 Chiara Teneggi et al., "Social Modulation of Peripersonal Space Boundaries," *Current Biology* 23 (March 4, 2013), pp. 406–411.

51 Michael Schaefer et al., "Close to You: Embodied Simulation for Peripersonal Space in Primary Somatosensory Cortex," *PLoS ONE* 7:8 (2012), e42308.

52 See Stamps, "Visual Permeability, Locomotive Permeability, Safety, and Enclosure," pp. 587–619; Stamps, "Effects of Permeability on Perceived Enclosure and Spaciousness," pp. 864–886. See also Vartinian et al., "Architectural Design and the Brain," pp. 10–18.

53 Vartanian et al., "Impact of Contour on Aesthetic Judgments and Approach-Avoidance Decisions in Architecture," p. 10451.

54 John Goodbun, "The Architecture of the Extended Mind: Towards a Critical Urban Ecology" (Ph.D. diss., University of Westminster, 2011), p. 192.

55 Isabella Pasqualini et al., "'Seeing' and 'Feeling' Architecture: How Bodily Self-Consciousness Alters Architectonic Experience and Affects the Perception of Interiors," *Frontiers in Psychology* 4:354 (2013), p. 9. Doi:10.3389/fpsyg.2013.00354 (italics in original). See also Isabella Pasqualini, "Architectonic Inception—Avatar Induces Body Expansion and Space Compression in Augmented Interiors."

56 See Vittorio Gallese, "The Roots of Empathy: The Shared Manifold Hypothesis and the Neural Basis of Intersubjectivity," *Psychopathology* 36:4 (2003), pp. 171–180. See also Dan Zahavi, *Subjectivity and Selfhood: Investigating the First-Person Perspective* (Cambridge, MA: MIT Press, 2005).

57 Suzanne Langer, *Mind: An Essay on Human Feeling* (Baltimore: The Johns Hopkins University Press, 1967), p. 160; *Feeling and Form: A Theory of Art Development from Philosophy in a New Key* (New York: Charles Scribner's Sons, 1953), p. 99.

58 Richard Etlin, "Aesthetics and the Spatial Sense of Self," *Journal of Aesthetics and Art Criticism* 56:1 (1998), pp. 1–19.

Chapter 7

1. Sinclair Gauldie, *Architecture: The Appreciation of the Arts* (New York: Oxford University Press, 1969), p. 182.
2. Jeff Malpas, *Place and Experience: A Philosophical Topography* (Cambridge: Cambridge University Press, 1999), pp. 19–43.
3. *Existence, Space & Architecture* was a transitional work of Norberg-Schulz, between the largely semiotic and methodological approach of *Intentions in Architecture* (1965) and *Genius Loci*, which carried the subtitle "Towards a Phenomenology of Architecture."
4. Kenneth Frampton, "On Reading Heidegger," *Oppositions* 4 (1974), Editorial.
5. Edward Relph, *Place and Placelessness* (Los Angeles: Sage, 1976), pp. 51–55, 140.
6. Gauldie, *Architecture*, p. 182.
7. Malpas, *Place and Experience*, pp. 31–32.
8. Jeff Malpas, "The Remembrance of Place," jeffmalpas.com/wp-content/uploads/2013/03/The-Remembrance-of-Place.pdf, p. 3.
9. Martin Heidegger, "Building, Dwelling, Thinking," in David Farrell Kress (ed.) *Basic Writings* (New York: Harper & Rowe, 1977), pp. 330 & 324.
10. Ibid., p. 332.
11. Christopher Tilley, *A Phenomenology of Landscape Places, Paths and Monuments* (Oxford: Berg, 1994), pp. 38, 47.
12. Tilley, *The Materiality of Stone*, p. 25.
13. Carsten Harries, *The Ethical Function of Architecture* (Cambridge, MA: MIT Press, 1998), p. 154.
14. Jacques-François Blondel, *Cours d'Architecture ou traité de la décoration, Distribution & Construction de bâtiments* (Paris: Desaint, 1771–77), I: pp. 373–374.
15. Nicolas Le Camus De Mézières, *The Genius of Architecture; or, The Analogy of That Art with Our Sensations*, trans. David Britt (Santa Monica, CA: Getty Publications, 1992), p. 95.
16. Ibid., p. 136.
17. Ibid., p. 71.
18. Semper, *Style in the Technical and Tectonic Arts*, pp. 439n.85.
19. Gernot Böhme, *Für eine ökologische Naturästhetik* (Frankfurt: Edition Suhrkamp, 1989).
20. Gernot Böhme, "Atmosphere as a Fundamental Concept of a New Aesthetics," *Thesis Eleven* 36 (1993), pp. 117–118.
21. Gernot Böhme, "Atmosphere as the Subject Matter of Architecture," in Philip Ursprung (ed.) *Herzog & DeMeuron: Natural History* (Montreal: Canadian Centre for Architecture, 2002), p. 402 (author's emphasis).
22. Gernot Böhme, "Atmosphere as Mindful Physical Presence in Space," *OASE Journal for Architecture* 91 (2013), p. 27.

23 Thomas Thiis-Evensen, *Archetypes in Architecture* (Oslo: Norwegian University Press, 1987), p. 387.

24 Harries, *The Ethical Function of Architecture*, p. 125.

25 Zumthor, *Atmospheres*, p. 17.

26 Juhani Pallasmaa, "On Atmosphere," in Peter MacKeith (ed.) *Encounters 2: Architectural Essays* (Helsinki: Rakennustieto Publishing, 2012), p. 240.

27 Tonino Griffero, "Architectural Affordances: The Atmospheric Authority of Spaces," in Philip Tidwell (ed.) *Architecture and Atmosphere* (Helsinki: Tapio Wirkkata-Rut Bryk Foundation, 2014), p. 26.

28 Ibid., p. 38.

29 Gernot Böhme, "Atmospheres: New Perspectives for Architecture and Design," in Philip Tidwell (ed.) *Architecture and Atmosphere*, p. 8.

30 Jean-Paul Thibaud, "Installing an Atmosphere," in Philip Tidwell (ed.) *Architecture and Atmosphere*, pp. 57–58.

31 Pérez-Gómez, *Attunement*, pp. 26 & 180.

32 Van Eyck, "Kaleidoscope of the Mind."

33 The seminal texts for biophilic design are Stephen Kellert, *Buildings for Life: Designing and Understanding the Human-Nature Connection* (Washington, DC: Island Press, 2005); Stephen Kellert et al., *Biophilic Design: The Theory, Science, and Practice of Bring Buildings to Life* (Hoboken, NJ: John Wiley & Sons, 2008); Timothy Beatley, *Biophilic Cities: Integrating Nature into Urban Design and Planning* (Washington, DC: Island Press, 2011).

34 See Jay Appleton, *The Experience of Landscape* (New York: John Wiley & Sons, 1975), p. vii.

35 The model was first presented in *The Nature of Experience: A Psychological Perspective* (New York: Cambridge University Press, 1989).

36 Roger S. Ulrich, "Visual Landscapes and Psychological Well-Being," *Landscape Research* 4:1 (1979), p. 21; "Natural Versus Urban Scenes: Some Psychophysiological Effects," *Environment and Behavior* 13:5 (September 1981), p. 546.

37 Roger S. Ulrich, "Biophilia, Biophobia, and Natural Landscapes," in *The Biophilic Hypothesis*, p. 94.

38 Andrea Faber Taylor et al., "Growing Up in the Inner City: Green Spaces as Places to Grow," *Environment and Behavior* 30:1 (1998), pp. 3–27; Frances Kuo & William Sullivan, "Environment and Crime in the Inner City: Does Vegetation Reduce Crime?" *Environment and Behavior* 33:3 (2001), pp. 343–367; Frances Kuo, "Coping with Poverty: Impacts of Environment and Attention in the Inner City," *Environment and Behavior* 33:1 (2001), pp. 5–34; Meghan T. Holtan et al., "Social Life under Cover: Tree Canopy and Social Capital in Baltimore, Maryland," *Environment and Behavior* 1:24 (2014); Austin Troy et al., "The Relationship between Tree Canopy and Crime Rates across an Urban-Rural Gradient in the Greater Baltimore Region," *Landscape and Urban Planning* 106 (2012), pp. 262–270; Amanda W. Vermuri et al., "A Tale of Two Scales: Evaluating the Relationship among Life Satisfaction, Social Capital, Income, and the Natural Environment at Individual and Neighborhood Levels in Metropolitan Baltimore," *Environment*

and Behavior 43:1 (2011), pp. 3–25; Catherine Ward Thompson et al., "More Green Space Is Linked to Less Stress in Deprived Communities: Evidence from Salivary Cortisol Patterns," *Landscape and Urban Planning* 105 (2012), pp. 221–229; Jenny J. Roe et al., "Green Space and Stress: Evidence from Cortisol Measures in Deprived Urban Communities," *International Journal of Environmental Research and Public Health* 10 (2013), pp. 4086–4103; Ronald Glaser & Janice Kiecolt-Glaser, "Stress-Induced Immune Dysfunction: Implications for Health," *Nature Reviews: Immunology* 5 (March 2005), pp. 243–251; Theodore Robles et al., "A New Look at Chronic Stress, Depression, and Immunity," *Current Directions in Psychological Science* 14:2 (2005), pp. 111–115.

39 Notable research studies are J. Maas et al., "Morbidity Is Related to a Green Living Environment," *Journal of Epidemiological Community Health* 63 (2009), pp. 967–973; Thomas Astell-Burt et al., "Does Access to Neighbourhood Green Space Promote a Healthy Duration of Sleep? Novel Findings from a Cross-Sectional Study of 259 319 Australians," *BMJ Open* (2013); T. Sugiyama et al., "Associations of Neighbourhood Greenness with Physical and Mental Health: Do Walking, Social Coherence and Local Social Interaction Explain the Relationships?" *Journal of Epidemiological Community Health* 62 (2008); D. Nutsford et al., "An Ecological Study Investigating the Association between Access to Urban Green Space and Mental Health," *Public Health* (2013). http://dx.doi.org/10.1016/j.puhe.2013.08.016; Ulrika Stigsdotter et al., "Health Promoting Outdoor Environments—Associations between Green Space, and Health, Health-Related Quality of Life and Stress Based on a Danish National Representative Survey," *Scandinavian Journal of Public Health* (April 22, 2010).

40 See Chun-Yen Chang et al., "Psychophysiological Responses and Restorative Values of Wilderness Environments," *USDA Forest Service Proceedings RMRS-P-49* (2007), pp. 479–484. Chun-Yen Chang et al., "Psychophysiological Responses and Restorative Values of Natural Environments in Taiwan," *Landscape and Urban Planning* 85 (2008), pp. 79–84.

41 Qing Li, "Effect of Forest Bathing Trips on Human Immune Function," pp. 9–17. Qing Li, "Phytoncides (Wood Essential Oils) Induce Human Natural Killer Cell Activity," *Immunopharmacology and Immunotoxicology* 28 (2006), pp. 319–333.

42 Grant Hildebrand, *The Wright Space: Pattern & Meaning in Frank Lloyd Wright's Houses* (Seattle: University of Washington Press, 1991).

43 Grant Hildebrand, *Origins of Architectural Pleasure* (Seattle: University of Washington Press, 1999).

44 See Jan Gehl, *Cities for People* (Washington: Island Press, 2010).

45 Ellard, *Places of the Heart,* pp. 107–124.

46 See Colleen Merrifield & James Danckert, "Characterising the Psychophysiological Signature of Boredom," *Experimental Brain Research* 232:2 (2014), pp. 481–491.

47 See Thomas Herzog et al., "Houses of Worship as Restorative Environments," *Environment and Behavior* 42:4 (2010), pp. 395–419; Pierre

Ouellette et al., "The Monastery as a Restorative Environment," *Journal of Environmental Psychology* 25 (2005), pp. 175–188.

48 Julio Bermudez et al. "Externally-Induced Meditative States: An Exploratory Fmri Study of Architects' Responses to Contemplative Architecture," *Frontiers of Architectural Research* (June 2017). http://dx.doi.org/10.1016/j.foar.2017.02.002, p. 10.

49 Jussi Tarveinen et al., "The Way Films Feel: Aesthetic Features and Mood in Film," *Psychology of Aesthetics, Creativity, and the Arts* 9:3 (2015), 254–265.

50 Sjoerd Ebisch et al., "The Sense of Touch: Embodied Simulation in a Visuotactile Mirroring Mechanism for Observed Animate or Inanimate Touch," *Journal of Cognitive Neuroscience* 20:9 (2008), p. 1621.

51 Juhani Pallasmaa, *The Thinking Hand: Existential and Embodied Wisdom in Architecture* (Chichester: John Wiley and Sons, 2009), pp. 101–102.

52 Marco Frascari, "The Tell-the-Tale Detail," *VIA* 7 (1984), p. 31.

53 Ibid., p. 29.

54 Kenneth Frampton, *Studies in Tectonic Culture: The Poetics of Construction in Nineteenth and Twentieth Century Architecture* (Cambridge, MA: MIT Press, 1995), p. 299.

55 Tim Ingold, *Making: Anthropology, Archaeology, Art and Architecture* (London: Routledge, 2013), p. 6.

56 Joseph Brodsky, "A Cat's Meow," in *On Grief and Reason* (New York: Farrar, Straus and Giroux, 1997), p. 301.

57 Ingold, *Making*, pp. 69 & 115.

58 Ibid., 128.

59 Elvin Karana et al., "Meanings of Materials through Sensorial Properties and Manufacturing," *Materials and Design* 30 (2009), pp. 2778–2784; "A Tool for Meaning Driven Materials Selection," *Materials and Design* 31 (2010), pp. 2932–2941.

60 Anna Fenko et al., "Looking Hot or Feeling Hot: What Determines the Product Experience of Warmth," *Materials and Design* 31 (2010), pp. 1325–1331.

61 Frampton, *Studies in Tectonic Culture*, p. 2.

62 Richard Sennett, *The Craftsman* (New Haven: Yale University Press, 2008), p. 7.

63 Arendt, *The Human Condition*.

64 Colin Rowe, "Introduction," in *Five Architects: Eisenman, Graves, Gwathmey, Hejuk, Meier* (New York: Oxford University Press, 1975), p. 4.

65 Roger Scruton, *The Aesthetics of Architecture* (Princeton, NJ: Princeton University Press, 1979), p. 205.

66 Ibid., p. 220.

67 Ibid., p. 233.

68 Edward R. Ford, *The Architectural Detail* (New York: Princeton Architectural Press, 2011), p. 268.

69 Ibid., p. 279. See Zumthor, *Atmospheres*, pp. 49–53.

70 Ford, *The Architectural Detail*, p. 309.

71 Pallasmaa, *The Thinking Hand*, p. 115.
72 Goodbun, "The Architecture of the Extended Mind," p. 182.
73 Bruce Metcalf, "Culture and Art, Culture and Biology," in Peter Dormer (ed.) *The Culture of Craft* (Manchester: Manchester University Press, 1997), pp. 75 & 80.

Chapter 8

1 Olaf Blanke & Thomas Metzinger, "Full-Body Illusions and Minimal Phenomenal Selfhood," *Trends in Cognitive Sciences* 13:1 (2008), Abstract.
2 Diedrich Mania & Ursula Mania, "The Natural and Socio-Cultural Environment of *Homo erectus* at Bilzingsleben, Germany," in Clive Gamble & Martin Porr (eds.) *The Hominid Individual in Context: Archaeological Investigations of Lower and Middle Palaeolithic landscapes, Locales and Artefacts* (London: Routledge, 2005), pp. 98–114.
3 Henry De Lumley, (*sous la direction de*), *Terra Amata: Nice, Alpes-Maritimes, France* (Paris: CNRS, 2009).
4 Josef Vallverdú et al., "Sleeping Activity Area with the Site Structure of Archaic Human Groups: Evidence from Abric Romaní Level N Combustion Activity Areas," *Current Anthropology* 51:1 (February 2010), pp. 137–145.
5 Vitruvius, *Ten Books on Architecture*, trans. Ingrid D. Rowland (New York: Cambridge University Press, 1999), Bk.2:1, p. 34.
6 Aristotle, *Politics*, 1253 ^{a}3–4.
7 Charles Darwin, *The Descent of Man and Selection in Relation to Sex*, 2nd edn. (New York: Lovell, Coryell & Company, 1874), p. 123.
8 See Joseph Rykwert, *On Adams House in Paradise: The Idea of the Primitive Hut in Architectural History* (New York: Museum of Modern Art, 1972). The "Laugierian moment," refers to Marc-Antoine Laugier's introductory remarks in *An Essay on Architecture*, trans. Wolfgang & Anni Hermann (Los Angeles: Hennessey & Ingalls).
9 All dates presented here and below are from the Smithsonian National Museum of Natural History. Http://humanorigins.si.edu/evidence/human-fossils/species.
10 Leslie Aiello & Peter Wheeler, "The Expensive-Tissue Hypothesis: The Brain and the Digestive System in Human and Primate Evolution," *Current Anthropology* 36:2, pp. 199–221.
11 Richard Wrangham, *Catching Fire: How Cooking Made Us Human* (London: Basic Books, 2009); Rachel Carmody & Richard Wrangham, "The Energetic Significance of Cooking," *Evolutionary Anthropology* 57:4 (2009), pp. 379–391.
12 Morten Kringelbach, "Food for Thought: Hedonic Experience beyond Homeostasis in the Human Brain," *Neuroscience* 126 (2004), pp. 807–819.
13 Peter Wheeler, "The Thermoregulatory Advantages of Heat-Storage in Shade-Seeking Behavior to Hominids Foraging in Equatorial Savanna Environments," *Journal of Human Evolution* 26:4 (1994), pp. 339–350.

14. Ikiki & Taoka, "Triadic (ecological, neural, cognitive) Niche Construction."
15. Michael Arbib, "From Monkey-Like Action Recognition to Human Language: An Evolutionary Framework for Neurolinguistics," *Behavioral and Brain Sciences* 28, pp. 105–167.
16. See Alison Wray, "Protolanguage as a Holistic System for Social Interaction," *Language & Communication* 18 (1998), pp. 47–67; see also Maggie Tallerman, "Did our Ancestors Speak a Holistic Protolanguage?" *Lingua* 117 (2007), pp. 579–604.
17. John Gamble, John Gowlett & Robin Dunbar, *Thinking Big: How the Evolution of Social Life Shaped the Human Mind* (London: Thames & Hudson, 2014), pp. 144–145.
18. Ann MacLarnon & Gwen Hewitt, "The Evolution of Human Speech: The Role of Enhanced Breathing Control," *American Journal of Physical Anthropology* 109 (1999), pp. 341–363.
19. I. Martinez et al., "Auditory Capacities in Middle Pleistocene Humans from the Sierra de Atapuerca in Spain," *Proceedings of the National Academy of Sciences* 101 (July 6, 2004), pp. 9976–9981.
20. Steven Mithen, *The Singing Neanderthals: The Origins of Music, Language, Mind, and Body* (Cambridge, MA: Harvard University Press, 2007), pp. 69–74.
21. Donald, *A Mind So Rare: The Evolution of Human Consciousness*, p. 15.
22. Marek Kohn & Steven Mithen, "Handaxes: Products of Sexual Selection?" *Antiquity* 73:281 (September 1999), pp. 518–527.
23. Stephen Edwards, "Nonutilitarian Activities in the Lower Paleolithic: A Look at the Two Kinds of Evidence," *Current Anthropology* 19:1 (1978), pp. 135–137.
24. Robert Bednarik, "A Figurine from the African Acheulian," *Current Anthropology* 44:3 (June 2003), pp. 405–413.
25. Francesco d'Errico & April Nowell, "A New Look at the Berekhat Ram Figurine: Implications for the Origins of Symbolism," *Cambridge Archaeological Journal* 10:1 (2000), pp. 146, 123–167.
26. Jean-Jacques Hublin et al., "New fossils from Jebel Irhoud, Morocco and the pan-African origin of *Homo sapiens*," *Nature* 546 (June 8, 2017), pp. 289–292.
27. Chris Stringer & Julia Galway-Witham, "On the Origin of Our Species," *Nature* 546 (June 8, 2017), pp. 212–214.
28. Christopher Henshilwood et al., "A 100,000-Year-Old Ochre-Processing Workshop at Blombos Cave, South Africa," *Science* 334 (October 14, 2011), pp. 219–222.
29. Christopher Henshilwood et al., "Engraved Ochres from the Middle Stone Age Levels at Blombos Cave, South Africa," *Journal of Human Evolution* 57 (2009), pp. 27–47.
30. Polly Wiessner, "Embers of Society: Firelight Talk among the Ju/'hoansi Bushman," *Proceedings of the National Academy of Sciences* 111:39 (September 30, 2014), pp. 14027–14035.
31. Robin Dunbar, "Neocortex Size as a Constraint on Group Size in Primates," *Journal of Human Evolution* 20 (1998), pp. 469–493.

32. See Gamble, Gowlett, & Dunbar, *Thinking Big*.
33. Ibid., pp. 65–72.
34. Michael Tomasello, *Origins of Human Communication* (Cambridge, MA: Harvard University Press, 2008).
35. Michael Tomasello, *The Cultural Origins of Human Cognition* (Cambridge, MA: Harvard University Press, 1999), p. 5.
36. Michael Tomasello, *A Natural History of Human Thinking* (Cambridge, MA: Harvard University Press, 2014), pp. 141–143.
37. Kim Sterelny, *The Evolved Apprentice: How Evolution Made Humans Unique* (Cambridge, MA: MIT Press, 2012), p. 122.
38. Donald, *A Mind So Rare: The Evolution of Human Consciousness*, p. 212.
39. Umberto Castiello et al., "Wired to be Social: The Ontogeny of Human Interaction," *PLoS ONE* 5:10 (October 2010), e 13199.
40. Colwyn Trevarthen & Kenneth Aitken, "Infant Intersubjectivity: Research, Theory, and Clinical Applications," *Journal of Child Psychology and Psychiatry* 42:1 (2001), pp. 3–48.
41. Ruth Feldman, "Parent-Infant Synchrony: A Biobehavioral Model of Mutual Influences in the Formation of Affiliative Bonds," *Monographs of the Society for Research in Child Development* 77:2 (2012), Abstract.
42. Ruth Feldman, "Parent-Infant Synchrony and the Construction of shared Timing; Physiological Precursors, Developmental Outcomes, and Risk Conditions," *Journal of Child Psychology and Psychiatry* 48:3 (2007), pp. 329–354.
43. Colwyn Trevarthen, "First things first: infants make good use of the sympathetic rhythm of imitation, without reason or language," *Journal of Child Psychotherapy* 31:1 (2005), pp. 91–113. See also "What Is It Like to Be a Person Who Knows Nothing? Defining the Active Intersubjective Mind of a Newborn Human Being," *Infant and Child Development* 20 (2011a), pp. 119–135.
44. Daniel Siegel, *The Developing Mind: How Relationships and the Brain Interact to Shape Who We Are* (New York: The Guilford Press, 2012), p. 308.
45. Stephen Malloch, "Mothers and Infants and Communicative Musicality," *Musicae Scientiae*, Special Issue 1999–2000, pp. 29–57.
46. Ann Fernald, "Intonation and Communicative Intent in Mother's Speech to Infants: Is the Melody the Message?" *Child Development* 60 (1989), pp. 1497–1510; "Prosody in Speech to Children: Prelinguistic and Linguistic Functions," *Annals of Child Development* 8 (1991), pp. 43–80.
47. Colwyn Trevarthan, "Born for Art, and the Joyful Companionship of Fiction," in Darcia Narvaez, Jaak Panksepp, Allan Schore, & Tracy Gleason (eds.) *Human Nature, Early Experience and the Environment of Evolutionary Adaptedness* (Oxford: Oxford University Press, 2012).
48. Ellen Dissanayake, *Art and Intimacy: How the Arts Began* (Seattle: University of Washington Press, 2000).
49. Ellen Dissanayake, "Root, Lead, Blossom, or Bole: Concerning the Origin and Adaptive Function of Music," in Stephen Malloch & Colwyn Trevarthen (eds.)

Communicative Musicality: Exploring the Basis of Human Companionship (Oxford: Oxford University Press, 2009), p. 23.

50 Sandra Trehub & E. G. Schellenberg, "Musical Predispositions in Infancy: An Update," in I. Peretz & R. Zatorre (eds.) *The Cognitive Neuroscience of Music* (Oxford: Oxford University Press, 1995), pp. 3–20; Sandra Trehub & Laurel J. Trainor, "Singing to Infants: Lullabies and Playsongs," *Advances in Infancy Research* 12 (1998), pp. 43–77.

51 Wei Gao et al., "Evidence on the emergence of the brain's default network from 2-week-old to 2-year-old healthy pediatric subjects," *Proceedings of the National Academy of Sciences* 106:16 (April 21, 2009), pp. 6790–6796.

52 Allan Schore, "Attachment, Affect Regulation, and the Developing Right Brain: Linking Developmental Neuroscience to Pediatrics," *Pediatrics in Review* 26:6 (June 2005), p. 208.

53 Narvaez, *Neurobiology and the Development of Human Morality*, pp. 114–116.

54 See Sandra Kahler & B. J. Freeman, "Analysis of Environmental Deprivation: Cognitive and Social Development in Romanian Orphans," *Journal of Child Psychological Psychiatry* 33:4 (1994), pp. 769–781; Michael Rutter et al., "Quasi-autistic Patterns following Severe Early Global Privation," *Journal of Child Psychology and Psychiatry* 40:4 (1999), pp. 537–549; Michael Rutter et al., "Effects of Profound Early Institutional Deprivation: An Overview of Findings from a UK Longitudinal Study of Romanian Adoptees," *European Journal of Developmental Psychology* 4:3 (2007), pp. 332–350; Harry Chugani et al., "Local Brain Functional Activity Following Early Deprivation: A Study of Postinstitutionalized Romanian Orphans," *NeuroImage* 14 (2001), pp. 1290–1301; Katia McLaughlin et al., "Causal Effects of the Early Caregiving Environment on Development of Stress Response Systems in Children," *Proceedings of the National Academy of Science* 112:18 (May 5, 2015), pp. 5637–5642.

55 See Rosenzweig et al., "Effects of Environmental Complexity and Training on Brain Chemistry and Anatomy"; Van Praag et al., "Neural Consequences of Environmental Enrichment"; Sampedro-Piquero et al., "Effects of Environmental Enrichment on Anxiety Responses, Spatial Memory and Cytochrome C Oxidase Activity in Adult Rats"; Costa-Goes et al., "Environmental Enrichment for Adult Rats: Effects on Train and State Anxiety"; Mármol et al., "Anti-Oxidative Effects Produced by Environmental Enrichment in the Hippocampus and Cerebral Cortex of Male and Female Rats"; Hannel, "Review: Environmental Enrichment and Brain Repair."

Chapter 9

1 Vesely, *Architecture in the Age of Divided Representation*, p. 373.

2 Jean Molino, "Toward an Evolutionary Theory of Music and Language," in N. L. Wallin, B. Meerke & S. Brown (eds.) *The Origins of Music* (Cambridge, MA: MIT Press, 2001), pp. 165–176.

3   Jerome Lewis, "A Cross-Cultural Perspective on the Significance of Music and Dance to Culture and Society: Insight from BaYaka Pygmies," in Michael A. Arbib (ed.) *Language, Music, and the Brain* (Cambridge, MA: MIT Press, 2013), Abstract.
4   Langer, *Feeling and Form*, p. 204.
5   Ibid., p. 203.
6   Ibid., p. 176.
7   Carol Krumhansl, "Music: A Link between Cognition and Emotion," *Current Directions in Psychological Science* 11:2 (April 2002), pp. 45–50.
8   Jaak Panksepp & Colwyn Trevarthen, "The Neuroscience of Emotion in Music," in Stephen Malloch & Colwyn Trevarthen (eds.) *Communicative Musicality* (Oxford: Oxford University Press, 2009), pp. 106–108.
9   Ibid., p. 109.
10 Ibid., p. 115.
11 Anne Blood & Robert Zatorre, "Intensely Pleasurable Responses to Music Correlate with Activity in Brain Regions Implicated in Reward and Emotion," *Proceedings of the National Academy of Sciences* 98:20 (September 25, 2001), pp. 11818–11823.
12 James, *The Principles of Psychology*, 2 vols., II:428.
13 Ibid.
14 Ellen Dissanayake, "Bodies Swayed to Music: The Temporal Arts as Integral to Ceremonial Ritual," *Communicative Musicality*, p. 537.
15 Joseph Rykwert, *The Idea of the Town: An Anthropology of Urban Form in Rome, Italy, and the Ancient World* (Princeton: Princeton University Press, 1976). See also Numa Denis Fustel De Coulanges, *The Ancient City: A Study of the Religion, Laws, and Institutions of Greece and Rome* (Mineola, NY: Dover Publications, 2006).
16 Pausanias, *Guide to Greece* (New York: Penguin Books, 1979), Bk4; sec. 27.
17 Rykwert, *The Idea of the Town*, pp. 44–48.
18 Indra Kagins McEwen, *Vitruvius: Writing the Body of Architecture* (Cambridge, MA: MIT Press, 2003), pp. 30 & 166.
19 Cicero, *De Legibus*, trans. Clinton Walker Keyes (Cambridge, MA: Harvard University Press, 1977), II:32.
20 Vitruvius, *Ten Books on Architecture*, Bk3, ch.4.
21 de Coulanges, *The Ancient City*, p. 212.
22 Malcolm Quantrill, *The Environmental Memory: Man and Architecture in the Landscape of Ideas* (New York: Schocken Books, 1987), p. 90.
23 Hans-Georg Gadamer, "The Relevance of the Beautiful," in *The Relevance of the Beautiful and Other Essays*, trans. by Nicholas Walker (New York: Cambridge University Press, 1986), pp. 35–36.
24 Ibid., p. 53.
25 Wendy James, *The Ceremonial Animal: A New Portrait of Anthropology* (Oxford: Oxford University Press, 2005), pp. 6–7.

26 Pérez-Gómez, *Attunement: Architectural Meaning after the Crisis of Modern Science*, p. 229.
27 Friedrich Schiller, *On the Aesthetic Education of Man in a Series of Letters*, trans. by Reginald Snell (New York: Frederick Ungar Publishing, 1977), p. 76.
28 Joseph Rykwert, "The Necessity of Artifice," in *The Necessity of Artifice* (New York: Rizzoli, 1982), pp. 58–59.
29 Gadamer, *Truth and Method*, p. 102.
30 Ibid., pp. 104–105.
31 Ibid., pp. 128–129.
32 Semper, *Style in the Technical and Tectonic Arts; or, Practical Aesthetics*.
33 David Leatherbarrow, *Architecture Oriented Otherwise* (New York: Princeton Architectural Press, 2014); Gehl, *Cities for People*.
34 See Chatterjee, *The Aesthetic Brain*; Martin Skov & Oshin Vartanian (eds.) *Neuroaesthetics* (Amityville, NY: Baywood Publishing Company, 2009).
35 Brown et al., "Naturalizing Aesthetics."
36 Dissanayake, *Art and Intimacy*, pp. 209–216.
37 Richard O. Prum, "Coevolutionary Aesthetics in Human and Biotic Artworlds," *Biological Philosophy* 28 (2013), p. 813.
38 Ibid., p. 814.
39 Gadamer, *Truth and Method*, p. 102.
40 Hans-Georg Gadamer, *The Relevance of the Beautiful*, p. 16.
41 Ibid., p. 53.
42 Ibid., p. 50.
43 Gernot Böhme, "On Beauty," *The Nordic Journal of Aesthetics* 39 (2010), p. 30.
44 Ibid., p. 31.
45 Gadamer, *The Relevance of the Beautiful*, p. 39.
46 Gadamer, *Truth and Method*, p. 156.
47 Ibid., p. 158.
48 Scarry, *On Beauty and Being Just*.
49 Alberto Pérez-Gómez, *Built upon Love: Architectural Longing after Ethics and Aesthetics* (Cambridge, MA: MIT Press, 2006), p. 18.
50 Alberto Pérez-Gómez, *Attunement*, p. 9.
51 Roger Scruton, *The Soul of the World* (Princeton: Princeton University Press, 2014), p. 138.
52 Ibid., p. 139.
53 Narvaez, *Neurobiology and the Development of Human Morality*, pp. 238–240.
54 Harries, *The Ethical Function of Architecture*, p. 4.
55 Ibid., p. 364.
56 Ibid.

57 Bermudez et al., "Externally-Induced Meditative States."
58 Iain McGilchrist, "Tending the World," in Sarah Robinson & Juhanni Pallasmaa (eds.) *Mind in Architecture: Neuroscience, Embodiment, and the Future of Design* (Cambridge, MA: MIT Press, 2016), p. 115.
59 Vesely, *Architecture in the Age of Divided Representation*, pp. 365–366.
60 Ibid., p. 371.
61 Ibid., p. 368.
62 Ibid., p. 373.
63 Ibid., p. 374.

Select Bibliography

Aguirre, Geoffrey K. et al. (August 1998) "An Area within Human Ventral Cortex Sensitive to 'Building' Stimuli: Evidence and Implications," *Neuron* 21, 373–383.

Aiello, Leslie C. & Wheeler, Peter. (1995) "The Expensive-Tissue Hypothesis: The Brain and the Digestive System in Human and Primate Evolution," *Current Anthropology* 36:2 (April), 199–221.

Aimone, James B. & Gage, Fred. (2011) "Modeling New Neuron Function: A History of using Computational Neuroscience to Study Adult Neurogenesis," *European Journal of Neuroscience* 33, 1160–1169.

Albright, Thomas. (August 23, 1996) "An Excellent Lightness," *Science* 273, 1055–1056.

Albright, Thomas & Stoner, Gene. (2002) "Contextual Influence on Visual Processing," *Annual Review of Neuroscience* 25, 339–379.

Alexander, Christopher. (1964) *Notes of the Synthesis of Form*. Cambridge, MA: Harvard University Press.

Alexander, Christopher et al. (1977) *A Pattern Language: Towns, Buildings, Construction*. New York: Oxford University Press.

Alexander, Christopher. (2002–2005) *The Nature of Order: An Essay on the Art of Building and the Nature of the Universe*. Berkeley: The Center for Environmental Structure. Vol. I (2002), Vol. II (2002), Vol. III (2005), Vol. IV (2004).

Appleton, Jay. (1975) *The Experience of Landscape*. New York: John Wiley & Sons.

Arbib, Michael A. (1989) *The Metaphorical Brain 2: Neural Networks and Beyond*. New York: Wiley & Sons.

Arbib, Michael A. (2005) "From Monkey-Like Action Recognition to Human Language: An Evolutionary Framework for Neurolinguistics," *Behavioral and Brain Sciences* 28, 105–167.

Arbib, Michael A. & Bonaiuto, James. (2012) "Multiple Levels of Spatial Organization: World Graphs and Spatial Difference Learning," *Adaptive Behavior* 20:4, 287–303.

Arbib, Michael A. (2014) "Language is Handy but is it Embodied?" *Neuropsychologia* 55, 57–70.

Ardrey, Robert. (1961) *African Genesis*. Madison: University of Wisconsin.

Ardrey, Robert. (1966) *The Territorial Imperative: A Personal Inquiry into the Animal Origins of Property and Nations*. New York: Antheum.

Arendt, Hannah. (1958) *The Human Condition*. Chicago: University of Chicago Press.

Aristotle. (1984) *The Complete Works of Aristotle*, 2 vols., (ed.) Johathan Barnes. Princeton: Princeton University Press.
Arnheim, Rudolf. (1954/1974) *Art and Visual Perception: A Psychology of the Creative Eye*. Berkeley and Los Angeles: University of California Press.
Arnheim, Rudolf. (1977) *The Dynamics of Architectural Form*. Berkeley: University of California Press.
Bangert, Marc et al. (2006) "Shared Networks for Auditory and Motor Processing in Professional Pianists: Evidence from fMRI conjunction," *NeuroImage* 30, 917–926.
Bannan, Nicholas. (2008) "Language out of Music: The Four Dimensions of Vocal Learning," *The Australian Journal of Anthropology* 19:3, 272–293.
Bar, Moshe & Neta, Maital. (2006) "Humans Prefer Curved Visual Objects," *Psychological Science* 17:8, 645–648.
Bar, Moshe & Neta, Maital. (2007) "Visual Elements of Subjective Preference Modulate Amygdala Activation," *Neuropsychologia* 45, 2191–2200.
Barret, Lisa Feldman. (2008) "The Experience of Emotion," *Annual Review of Psychology*, 58, 373–403.
Barsalou, Lawrence W. (1999) "Perceptual Symbol Systems," *Behavioral and Brain Sciences* 22, 577–660.
Barsalou, Lawrence W. (2008) "Grounded Cognition," *Annual Review of Psychology* 59, 617–645.
Barsalou, Lawrence W. (2010) "Grounded Cognition: Past, Present, and Future," *Topics in Cognitive Science* 2, 716–724.
Baumgarten, Alexander. (2007) *Aesthetica/Ästhetik*, 2 vols., (ed.) Dagmar Mirback. Hamburg: Felix Meiner Verlag.
Behrendt, Walter Curt. (2000/1927) *The Victory of the New Building Style*, trans. H. F. Mallgrave. Los Angeles: Getty Publications.
Bell, Clive. (1958) *Art*. New York: Capricorn Books.
Bell, Daniel. (1973) *The Cultural Contradictions of Capitalism*. New York: Basic Books.
Bengoetxea, Harkaitz et al. (2012) "Enriched and Deprived Sensory Experience Induces Structural Changes and Rewires Connectivity during the Postnatal Development of the Brain," *Neural Plasticity*. Doi:10:1155/2012/305693.
Berenson, Bernard. (1902) *The Florentine Painters of the Renaissance*. New York: G. P. Putnam's Sons.
Bermudez, Julio et al. (June 2017) "Externally-Induced Meditative States: An Exploratory fMRI Study of Architects' Responses to Contemplative Architecture," *Frontiers of Architectural Research*. http://dx.doi.org/10.1016/j.foar.2017.02.002
Biederman, Irving & Vessel, Edward. (May–June 2006) "Perceptual Pleasure and the Brain," *American Scientist* 94, 247–253.
Blackmore, Colin & Cooper, Grahame. (October 31, 1970) "Development of the Brain Depends on the Visual Environment," *Nature* 228, 477–478.
Blackmore, Sarah-Jayne. (2012) "Imaging Brain Development: The Adolescent Brain," *NeuroImage* 61, 397–406.
Blanke, Olaf. (August 2012) "Multisensory Brain Mechanisms of Bodily Self-Consciousness," *Nature Reviews: Neuroscience* 13, 556–571.

SELECT BIBLIOGRAPHY

Blanke, Olaf. (2016) "Embodiment and Bodily Self-Consciousness," *Empirical: Embodiment in Architecture and Neuroscience*, seminar May 4, 2016, http://archizoom.epfl.ch/empirical_en_1 (accessed June 2016).

Blanke, Olaf, & Metzinger, Thomas. (2008) "Full-Body Illusions and Minimal Phenomenal Selfhood," *Trends in Cognitive Sciences* 13:1, 7–13.

Blondel, Jacques-François. (1771–1777) *Cours d'architecture; ou Traité de la Décoration, Distribution & Construction de Bâtimens*. Paris: Chez Desaint.

Blood, Anne J. & Zatorre, Robert J. (2001) "Intensely Pleasurable Responses to Music Correlate with Activity in Brain Regions Implicated in Reward and Emotion," *Proceedings of the National Academy of Sciences* 98, 11818–11823.

Böhme, Gernot. (1989) *Für eine ökologische Naturästhetik*. Frankfurt: Edition Suhrkamp.

Böhme, Gernot. (1993) "Atmosphere as a Fundamental Concept of a New Aesthetics," *Thesis Eleven* 36, 113–126.

Böhme, Gernot. (1998) "Atmosphere as an Aesthetic Concept," *Daidalos: Berlin Architectural Journal* 68, 112–115.

Böhme, Gernot. (2002) "Atmosphere as the Subject Matter of Architecture," in Philip Ursprung (ed.) *Herzog & DeMeuron: Natural History*. Montreal: Canadian Centre for Architecture.

Böhme, Gernot. (2010) "On Beauty," *The Nordic Journal of Aesthetics* 39, 22–33.

Böhme, Gernot. (2013) "Atmosphere as Mindful Physical Presence in Space," *OASE Journal for Architecture* 91, 21–32.

Botvinick, Matthew & Cohen, Jonathan. (February 19, 1998) "Rubber hands 'feel' touch that eyes see," *Nature* 391, 756.

Boyd, Robert & Richerson, Peter. (1985) *Culture and the Evolutionary Process*. Chicago: University of Chicago Press.

Boyd, Robert & Richerson, Peter. (2005) *The Origin and Evolution of Cultures*. Oxford: Oxford University Press.

Bressani, Martin & Contandriopoulos, Chritina (eds.). (2017) *The Companions to the History of Architecture, Volume III, Nineteenth-Century Architecture*. New York: John Wiley & Sons.

Brodsky, Joseph. (1997) "An Immodest Proposal," in *On Grief and Reason*. New York: Farrar, Straus and Giroux.

Brown, Steven. (2001) "The 'Musilanguage' Model of Music Evolution," in N. L. Wallin, B. Meerke, & S. Brown (eds.) *The Origins of Music*. Cambridge, MA: MIT Press, 271–300.

Brown, Steven et al. (2011) "Naturalizing Aesthetics: Brain Areas for Aesthetic Appraisal across Sensory Modalities," *NeuroImage* 58, 250–258.

Calvo-Merino, B. et al. (2006) "Seeing or Doing? Influence of Visual and Motor Familiarity in Action Observation," *Current Biology* 16, 1905–1910.

Calvo-Merino, B. et al. (2008) "Towards a Sensorimotor Aesthetics of Performing Art," *Consciousness and Cognition* 17, 911–922.

Calvo-Merino, B. et al. (2010) "Experts See It All: Configural Effects in Action Observation," *Psychological Research* 74, 400–406.

Cassirer, Ernst. (1981) *Kant's Life and Thought*, trans. James Haden. New Haven: Yale University Press.

Castiello, Umberto et al. (2010) "Wired to be Social: The Ontogeny of Human Interaction," *PLoS ONE* 5:10 (October), e13199.

Chatterjee, Anjan. (2014) *The Aesthetic Brain*. Oxford: Oxford University Press.

Chermayeff, Serge & Alexander, Christopher. (1963/1965) *Community and Privacy: Toward a New Architecture of Humanism*. Garden City, NY: Anchor Books.

Cléry, Justine et al. (2015) "Neuronal bases of peripersonal and extrapersonal spaces, their plasticity and their dynamics: Knowns and unknowns," *Neuropsychologia* 20, 313–326.

Cloak, F. T. (1975) "Is a Cultural Ethology Possible?" *Human Ecology* 3:3, 161–182.

Clynes, Manfred. (1977) *Sentics, the Touch of Emotion*. New York: Doubleday Anchor.

Cole, Jonathan & Montero Barbara. (2007) "Affective Proprioception," *Janus Head* 9:2, 299–317.

Collingwood, R. G. (1974) *The Principles of Art*. London: Oxford University Press.

Colombetti, Giovanna. (2014) *The Feeling Body: Affective Science Meets the Enactive Mind*. Cambridge, MA: MIT Press.

Colombetti, Giovanna & Thompson, Evan. (2008) "The Feeling Body: Towards an Enactive Approach to Emotion," in W. F. Overton et al. (eds.) *Developmental Perspectives on Embodiment and Consciousness*. New York: Erlbaum, 45–68.

Dal Co, Francesco. (1990) *Figures of Architecture and Thought: German Architecture Culture 1880–1920*. New York: Rizzoli.

Darwin, Charles. (1874) *The Descent of Man and Selection in Relation to Sex*, 2nd edn. New York: Lovell, Coryell & Company.

Dawkins, Richard. (2006) *The Selfish Gene*. Oxford: Oxford University Press.

de Coulanges, Fustel & Denis, Numa. (1864/2006) *The Ancient City: A Study of the Religion, Laws, and Institutions of Greece and Rome*. Mineola, NY: Dover Publications.

Dehaene, Stanislas & Cohen, Laurent. (October 25, 2007), "Cultural Recycling of Cortical Maps," *Neuron* 56, 384–398.

Dehaene, Stanislas et al. (Decembere 3, 2010) "How Learning to Read Changes the Cortical Networks for Vision and Language," *Science* 330, 1359–1364.

Dewey, John. (1884) "The New Psychology," *Andover Review* 2, 278–289.

Dewey, John. (2005) *Art as Experience*. New York: A Perrigee Book.

Di Dio, Cinzia et al. (2007) "The Golded Beauty: Brain Response to Classical and Renaissance Sculptures," *PLoS One* 2:11, e1201. Doi:10:1371/journal.pone0001201.

Dissanayake, Ellen. (2000) *Art and Intimacy: How the Arts Began*. Seattle: University of Washington Press.

Donald, Merlin. (2001) *A Mind So Rare: The Evolution of Human Consciousness*. New York: W. W. Norton & Company.

Donald, Merlin. (2004) "The Definition of Human Nature," in Dai Rees & Steven Rose (eds.) *The New Brain Sciences: Perils and Prospects*. New York: Cambridge University Press.

Dormer, Peter (ed.). (1997) *The Culture of Craft*. Manchester: Manchester University Press.

Dunbar, Robin. (1992) "Neocortex Size as a Constraint on Group Size in Primates," *Journal of Human Evolution* 20, 469–493.

Dunbar, Robin. (1998) "The Social Brain Hypothesis," *Evolutionary Anthropology* 6, 178–190

Dunbar, Robin. (2012) "The Social Brain Meets Neuroimaging," *Trends in Cognitive Sciences* 16:2, 101–102.

Durham, William H. (1976) "The Adaptive Significance of Cultural Behavior," *Human Ecology* 4:2, 89–121.
Durham, William H. (1978) "Toward a Coevolutionary Theory of Human Biology and Culture," in Arthur L. Caplan (ed.) *The Sociobiology Debate: Readings on the Ethical and Scientific Issues Concerning Sociobiology*. New York: Harper & Row.
Ebert, Thomas & Pantev, Christo. (1995) "Increased Cortical Representation of the Fingers of the Left Hand in String Players," *Science* 270:5234, 305–307.
Ebisch, Sjoerd J. H. et al. (2008) "The Sense of Touch: Embodied Simulation in a Visuotactile Mirroring Mechanism for Observed Animate or Inanimate Touch," *Journal of Cognitive Neuroscience* 20:9, 1611–1623.
Eckert, Michael & Abraham, Wickliffe. (2012) "Effects of Environmental Enrichment Exposure on Synaptic Transmission and Plasticity in the Hippocampus," *Current Topics in Behavioral Neuroscience* 15, 165–187.
Ehrenzweig, Anton. (1971) *The Hidden Order of Art*. Berkeley: University of California Press.
Eibl-Eibesfeldt, Irenäus. (1971) *Love and Hate: The Natural History of Behavior Patterns*, trans. Geoffrey Strachan. New York: Holt, Rinehart and Winston.
Ekstrom, Arne et al. (September 11, 2003) "Cellular Networks Underlying Human Spatial Navigation," *Nature* 425, 184–187.
Ellard, Colin. (2015) *Places of the Heart: The Psychogeography of Everyday Life*. New York: Bellevue Literary Press.
Epstein, Russell et al. (May 1999) "The Parahippocampal Place Area: Recognition, Navigation, or Encoding?" *Neuron* 23, 115–125.
Epstein, Russell. (2005) "A Cortical Basis of Visual Scene Processing," *Visual Cognition* 12:6, 954–978.
Epstein, Russell. (2008) "Parahippocampal and Retrosplenial Contributions to Human Spatial Navigation," *Trends in Cognitive Sciences* 12:10, 388–396.
Epstein, Russell. (2015) "Neural systems for landmark-based wayfinding in humans," *Philosophical Transactions of the Royal Society* 369:20120533, http://dx.doi.org/10.1098/rstb.2012.0533 (accessed November 2015).
Epstein, Russell & Kanwisher, Nancy. (April 9, 1998) "A Cortical Representation of the Local Visual Environment," *Nature* 392, 598–601.
Etlin, Richard A. (1998) "Aesthetics and the Spatial Sense of Self," *Journal of Aesthetics and Art Criticism* 56:1, 1–19.
Etlin, Richard A. (2000) "Louis Sullivan: The Life-Enhancing Symbiosis of Music, Language, Architecture, and Ornament," in Marles Kronegger (ed.) *The Orchestration of the Arts—A Creative Symbiosis of Existential Powers*. Dordrecht: Kluwer Academic Publishers.
Feldman, Ruth. (2007) "Parent-Infant Synchrony and the Construction of Shared Timing; Physiological Precursors, Developmental Outcomes, and Risk Conditions," *Journal of Child Psychology and Psychiatry* 48:3, 329–354.
Feldman, Ruth. (2012) "Parent-Infant Synchrony: A Biobehavioral Model of Mutual Influences in the Formation of Affiliative Bonds," *Monographs of the Society for Research in Child Development* 77:2, 42–51.
Fernald, Anne. (1989) "Intonation and Communicative Intent in Mother's Speech to Infants: Is the Melody the Message?" *Child Development* 60, 1497–1510.
Fernald, Anne. (1991) "Prosody in Speech to Children: Prelinguistic and Linguistic Functions," *Annals of Child Development* 8, 43–80.

Ford, Edward. (2011) *The Architectural Detail*. New York: Princeton Architectural Press.
Frampton, Kenneth. (1974) "On Reading Heidegger," *Oppositions* 4.
Frampton, Kenneth. (1983) "Towards a Critical Regionalism: Six Points for an Architecture of Resistance," in Hal Foster (ed.) *The Anti-Aesthetic: Essays on Postmodern Culture*. Seattle: Bay Press.
Frampton, Kenneth. (1995) *Studies in Tectonic Culture: The Poetics of Construction in Nineteenth and Twentieth Century Architecture*. Cambridge, MA: MIT Press.
Frascari, Marco. (1984) "The Tell-the-Tale Detail," *VIA* 7, 23–37.
Freedberg, David & Gallese, Vittorio. (2007) "Motion, Emotion and Empathy in Esthetic Experience," *Trends in Cognitive Sciences* 11:5, 197–203.
Freeman, Walter. (2000) "Emotion is Essential to All Intentional Behaviors," UC Berkely Previously Published Works. Http://escholarship.org/uc/item/7t10x8mm.
Gadamer, Hans-Georg. (1986) *The Relevance of the Beautiful and Other Essays*, trans. Nicholas Walker. New York: Cambridge University Press.
Gadamer, Hans-Georg. (1999) *Truth and Method*, 2nd edn. trans. Joel Weinsheimer & Donald Marshall. New York: Continuum.
Gage, Fred. (2003) "Brain, Repair Yourself," *Scientific American* 239:3, 47–54.
Gaissert, Nina et al. (2011) "Similarity and Categorization: From Vision to Touch," *Acta Psychologica* 138, 219–230.
Gallagher, Shaun. (2005) *How the Body Shapes the Mind*. Oxford: Clarendon Press.
Gallese, Vittorio. (2003) "The Manifold Nature of Interpersonal Relations: The Quest for a Common Mechanism," *Philosophical Transactions of the Royal Society London B* 358, 517–528.
Gallese, Vittorio. (2005) "Embodied Simulation: From Neurons to Phenomenal Experience," *Phenomenology of Cognitive Science* 4, 23–48.
Gallese, Vittorio. (2016) "The Multimodal Nature of Visual Perception: Facts and Speculations," *Gestalt Theory* 38:2/3, 127–140.
Gallese, Vittorio. (2017) "Visions of the Body: Embodied Simulation and Aesthetic Experience," Franklin Humanities Institute, Duke University.
Gallese, Vittorio & Sinigaglia, C. (November 2011) "What is so special about embodied simulation?" *Trends in Cognitive Sciences* 15:11, 512–519.
Gallese, Vittorio & Ebisch, Sjoerd. (2013) "Embodied Simulation and Touch: The Sense of Touch in Social Cognition," *Phenomenology and Mind* 4, 269–291.
Gamble, Clive, Gowlett, John, & Dunbar, Robin. (2014) *Thinking Big: How the Evolution of Social Life Shaped the Human Mind*. London: Thames & Hudson.
Gans, Herbert. (1962) *The Urban Villagers: Group and Class in the Life of Italian Americans*. New York: The Free Press.
Gao, Wei et al. (April 21, 2009) "Evidence on the Emergence of the Brain's Default Network From 2-Week Old to 2-Year Old Healthy Pediatric Subjects," *Proceedings of the National Academy of Sciences* 106:16, 6790–6796.
Gauldie, Sinclair. (1969) *Architecture: The Appreciation of the Arts*. New York: Oxford University Press.
Geertz, Clifford. (1973) *The Interpretation of Cultures: Selected Essays*. New York: Basic Books.
Gehl, Jan. (2010) *Cities for People*. Washington, DC: Island Press.

Gibson, James. (1950) *The Perception of the Visual World.* Boston: Houghton Mifflin Company.
Gibson, James. (1966) *The Senses Considered as Perceptual Systems.* Boston: Houghton Mifflin Company.
Gibson, James. (1986) *The Ecological Approach to Visual Perception.* Hillsdale, NJ: Lawrence Erlbaum Associates.
Giedion, Sigfried. (1928/1995) *Building in France, Building in Iron, Building in Ferro-Concrete,* trans. J. Duncan Berry. Santa Monica: Getty Publications.
Giedion, Sigfried. (1949) *Space, Time and Architecture: The Growth of a New Tradition.* Cambridge MA: Harvard University Press.
Goel, Vinod. (April 2014) "Creative Brains: Designing in the Real World," *Frontiers in Human Neuroscience* 8, Article, 241.
Goethe, Wolfgang. (1980) "Palladiio," in ed. and trans. John Gage. *Goethe on Art.* London: Scolar Press.
Goldstein, Kurt. (1934/2000) *The Organism: A Holistic Approach to Biology Derived from Pathological Data in Man.* New York: Zone Books.
Gombrich, Ernst. (1979) *The Sense of Order: A Study in the Psychology of Decorative Art.* Ithaca: Cornell University Press.
Gombrich, Ernst. (1982) "The Mask and the Face: The Perception of Physiognomic Likeness in Life and in Art," in *The Image and the Eye: Further Studies in the Psychology of Pictorial Representation.* Ithaca: Cornell University Press.
Goodbun, John. (2011) "The Architecture of the Extended Mind: Towards a Critical Urban Ecology," (Ph.D. diss., University of Westminster).
Gottlieb, Gilbert. (2007) "Probabilistic Epigenesis," *Developmental Science* 10:1, 1–11.
Griffero, Tonino. (2014) "Architectural Affordances: The Atmospheric Authority of Spaces," in Philip Todwell (ed.) *Architecture and Atmosphere.* Helsinki: Tapio Wirkkata-Rut Bryk Foundation.
Groh, Jennifer. (2014) *Making Space: How the Brain Knows Where Things Are.* Cambridge, MA: Harvard University Press.
Gumbrecht, Hans Ulrich. (2004) *Production of Presence: What Meaning Cannot Convey.* Stanford: Stanford University Press.
Gutman, Robert. (1966) "The Questions Architects Ask," *Transactions of the Bartlett Society* 4, 47–82.
Gutman, Robert. (1968) "What Architectural Schools Expect from Sociology," *Journal of Architectural Education* 22:2/3, 13–20.
Gutman, Robert (ed.). (1972) *People and Buildings.* New York: Basic Books.
Habermas, Jürgen. (1989) "Modern and Postmodern Architecture," in trans. Shierry Weber Nicholsen, *The New Conservatism: Cultural Criticism and the Historians' Debate.* Cambridge, MA: MIT Press.
Hafting, Torkel et al. (August 11, 2005) "Microstructure of a Spatial Map in the Entorhinal Cortex," *Nature* 436:11, 801–806.
Hall, Edward T. (1966) *The Hidden Dimension.* Garden City NY: Doubleday & Company.
Harries, Karsten. (1998) *The Ethical Function of Architecture.* Cambridge, MA: MIT Press.
Hart, Robert Lamb. (2015) *A New Look at Humanism: In Architecture, Landscapes and Urban Design.* California: Meadowlark Publishing.

Heidegger, Martin. (1962) *Being and Time*, trans. John Macquarrie & Edward Robinson. New York: Harper & Row.
Heidegger, Martin. (1977) *Basic Writings*, (ed.) David Farrell Kress. New York: Harper & Rowe.
Hekkert, Paul. (2006) "Design Aesthetics: Principles of Pleasure in Design," *Psychology Science* 48:2, 157–172.
Hekkert, Paul et al. (2003) "'Most Advanced, yet Acceptable': Typicality and Novelty as Joint Predictors of Aesthetic Preference in Industrial Design," *British Journal of Psychology* 94, 111–124.
Henshilwood, Christopher et al. (2009) "Engraved Ochres from the Middle Stone Age Levels at Blombos Cave, South Africa," *Journal of Human Evolution* 57, 27–47.
Henshilwood, Christopher et al. (2011) "A 100,000-Year-Old Ochre-Processing Workshop at Blombos Cave, South Africa," *Science* 334:(14 October), 219–222.
Herder, Johann Gottfried. (1803) *Outlines of a Philosophy of the History of Man*, trans. T. Churchill. London: J. Johnson.
Herrmann, Wolfgang. (1973) *The Theory of Claude Perrault*. London: Zwimmer.
Hildebrand, Adolf. (1893) "The Problem of Form in the Fine Arts," in Mallgrave & Ikonomou (trans. & eds.) *Empathy, Form, and Space: Problems in German Aesthetics, 1873–1893*. Santa Monica: Getty Publications.
Hildebrand, Grant. (1991) *The Wright Space: Patterns and Meaning in Frank Lloyd Wright's Houses*. Seattle: University of Washington Press.
Hildebrand, Grant. (1999) *Origins of Architectural Pleasure*. Seattle: University of Washington Press.
Hillier, Bill. (1973) "In Defense of Space," *RIBA Journal*, 80:11, 540–544.
Hillier, Bill. (1996) *Space Is the Machine: A Configurational theory of Architecture*. Cambridge: Cambridge University Press. Electronic version published by Space Syntax in 2007.
Hillier, Bill et al. (1976) "Space Syntax," *Environment and Planning B: Planning and Design* 3, 147–185.
Hitchcock, Henry-Russell & Johnson, Philip. (1966/1932) *The International Style*. New York: W. W. Norton & Company.
Horkheimer, Max & Adorno, Theodor. (1944/1989) *Dialectic of Enlightenment*, trans. John Coming. New York: Continuum.
Hubel D. H. & Wiesel, T. N. (1970) "The Period of Susceptibility to the Physiological Effects of Unilateral Eye Closure in Kittens," *Journal of Physiology* 206:2, 419–436.
Hublin, Jean-Jacques et al. (June 8, 2017) "New Fossils from Jebel Irhoud, Morocco and the pan-African Origin of *Homo sapiens*," *Nature* 546, 289–292.
Ihde, Don. (2007) *Listening and Voice, Phenomenologies of Sound*, 2nd edn. Albany: State University of New York Press.
Ingold, Tim. (2000) *The Perception of the Environment: Essays on Livelihood, Dwelling and Skill*. London: Routledge.
Ingold, Tim. (2004) "CULTURE ON THE GROUND: The World Perceived Through the Feet," *Journal of Material Culture* 9:3, 315–340.
Ingold, Tim. (2013) *Making: Anthropology, Archaeology, Art and Architecture*. London: Routledge.

Iriki, Atsushi. (2006) "The Neural Origins and Implications of Imitation, Mirror Neurons and Tool use," *Current Opinion in Neurobiology* 16, 660–1667.
Iriki, Atsushi & Taoka, Miki. (2011) "Triadic (ecological, neural, cognitive) Niche Construction: A Scenario of Human Brain Evolution Extrapolating Tool Use and Language from the Control of Reaching Actions," *Philosophical Transactions of the Royal Society B: Biological Sciences* 367, 10–23.
Jacobs, Jane. (1961) *The Death and Life of Great American Cities*. New York: Random House.
James, Wendy. (2005) *The Ceremonial Animal: A New Portrait of Anthropology*. Oxford: Oxford University Press, 2005, pp. 6–7.
James, William. (1890/1950) *The Principles of Psychology*, 2 vols. New York: Dover.
Jelić, Andrea et al. (March 2016) "The Enactive Approach to Architectural Experience: A Neurophysiological Perspective on Embodiment, Motivation, and Affordances," *Frontiers in Psychology* 7:481. Doi: 10:3389/fpsyg.2016.00481.
Johnson, Mark. (2007) *The Meaning of the Body: Aesthetics of Human Understanding*. Chicago: University of Chicago Press.
Junghanns, Kurt. (1982) *Der Deutsche Werklbund: Sein erstes Jahrzehnt*. Berlin: Henschelverlage Kunst und Gesellschaft.
Kalkatechi, Mina. (2016) "A Forgotten Chapter of the Bauhaus: Psycho-Physiological Aesthetics and the Inception of Modern Design Theory," Ph.D. diss. Illinois Institute of Technology.
Kant, Immanuel. (1977) *Kritik der Urteilskraft, Werke in zwölf Bänden*, vol. 10. Frankfurt. www.wissensnavigator.com/documents/kritikderurteilskraft.pdf.
Kaplan, Stephen & Kaplan, Rachael. (1982) *Cognition and Environment: Functioning in an Uncertain World*. New York: Praeger.
Kaplan, Stephen & Kaplan, Rachael. (1989) *The Nature of Experience: A Psychological Perspective*. New York: Cambridge University Press.
Kaplan, Stephen & Kaplan, Rachael & Ryan, Robert. (1998) *With People in Mind: Design and Management of Everyday Nature*. Washington, DC: Island Press.
Kellert, Stephen R. (2005) *Buildings for Life: Designing and Understanding the Human-Nature Connection*. Washington, DC: Island Press.
Kellert, Stephen R & Wilson, Edward O. (eds.) (1993) *The Biophilic Hypothesis*. Washington, DC: Island Press.
Kellert, Stephen R., Heerwagen, Judith H., & Mador, Martin L. (2008) *Biophilic Design: The Theory, Science, and Practice of Bringing Buildings to Life*. Hoboken, NJ: John Wiley & Sons.
Kempermann, Gerd & Gage, Fred. (1999) "New Nerve Cells for the Adult Brain," *Scientific American* 280:5, 48–53.
Keysers, Christian. (2011) *The Empathic Brain: How the discovery of mirror neurons changes our understanding of human nature*. Social Brain Press.
Keysers, Christian et al. (April 22, 2004) "A Touching Sight: SII/PV Activation during the Observation and Experience of Touch," *Neuron* 42, 335–346.
Klemm, Gustav. (1843–1852) *Allgemeine Cultur-Geschichte der Menschheit*. Leipzig: Teubner.
Knight, Richard Payne. (1805) *An Analytical Inquiry into the Principles of Taste*. London: Mews-Gate & J. White.
Koestler, Arthur. (1969) *The Act of Creation*. New York: The Macmillan Company.

Kohn, Marek & Mithen, Steven. (1999) "Handaxes: Products of Sexual Selection?" *Antiquity* 73:281(September), 518–527.
Kolb, Bryan et al. (2003) "Brain Plasticity and Behavior," *Current Directions in Psychological Science* 12:1, 1–4.
Kosslyn, Stephen et al. (September 2001) "Neural Foundations of Imagery," *Nature Reviews: Neuroscience* 2, 635–642.
Kourtzi, Zoe & DiCarlo, James. (2006) "Learning and Neural Plasticity in Visual Object Recognition," *Current Opinion in Neurobiology* 16, 152–58.
Kringelbach, Morten & Berridge, Ken (eds.). (2010) *Pleasures of the Brain*. Oxford: Oxford University Press.
Krumhansl, Carol. (1997) "An Exploratory Study of Musical Emotions and Psychophysiology," *Canadian Journal of Experimental Psychology* 52:4, 336–352.
Krumhansl, Carol. (April 2002) "Music: A Link between Cognition and Emotion," *Current Directions in Psychological Science* 11:2, 45–50.
Lalande, Kevin et al. (2001) "Cultural Niche Construction and Human Evolution," *Journal of Evolutionary Biology* 14, 22–33.
Lalande, Kevin et al. (February 2010) "How Culture Shaped the Human Genome: Bringing Genetics and the Human Sciences Together," *Genetics* 11, 137–148.
Langer, Suzanne. (1953) *Feeling and Form: A Theory of Art Development from Philosophy in a New Key*. New York: Charles Scribner's Sons.
Langer, Suzanne. (1967) *Mind: An Essay on Human Feeling*. Baltimore: The Johns Hopkins University Press.
Latham, Robert & Forbes, Edward. (1854) *The Natural History Department of the Crystal Palace Described*. London: Crystal Palace Library.
Leatherbarrow, David. (2009) *Architecture Oriented Otherwise*. New York: Princeton Architectural Press.
Leatherbarrow, David & Eisenschmidt, Alexander (eds.). (2017) *The Companions to the History of Architecture, Volume IV, Twentieth-Century Architecture*. New York: John Wiley & Sons.
Le Camus de Mézières, Nicolas. (1780/1992) *The Genius of Architecture; or, The Analogy of That Art with Our Sensations*, trans. David Britt. Santa Monica, CA: Getty Publications.
Lee, Vernon & Anstruther-Thomson. (1912) *Beauty and Ugliness and Other Studies in Psychological Aesthetics*. London: John Lane.
Lenggenhager, Bigna et al. (August 24, 2007) "Video Ergo Sum: Manipulating Bodily Self-Consciousness," *Science* 317, 1096–1099.
Lenggenhager, Bigna et al. (2009) "Spatial Aspects of Bodily Self-Consciousness," *Consciousness and Cognition* 18, 110–117
Levitin, Daniel. (February 23, 2008), "The Illusion of Music," *New Scientist* 197:2644, 34–37.
Levitin, Daniel & Tirovolas, Anna. (2009) "Current Advances in the Cognitive Neuroscience of Music," *Annals of the New York Academy of Sciences* 1156, 211–231.
Lewis, Jerome. (2013) "A Cross-Cultural Perspective on the Significance of Music and Dance to Culture and Society: Insight from BaYaka Pygmies," in Michael A. Arbib (ed.) *Language, Music, and the Brain*. Cambridge, MA: MIT Press.

Li, Fuzhong, et al. (2005) "Improving Physical Function and Blood Pressure in Older Adults through Cobblestone Mat Walking: A Randomized Trial," *Journal of the American Geriatrics Society* 53:8, 1305–1312.
Li, Qing. (2010) "Effect of Forest Bathing Trips on Human Immune Function," *Environmental Health and Preventative Medicine* 15, 9–17.
Li, Qing et al. (2006) "Phytoncides (Wood Essential Oils) Induce Human Natural Killer Cell Activity," *Immunopharmacology and Immunotoxicology* 28, 319–333.
Loos, Adolf. (1910) "Architecture," *Midgard: Journal of Architectural Theory and Criticism* 1:1, 49–56.
Lumley, Henry de (*sous la direction de*). (2009) *Terra Amata: Nice, Alpes-Maritimes, France*. Paris: CNRS.
Lumsden, Charles & Wilson, Edward O. (1981) *Genes, Mind, and Culture: The Coevolutionary Process*. Hackensack, NJ: World Scientific.
MacLarnon, Ann & Hewitt, Gwen. (1999) "The Evolution of Human Speech: The Role of Enhanced Breathing Control," *American Journal of Physical Anthropology* 109, 341–363.
Maguire, Eleanor. (2001) "The Retrosplenial Contribution to Human Navigation: A Review of Lesion and Neuroimaging Findings," *Scandinavian Journal of Psychology* 42, 225–238.
Maguire, Eleanor & Mullally, Sinéad. (2013) "The Hippocampus: A Manifesto for Change," *Journal of Experimental Psychology* 142:4, 1180–1189.
Maguire, Eleanor et al. (September 15, 1997) "Recalling Routes around London: Activation of the Right Hippocampus in Taxi Drivers," *Journal of Neuroscience* 17:18, 7103–7110.
Mallgrave, Harry Francis. (2013) *Architecture and Embodiment: The Implications of the New Sciences and Humanities for Design*. London: Routledge.
Mallgrave, Harry Francis & Ikonomou, Eleftherios. (1994) *Empathy, Form, and Space: Problems in German Aesthetics, 1873–1893*. Santa Monica: Getty Publications.
Mallgrave, Harry Francis & Goodman, David. (2011) *An Introduction to Architectural Theory: 1968 to the Present*. Chichester: Wiley-Blackwell.
Malloch, Stephen. (1999) "Mothers and Infants and Communicative Musicality," *Musicae Scientiae*, Special Issue 1999–2000, 29–57.
Malloch, Stephen & Trevarthen, Colwyn. (2010) *Communicative Musicality: Exploring the Basis of Human Companionship*. Oxford: Oxford University Press.
Malnar, Joyce Monice & Vodvarka, Frank. (2004) *Sensory Design*. Minneapolis: University of Minnesota Press.
Malpas, Jeff. (1999) *Place and Experience: A Philosophical Topography*. Cambridge: Cambridge University Press.
Malpas, Jeff. (2013) "The Remembrance of Place," jeffmalpas.com/wp-content/uploads/2013/03/The-Remembrance-of-Place.pdf.
Mania, Dietrich & Mania, Ursula. (2005) "The Natural and Socio-Cultural Environment of Homo Erectus at Bilzingsleben, Germany," in Clive Gamble & Martin Porr (eds.) *The Hominid Individual in Context: Archaeological investigations of Lower and Middle Palaeolithic Landscapes, Locales and Artefacts*. London: Routledge.

McEwen, Indra Kagis. (2003) *Vitruvius: Writing the Body of Architecture*. Cambridge, MA: MIT Press.

McGilchrist, Iain. (2009) *The Master and his Emissary: The Divided Brain and the Making of the Western World*. New Haven: Yale University Press.

Merleau-Ponty, Maurice. (1962) *The Phenomenology of Perception*, trans. Colin Smith. London: Routledge & Kegan Paul.

Merleau-Ponty, Maurice. (1968) *The Visible and the Invisible*, (ed.) Claude Lefort, trans. Alphonso Lingis. Evanston: Northwestern University Press.

Mithen, Steven. (2007) *The Singing Neanderthals: The Origins of Music, Language, Mind, and Body*. Cambridge, MA: Harvard University Press.

Molino, Jean. (2001) "Toward an Evolutionary Theory of Music and Language," in N. L. Wallin, B. Meerke, & S. Brown (eds.) *The Origins of Music*. Cambridge, MA: MIT Press, 165–176.

Montagu, M. F. Ashley. (1962/1964) *The Humanization of Man: Our Changing Conception of Human Nature*. New York: Grove Press.

Montagu, M. F. Ashley. (1962/1972) *Culture and the Evolution of Man*. New York: Oxford University Press.

Montero, Barbara. (2006) "Proprioception as an Aesthetic Sense," *Journal of Aesthetics and Art Criticism* 64:2, 231–242.

Morris, Desmond. (1967) *The Naked Ape: A Zoologist's Study of the Human Animal*. New York: McGraw-Hill.

Mullally, Sinéad & Maguire, Eleanor. (2014) "Memory, Imagination, and Predicting the Future: A Common Brain Mechanism," *The Neuroscientist* 20:3, 220–234.

Mumford, Eric. (2000) *The CIAM Discourse on Urbanism, 1928–1960*. Cambridge, MA: MIT Press.

Muthesius, Hermann. (1994/1902) *Style-Architecture and Building-Art*, trans. Stanford Anderson. Santa Monica: Getty Publications.

Nanda, Upali & Jansen, Ben. (2012) "Image and Emotion: From Outcomes to Brain Behavior," *HERD* 5:4, 40–59.

Nanda, Upali et al. (2013) "Lessons from Neuroscience: Form Follows Function, Emotions Follow Form," *Intelligent Buildings International* 5:1, 61–68. http://dx.doi.ort/10.1080/17508975.2013.807767.

Narvaez, Darcia. *Neurobiology and the Development of Human Morality: Evolution, Culture, and Wisdom*. (New York: W. W. Norton & Company).

Neisser, Ulrich. (1976) *Cognition and Reality: Principles and Implications of Cognitive Psychology*. San Francisco: W. H. Freeman.

Neutra, Richard. (1954) *Survival through Design*. New York: Oxford University Press.

Noë, Alva. (2004) *Action in Perception*. Cambridge, MA: MIT Press.

Odling-Smee F. John et al. (2003) *Niche Construction: The Neglected Process in Evolution*. Princeton: Princeton University Press.

O'Keefe J. & Dostrovsky, J. (1971) "The Hippocampus as a Spatial Map: Preliminary Evidence from Unit Activity in the Freely-Moving Rat," *Brain Research* 34:17, 171–175.

O'Keefe J. & Nadel, Lynn. (1978) *The Hippocampus as a Cognitive Map*. Oxford: Oxford University Press.

Oliva, Aude & Torralba, Antonio. (2006) "Building the Gist of a Scene: The Role of Global Image Features in Recognition," *Progress in Brain Research* 155, 23–36.

O'Regan, J. Keven & Noë, Alva. (2000) "A Sensorimotor Account of Visions and Visual Consciousness," *Behavioral and Brain Sciences* 24, 939–1031.

Oud, J. J. P. (1928) "Architecture and the Future," *The Studio* 98, 403–405, 453.

Oyama, Susan. (1985/2000) *The Ontogeny of Information: Developmental Systems an Evolution*. Durham, NC: Duke University Press.

Oyama, Susan. (1991) "Bodies and Minds: Dualism in Evolutionary Theory," *Journal of Social Issues* 47:3, 27–42.

Oyama, Susan. (1996) "HUMAN HISTORY, History, or History?" *Cultural Dynamics* 8:3, 353–361

Oyama, Susan. (2000) *Evolution's Eye: A Systems View of the Biology-Culture Divide*. Durham: Duke University Press.

Oyama, Susan et al. (eds.) (2001) *Cycles of Contingency: Developmental Systems and Evolution*. Cambridge, MA: MIT Press.

Pallasmaa, Juhani. (2006) "An Architecture of the Seven Senses," in Steven Holl et al. (eds.) *Questions of Perception: Phenomenology of Architecture*. San Francisco: William Stout Publishers.

Pallasmaa, Juhani. (2009) *The Thinking Hand: Existential and Embodied Wisdom in Architecture*. Chichester: John Wiley and Sons.

Pallasmaa, Juhani. (2012) *Encounters 1: Architectural Essays*, (ed.) Peter MacKeith. Helsinki: Rakennustieto Publishing.

Pallasmaa, Juhani. (2012) *Encounters 2: Architectural Essays*, (ed.) Peter MacKeith. Helsinki: Rakennustieto Publishing.

Panksepp, Jaak. (1998a) "The Periconscious Substrates of Consciousness: Affective States and the Evolutionary Origins of the Self," *Journal of Consciousness Studies* 5:5–6, 566–582.

Panksepp, Jaak. (1998b) *Affective Neuroscience: The Foundations of Human and Animal Emotions*. Oxford: Oxford University Press.

Pasqualini, Isabella et al. (2013) "'Seeing' and 'Feeling' Architecture: How Bodily Self-Consciousness Alters Architectonic Experience and Affects the Perception of Interiors," *Frontiers in Psychology* 4:354. Doi:10.3389/fpsyg.2013.00354.

Patel, Anirrudh. (2010) *Music, Language, and the Brain*. New York: Oxford University Press.

Paul, Sherman. (1962) *Louis Sullivan: An Architect in American Thought*. Englewood Cliffs, NJ: Prentice-Hall.

Pausanias. (1979) *Guide to Greece*. New York: Penguin Books.

Payne, Alina. (2012) *From Ornament to Object: Genealogies of Architectural Modernism*. New Haven: Yale University Press.

Pérez-Gómez, Alberto. (2006) *Built upon Love: Architectural Longing after Ethics and Aesthetics*. Cambridge, MA: MIT Press.

Pérez-Gómez, Alberto. (2015) "Place and Architectural Space," in Jeff Malpas (ed.) *The Intelligence of Place: Topographies and Poetics*. London: Bloomsbury.

Pérez-Gómez, Alberto. (2016) *Attunement: Architectural Meaning after the Crisis of Modern Science*. Cambridge, MA: MIT Press.

Porteous, J. Douglas. (1990) *Landscapes of the Mind: Worlds of Sense and Metaphor*. Toronto: University of Toronto Press.

Portoghesi, Paolo. (December 1958) "Dal Neorealismo al Neoliberty," *Communità* 65.

Prum, Richard O. (2013) "Coevolutionary Aesthetics in Human and Biotic Artworlds," *Biological Philosophy* 28, 811–832.

Pulvermüller, Friedemann. (July 2005) "Brain Mechanisms Linking Language and Action," *Nature Reviews Neuroscience* 6, 576–582.

Quantrill, Malcolm. (1987) *The Environmental Memory: Man and Architecture in the Landscape of Ideas*. New York: Schocken Books.

Ramachandran, V. S. & Hirstein, William. (1999) "The Science of Art: A Neurological Theory of Aesthetic Experience," *Journal of Consciousness Studies* 6:6–7, 15–51.

Rasmussen, Steen Eiler. (1959) *Experiencing Architecture*. Cambridge, MA: MIT Press.

Redies, Christoph. (2007) "A Universal Model of Esthetic Perception Based on the Sensory Coding of Natural Stimuli," *Spatial Vision* 27, 97–117.

Relph, Edward. (1976) *Place and Placelessness*. Los Angeles: Sage.

Richerson, Peter & Boyd, Robert. (2005) *Not by Genes Alone: How Culture Transformed Human Evolution*. Chicago: University of Chicago Press.

Rizzolatti, Giocomo et al. (July 11, 1997) "The Space Around Us," *Science* 277, 190–191.

Rizzolatti, Giocomo & Arbib, Michael. (1998) "Language within our grasp," *Trends in Neuroscience* 21:188, 169–192.

Rizzolatti, Giocomo & Matelli, Massimo. (2003) "Two different streams form the dorsal visual system: anatomy and functions," *Experimental Brain Research* 153, 146–157.

Rizzolatti, Giocomo & Craighero, Laila. (2004) "The Mirror-Neuron System," *Annual Review of Neuroscience* 27, 169–192.

Rizzolatti, Giocomo & Sinigaglia, Corrado. (2008) *Mirrors in the Brain: How Our Minds Share Actions and Emotions*, trans. Frances Anderson. Oxford: Oxford University Press.

Robinson, Sarah. (2011) *Nesting: Body, Dwelling, Mind*. Richmond: William Stout Publishers.

Robinson, Sarah. (2015) "John Dewey and the Dialogue between Architecture and Neuroscience," *arq* 19:3. Doi:10:1017/S1359135515000627.

Robinson, Sarah & Pallasmaa, Juhani. (2015) *Mind in Architecture: Neuroscience, Embodiment, and the Future of Design*. Cambridge, MA: MIT Press.

Rogers, Ernesto Nathan. (1953) Editorial "Continuità," *Casabella-Continuità* 199:2 (December).

Rogers, Ernesto Nathan. (1957) Editorial "Continuità o crisi," *Casabella-Continuità* 215 (April–May).

Rogers, Ernesto Nathan. (1959) "The Evolution of Architecture: Reply to the Caretaker of Frigidaires," *Casabella-Continuità* 228 (June).

Rooney, Kevin. (2015) "Vision and the Experience of Built Environments: Two Visual Pathways of Awareness and Embodiment in Architecture," (Ph.D. diss., Kansan State University).

Rossi, Aldo. (1982) *The Architecture of the City*, trans. Diane Ghirado & Joan Ockman. Cambridge, MA: MIT Press.

Rowe, Colin. (1975) "Introduction," in *Five Architects: Eisenman, Graves, Gwathmey, Hejuk, Meier*. New York: Oxford University Press.

Ruyle, Eugene E. (1973) "Genetic and Cultural Pools: Some Suggestions for a Unified Theory of Biocultural Evolution," *Human Ecology* 1:3, 201–215.

Rykwert, Joseph. (1972) *On Adam's House in Paradise: The Idea of the Primitive Hut in Architectural History*. New York: Museum of Modern Art.

Rykwert, Joseph. (1976) *The Idea of the Town: An Anthropology of Urban Form in Rome, Italy, and the Ancient World*. Princeton: Princeton University Press.
Rykwert, Joseph. (1982) *The Necessity of Artifice*. New York: Rizzoli.
Sabatino, Michelangelo. (2010) *Pride in Modesty: Modernist Architecture and the Vernacular Tradition in Italy*. Toronto: University of Toronto Press.
Sabatino, Michelangelo. (2013) "Toward a Regionalist Modernism: Italian Architecture and the Vernacular," in Leen Meganick, Linda Van Santvoort, Jan De Maeyer (eds.) *Regionalism and Modernity: Architecture in Western Europe, 1914–1940*. Leuven: Leuven University Press.
Saxe, Rebecca. (2006) "Unique Human Social Cognition," *Current Opinion in Neurobiology* 16, 235–239.
Sbriscia-Fioretti, Beatrice et al. (2013) "ERP Modulation during Observation of Abstract Paintings by Franz Kline," *Plos One* 8:10, e75241.
Scaff, Lawrence. (1995) "Social theory, Rationalism and the Architecture of the City: Fin-de-siècle Thematics," *Theory, Culture & Society* 12, 63–85. London: Sage.
Scaff, Lawrence. (2000) "Weber on the Cultural Situation of the Modern Age," in S. Turner (ed.) *The Cambridge Companion to Max Weber* Cambridge: Cambridge University Press.
Scarry, Elaine. (1999) *On Beauty and Being Just*. Princeton: Princeton University Press.
Schafer, R. Murray. (1977/1994) *Our Sonic Environment and The Soundscape: The Tuning of the World*. Rochester VT: Destiny Books.
Schellenberg, E. Glenn. (2004) "Music Lessons Enhance IQ," *Psychological Science* 15:8, 511–514.
Schiller, Friedrich. (1977) *On the Aesthetic Education of Man*, trans. Reginald Snell. New York: Frederick Ungar Publishing.
Schlaug, Gottfried. (1995) "Increased Corpus Callosum Size in Musicians," *Neuropsychologia* 33:8, 1047–1055.
Schore, Allan. (June 2005) "Attachment, Affect Regulation, and the Developing Right Brain: Linking Developmental Neuroscience to Pediatrics," *Pediatrics in Review* 26:6, 204–217.
Schwarzer, Mitchell. (August 1991) "The Emergence of Architectural Space: August Schmarsow's Theory of *Raumgestaltung*," *Assemblage* 15, 48–61.
Scruton, Roger. (1979) *The Aesthetics of Architecture*. Princeton: Princeton University Press.
Scruton, Roger. (2009a) "Why Beauty Matters," Https://vimeo.com/112655231.
Scruton, Roger. (2009b) *Beauty*. Oxford: Oxford University Press.
Scruton, Roger. (2014) *The Soul of the World*. Princeton: Princeton University Press.
Schwartz, Frederic J. (1996) *The Werkbund: Design Theory and Mass Culture before the First World War*. New Haven: Yale University Press.
Seamon, David. (1979) *A Geography of the Lifeworld*. New York: St. Martin's Press.
Seamon, David & Robert Mugerauer (eds.). (1985) *Dwelling, Place & Environment*. New York: Columbia University Press.
Segerstråle, Ullica. (2000) *Defenders of the Truth: The Battle for Science in the Sociobiology Debate and Beyond*. Oxford: Oxford University Press.

Semper, Gottfried. (1989) *Gottfried Semper: The Four Elements of Architecture and Other Writings*, trans. H. F. Mallgrave & Wolfgang Herrmann. New York: Cambridge University Press.

Semper, Gottfried. (2004) *Style in the Technical and Tectonic Arts; or, Practical Aesthetics*, trans. H. F. Mallgrave & Michael Robinson. Los Angeles: Getty Publication Programs.

Sennett, Riochard. (2008) *The Craftsman*. New Haven: Yale University Press.

Sheets-Johnstone, Maxine. (1999) "Emotion and Movement: A Beginning Empirical-Phenomenological Analysis of Their Relationship," *Journal of Consciousness Studies* 6:11–12, 259–277.

Sheets-Johnstone, Maxine. (2011) *The Primacy of Movement*, 2nd edn. Amsterdam: John Benjamins Publishing Company.

Siegel, Daniel. (2012) *The Developing Mind: How Relationships and the Brain Interact to Shape Who We Are*. New York: The Guilford Press.

Smail, Daniel Lord. (2008) *On Deep History and the Brain*. Berkeley: University of California Press.

Sperber, Ester. (October 2016) "The Wings of Daedalus: Toward a Relational Architecture," *Psychoanalytic Review* 103:5, 593–616.

Sperry, Roger. (1939) "Action Current Study in Movement Coordination," *The Journal of General Psychology* 20, 295–313.

Spiers, Hugo & Maguire, Eleanor. (2006a) "Thoughts, Behaviour, and Brain Dynamics during Navigation in the Real World," *NeuroImage* 31, 1826–1840.

Spiers, Hugo & Maguire, Eleanor. (June 2004) "A 'landmark' study on the neural basis of navigation," *Nature Neuroscience* 7:6, 572–574.

Spiers, Hugo & Maguire, Eleanor. (2007) "A Navigational Guidance System in the Human Brain," *Hippocampus* 17, 618–626.

Stamps, Arthur. (2005) "Visual Permeability, Locomotive Permeability, Safety, and Enclosure," *Environment and Behavior* 37:5, 587–619.

Stamps, Arthur. (2010) "Effects of Permeability on Perceived Enclosure and Spaciousness," *Environment and Behavior* 42:6, 864–886.

Sterelny, Kim. (2003) *Thought in a Hostile World: The Evolution of Human Cognition*. Malden, MA: Blackwell Publishing.

Sterelny, Kim. (2012) *The Evolved Apprentice: How Evolution Made Human Unique*. Cambridge, MA: MIT Press.

Stierli, Martino. (2007) "In the Academy's Garden: Robert Venturi, the Grand Tour and the Revision of Modern Architecture," *AA Files* 56, 42–55.

Straus, Erwin W. (1952) "The Upright Posture," *The Psychiatric Quarterly* 26:1, 529–561.

Stringer, Chris & Galway-Witham, Julia. (June 8, 2017) "On the Origin of Our Species," *Nature* 546, 212–214.

Sullivan, Louis H. (1947) *Kindergarten Chats and Other Writings*. New York: Wittenborn Art Books.

Sullivan, Louis H. (1988) *Louis Sullivan: The Public Papers*. (ed.) Robert Twombly. Chicago: University of Chicago Press.

Sütterlin, Christa. (2003) "From Sign and Schema to Iconic Representation: Evolutionary Aesthetics of Pictorial Art," in Eckart Voland & Karl Grammer (eds.) *Evolutionary Aesthetics*. Berlin Springer, 131–170.

Tafuri, Manfredo. (1968) *Theories and History of Architecture*. New York: Harper & Rowe.

Tafuri, Manfredo. (1989) *History of Italian Architecture, 1944–1985*, trans. Jessica Levine. Cambridge, MA: MIT Press.
Tarveinen, Jussi et al. (2015) "The Way Films Feel: Aesthetic Features and Mood in Film," *Psychology of Aesthetics, Creativity, and the Arts* 9:3, 254–265.
Thiis-Evensen, Thomas. (1987) *Archetypes in Architecture*. Oslo: Norwegian University Press.
Thompson, Evan. (2007) *Mind in Life: Biology, Phenomenology, and the Sciences of the Mind*. Cambridge, MA: Harvard University Press.
Thompson, Evan & Varela, F. (2001) "Radical Embodiment: Neural Dynamics and Consciousness," *Trends in Cognitive Sciences* 5:10 (February), 418–425.
Tidwell, Philip (ed.). (2013) *Architecture and Neuroscience*. Helsinki: Tapio Wirkkala-Rut Bryk Foundation.
Tidwell, Philip. (2014) *Architecture and Atmosphere*. Helsinki: Tapio Wirkkata-Rut Bryk Foundation.
Tilley, Christopher (ed.). (1996) *A Phenomenology of Landscape Places, Paths and Monuments*. Oxford: Berg.
Tilley, Christopher. (2004) *The Materiality of Stone: Explorations in Landscape Phenomenology*. Oxford: Berg.
Tomasello, Michael. (1999) *The Cultural Origins of Human Cognition*. Cambridge, MA: Harvard University press.
Tomasello, Michael. (2008) *Origins of Human Communication*. Cambridge, MA: MIT Press.
Tomasello, Michael. (2014) *A Natural History of Human Thinking*. Cambridge MA: Harvard University Press.
Trevarthen, Colwyn. (2005) "First things first: infants make good use of the sympathetic rhythm of imitation, without reason or language," *Journal of Child Psychotherpy* 31:1, 91–113.
Trevarthen, Colwyn. (2011) "What Is It Like to Be a Person Who Knows Nothing? Defining the Active Intersubjective Mind of a Newborn Human Being," *Infant and Child Development* 20, 119–135.
Trevarthen, Colwyn. (2012) "Born for Art, and the Joyful Companionship of Fiction," in Darcia Narvaez, Jaak Panksepp, Allan Schore, & Tracy Gleason (eds.) *Human Nature, Early Experience and the Environment of Evolutionary Adaptedness*. Oxford: Oxford University Press.
Trevarthen, Colwyn & Aitken, K. J. (2001) "Infant Intersubjectivity: Research, Theory, and Clinical Applications," *Journal of Child Psychology and Psychiatry* 42:1, 3–48.
Uexküll, Jakob von. (1934/2010) *A Foray into the Worlds of Animals and Humans*. Minneapolis: University of Minnesota Press.
Ulrich, Roger S. (1979) "Visual Landscapes and Psychological Well-being," *Landscape Research* 4:1, 17–23.
Ulrich, Roger S. (September 1981) "Natural versus Urban Scenes: Some Psychophysiological Effects," *Environment and Behavior* 13:5, 523–556.
Ulrich, Roger S. (1984) "View through a Window may Influence Recovery from Surgery," *Science* 224 (April 27, 1984), 420–421.
Umilta, M. Allesandra et al. (November 16, 2012) "Abstract Art and Cortical Motor Activation: An EEG Study," *Frontiers in Human Neuroscience*. Doi: 10.3389/fnhum.2012.00311.

Vallverdú, Josp et al. (2010) "Sleeping Activity Area with the Site Structure of Archaic Human Groups: Evidence from Abric Romaní Level N Combustion Activity Areas," *Current Anthropology* 51:1 (February), 137–145.
Van Eyck, Aldo. (1976) "Kaleidoscope of the Mind," *Miracles of Moderation*. Zürich: Eidgenössische Technische Hochschule.
Van Praag, Henriette et al. (December 2000) "Neural Consequences of Environmental Enrichment," *Nature Neuroscience* 1, 191–198.
Varela, Francisco, Thompson, Evan & Rosch, Eleanor. (1991) *The Embodied Mind: Cognitive Science and Human Experience*. Cambridge, MA: MIT Press.
Varela, Francisco. (1996) "Neurophenomenology: A Methodological Remedy for the Hard Problem," *Journal of Consciousness Studies* 3:4, 330–349.
Varki, Ajit et al. (2008) "Explaining Human Uniqueness: Genome Interactions with Environment, Behaviour and Culture," *Genetics* 9 (October), 749–763.
Vartanian, Oshin et al. (June 18, 2013) "Impact of Contour on Aesthetic Judgments and Approach-Avoidance Decisions in Architecture," *Proceedings of the National Academy of Sciences* 110:2, 10446–10453.
Vartanian, Oshin et al. (2015) "Architectural Design and the Brain: Effects of Ceiling Height and Perceived Enclosure on Beauty Judgments and Approach-Avoidance Decisions," *Journal of Environment Psychology* 41, 10–18.
Varela, Francisco J. (1996) "Neurophenomenology: A Methodological Remedy to the Hard Problem," *Journal of Consciousness Studies* 3, 330–350.
Varela, Francisco J, Thompson, Evan & Rosch, Eleanor. (1991) *The Embodied Mind: Cognitive Science and Human Experience*. Cambridge, MA: MIT Press.
Venturi, Robert. (1966) *Complexity and Contradiction in Architecture*. New York: Museum of Modern Art.
Vesely, Dalibor. (2004) *Architecture in the Age of Divided Representation: The Question of Creativity in the Shadow of Production*. Cambridge, MA: MIT Press.
Vitruvius. (1999) *Ten Books on Architecture*, trans. Ingrid D. Rowland. New York: Cambridge University Press.
von Uexküll, Jakob. (2010) *A Foray into the Worlds of Animals and Humans*, trans. Joseph D. O'Neil. Minneapolis, MN: University of Minnesota Press.
Wagner, Otto. (1988/1896) *Modern Architecture: A Guidebook for His Students to this Field of Art*, trans. H. F. Mallgrave. Santa Monica: Getty Publications.
Webber, Melvin. (1964) "The Urban Place and the Nonplace Urban Realm," in Weber et al. (eds.) *Explorations into Urban Structure*. Philadelphia: University of Pennsylvania Press.
Weber, Max. (1946) "Science as a Vocation," in *From Max Weber: Essays in Sociology*, trans. H. Gerth & C. W. Mills. New York: Oxford University Press.
Weber, Max. (1992) *The Protestant Ethic and the Spirit of Capitalism*. London: Routledge.
Weierrich, Mariann et al. (2010) "Novelty as a Dimension in the Affective Brain," *NeuroImage* 49, 2871–2878.
Weingarden, Lauren. (Winter 1985) "The Colors of Nature: Louis Sullivan's Architectural Polychromy and Nineteenth-Century Color Theory," *Winterthur Portfolio* 20:4, 243–260.
Wexler, Bruce E. (2008) *Brain and Culture: Neurobiology, Ideology, and Social Change*. Cambridge, MA: MIT Press.

Wheeler, Peter. (1994) "The Thermoregulatory Advantages of Heat-Storage and Shade-Seeking Behavior to Hominids Foraging in Equatorial Savanna Environments," *Journal of Human Evolution* 26:4, 339–350.
Whewell, William. (1856) "On the General Bearing of the Great Exhibition," *Lectures on the Progress of Arts and Science*. New York: A. S. Barnes & Co.
Whitman, Walt. (1982) *Complete Poetry and Collected Prose*. New York: The Library of America.
Wick, Rainer K. (2000) *Teaching at the Bauhaus*. Ostfildern-Rut: Hatje Cantz.
Wicker, Bruno et al. (2003) "Both of Us Disgusted in *My* Insula: The Common Neural Basis of Seeing and Feeling Disgust," *Neuron* 40, 655–664.
Wiessner, Polly. (September 30, 2014) "Embers of Society: Firelight Talk among the Ju/'hoansi Bushman," *Proceedings of the National Academy of Sciences* 111:39, 14027–14035.
Williamson, Scott et al. (2007) "Localizing Recent Adaptive Evolution in the Human Genome," *PLoS Genetics* 3:6, e90.
Wilson, Edward O. (1975/2000) *Sociobiology: The New Synthesis*. Cambridge, MA: Belknap Press.
Wilson, Edward O. (1978) "What Is Sociobiology," in Michael S. Gregory et al. (eds.) *Sociology and Human Nature: An Interdisciplinary Critique and Defense*. San Francisco: Jossey-Bass.
Wölfflin, Heinrich. (1888/1966) *Renaissance and Baroque*, trans. Kathrin Simon. Ithaca: Cornell University Press.
Wray, Alison. (1998) "Protolanguage as a Holistic System for Social Interaction," *Language & Communication* 18, 47–67.
Xenakis, Ioannis & Arnellos, Argyris. (September 2014) "Aesthetic perception and its minimal content: a naturalistic perspective," *Frontiers in Psychology* 5:1038, Abstract. Doi: 10.3389/fpsyg.2014.01038.
Zajonc, Robert. (2013) "Clive Bell's 'Significant Form' and the Neurobiology of Aesthetics," *Frontiers in Human Neuroscience* 7:730. DOI: 10.3389/fnhum.2013.00730.
Zatorre, Robert. (1999) "Brain Imaging Studies of Musical Perception and Musical Imagery," *Journal of New Music Research* 28:3, 229–236.
Zatorre, Robert et al. (1996) "Hearing in the Mind's Ear: PET Investigation of Musical Imagery and Perception," *Journal of Cognitive Neuroscience* 8, 29–46.
Zeisel, John. (2006) *Inquiry by Design: Environment/Behavior/Neuroscience in Architecture, Interiors, Landscape, and Planning*. New York: W. W. Norton & Company.
Zeki, Semir. (Spring 1998) "Art and the Brain," *Daedalus* 127:2, 71–103.
Zeki, Semir. (1999) *Inner Vision: An Exploration of Art and the Brain*. Oxford: Oxford University Press.
Zeki, Semir. (November 12, 2013) "Clive Bell's 'Significant Form' and the Neurobiology of Aesthetics," *Frontiers in Human Neuroscience*. Doi: 10.3389/fnhum.2013.00730.
Zumthor, Peter. (2006) *Atmospheres: Architectural Environments: Surrounding Objects*. Basel: Birkhäuser.
Zumthor, Peter. (2010) *Thinking Architecture*, 3rd edn. Basel: Birkhäuser.

Index

Aalto, Alvar 20, 51
Abric Romani 136
Academy of Neuroscience for Architecture 41
Adam, Robert & James 87
Adorno, Theodor 18, 21, 22, 24
aesthetic perception 85–97, 143–5
Aiello, Leslie 139
Albers, Josef 25
Alberti, Leon Battista 7, 85, 88, 101, 128, 131
Albright, Thomas 74
Alexander, Christopher 38, 39–40, 51
Algarotti, Francesco 23
amygdala 93–4
Anstruther-Thomson, Clementina 101
Appleton, Jay 123–4
Aquinas, Thomas 86
Arbib, Michael 46, 141
architecture
    as space 110–16
    definition of 9, 55–6
    design studios 7
    detailing 128–33
    as experience 2, 43–4, 55–6, 173–5
    as a language 1–2, 109
    materials 129–30
    practice (*praxis*) of 8, 170–2
    theory 1–2, 5, 8, 19, 22–4, 129–30, 132–3, 149, 172–5
Ardipithecus ramidus (Ardi) 138
Ardrey, Robert 29–30, 31, 33, 37
Arendt, Hannah 130, 172
Aristotle 137
Arnellos, Argyris 91
Arnheim, Rudolf 102, 104
art, visual, beginning of 143
atmosphere in architecture 120–3
attention deficit hyperactivity disorder 60

augury 159–60
Augustine 86
Australopithecus afarensis (Lucy) 138
Australopithecus africanus 29

Bachelard, Gaston 117
Bacon, Edmund 24
Badovici, John 1
Baird, George 28
Banham, Reyner 20–21
Barrett, Lisa 72
Bastian, Adolf 14
Bauhaus 45, 86
Baumgarten, Alexander 87
beauty 86–7, 89, 162, 164–5, 168–9
Behrendt, Walter Curt 86
Bell, Clive 102, 105
Bell, Daniel 24
Benjamin, Walter 18, 121
Berekhat Ram Figurine 144
Berenson, Bernard 101
Berlage, Hendrik 11
Bettini, Sergio 28
Bilzingsleben 135, 141
biophilic design 123–5
bipedalism 140–1
Blanke, Olaf 113, 135
Blombos cave 144–5
Blondel, François 92
Blondel, Jacques-François 120
Bloomer, Kent 117
Boas, Franz 15, 31
Böhme, Gernot 121–3, 127, 167
Bollnow, Otto Friedrich 117
Bond, James 66
border cells 80
Borromini, Francesco 106, 109, 131–2
Botticelli, Sandro 86
Botvinick, Matthew 112
Boucher de Perthes, Jacques 14

INDEX

Boxgrove 143
Boyd, Robert 34
Brain, human 57–9
   evolution of 145–7
   social development of 149–53
Brodsky, Joseph 86, 129
Brooks, Cleanth 25
Brown, Steven 89, 165
Bruhn, Ada 17
Brunelleschi, Filippo 7
Burke, Edmund 87, 92, 93

Callicrates 121
Canaletto, Giovanni Antonio 23
Casabella-continuità 20
Casals, Pablo 106
Cassirer, Ernst 87
Cavalli-Sforza, Luigi Luca 33
Chermayaff, Serge 39
Chomsky, Noam 40
CIAM (Congrès Internationaux d'Architecture Moderne) 19–21
Cicero 80, 159
Cloak, F. T. 33
Clynes, Manfred 99, 106
Cohen, Jonathan 112
Cole, Jonathan 72
Collingwood, R. G. 101
Colombetti, Giovanna 71–2, 91
constructivism 86
"contemplative" versus "ordinary" buildings 126
cooking, introduction of 139–40
Crane, David 24
creativity. *See* imagination
Crystal Palace, Sydenham 14
culture 4, 7–26
   cultural cognitive development 148–9

Dal co, Francesco 16
dance, origin of 143, 156–7
Danckert, James 125
Dante Alighieri 86
Dart, Raymond 29
Darwin, Charles 14, 137, 165
Davidoff, Paul 24, 37
Dawkins, Richard 33
de Chirico, Giorgio 22
De Fusco, Renato 28

Derrida, Jacques 26
De Stijl 86
Dewey, John 10, 17, 28, 44, 53, 90
Dilthey, Wilhelm 91
Dissanayake, Ellen 151, 158, 165
Dohrn, Wolf 16, 17
Donald, Merlin 54, 143, 148–9
Dunbar, Robin 146–7
Durham, William H. 33
Durkheim, Émile 28, 31, 40, 156

Eberhard, John 41
Eco, Umberto 28
Ehrenzweig, Anton 96
Eibl-Eibesfeldt, Irenäus 30, 33
Einstein, Albert 106
Eisenman, Peter 21
Eliot T. S. 25
Ellard, Colin 95, 125
embodied simulation 69–70, 107–10
embodiment 5, 45, 109–10
Emerson, Ralph Waldo 9
emotion 44, 53, 55, 108
   new models of 2–3, 70–4, 90–2
empathy (*Einfühlung*) 9, 16, 45–6, 53–4, 55, 67–8, 99–100, 104, 106
enactivism 52
enculturation 3, 54–5
environmental deprivation 60, 152–3
Environmental Design Research Association (EDRA) 38
environmental enrichment 62
Epicurus 88
Epson, William 25
ethos for design 168–73
Etlin, Richard 9, 116
evidence-based design 38
evolution 48
expensive-tissue hypothesis 139

Fechner, Gustav 71
feeling-for-form (*Formgefühl*) 9, 99–110
feeling-for-space (*Raumgefühl*) 9, 111–16
Feldman, Marcus 33
Feldman, Ruth 150
Fiedler, Conrad 111
fire, use of 139

Fontana, Lucio 110
Ford, Edward 131
forest bathing 125
Foucault, Michel 26
Frampton, Kenneth 117, 128
Frankfurt Institute for Social Research 18, 26
Frascari, Marco 128, 129
Freedberg, David 108–9
Freeman, Walter 63
Frey, Dagobert 117
Fuhlrott, Johann 14

Gabetti, Roberto 20
Gadamer, Hans-Georg 86, 91, 161–4, 166–9
Gallese, Vittorio 89, 108
Gans, Herbert 24–5, 37, 38
Gardella, Ignazio 20–1
Gauldie, Sinclair 117, 118
Geertz, Clifford 28–9, 31
Gehl, Jan 125, 163
gene/culture coevolution 33–5, 50
German Werkbund 16–18, 86
Gibson, James 46, 67, 107
Giedion, Sigfried 3, 19, 70, 86
gist, perception of 75
Goethe, Johann Wolfgang von 57
Goldstein, Kurt 44
Göller, Adolf 100–1
Gombrich, Ernst 74, 104
Goodbun, Jon 115, 131
Gottlieb, Gilbert 62
Gould, Stephen J. 33
Gray, Eileen 1
Great Exhibition of the Works of Industry, London 14
grid cells 79–80
Griffero, Tonino 122
Groh, Jennifer 80
Gropius, Walter 17
Grosse, Ernst 158
Gumbrecht, Hans Ulrich 97
Gurlitt, Cornelius 101
Gutman, Robert 37

Habermas, Jürgen 17
Hall, Edward T. 27, 37–8, 41, 65, 81–82, 113, 114, 117, 120

Hanson, Julienne 40
Harries, Karsten 119, 122, 169–70, 172
Harris, Britton 24
Hart, Robert Lamb 92
head-direction cells 79–80
hearing 82–4
Heidegger, Martin 2, 45, 117, 118, 119, 169, 172
Hekkert, Paul 95
Hellerau 16
Helmholtz, Hermann 71, 111
Herbart, Johann Friedrich 71
Herder, Johann Gottfried 8, 99, 106
hermeneutics 5, 45, 91, 175
Herzog & de Meuron 96
Hildebrand, Adolf 111
Hildebrand, Grant 125
Hillier, Bill 40–1
hippocampus 58, 80–1, 93
Hitchcock, Henry-Russell 86
Holl, Steven 44
Homo erectus 135, 139–41, 142, 147
Homo heidelbergensis (Heidelbergs) 136, 141–4, 148
Homo sapiens 32, 141, 144–5
  as social animal 137–45
Horkheimer, Max 18, 21, 22, 24
Hume, David 87
Husserl, Edmund 44–5, 53, 89

Ihde, Don 83
imagination (creativity) 81, 96–7, 132
Ingold, Tim 51, 66, 129
Iriki, Atsushi 140
Ishikawa, Sara 39
Isidore of Miletus 7
Isola, Aimaro 20
Ittelson, William 38

Jacobs, Jane 36, 38
James, Wendy 161–2
James, William 71, 96, 158, 167
Jammer, Max 117
Jäncke, Lutz 64
Jaques-Dalcroze, Émil 17
Jeanneret, Albert 17
Jelić, Andrea 89
Jencks, Charles 28
Johns, Jasper 25

INDEX

Johnson, Mark 90
Johnson, Philip 86
Jones, Owen 14

Kahn, Louis 24, 25, 97
Kames, Lord 87
Kant, Immanuel 71, 87–8
Kanwisher, Nancy 77
Kaplan, Stephen & Rachel 124
Kepes, György 25, 36
Klemm, Gustav 14
Kline, Franz 110
Knight, Richard Payne 92, 93
Koenig, Giovanni Klaus 28
Koestler, Arthur 96
Kosslyn, Stephen 95–6
Kringelbach, Morten 140
Krumhansl, Carol 157

Labrouste, Henri 155
Lange, Carl 71
Langer, Suzanne 156–7
language, origin of 141–2
Lartet, Édward 14
Laugier, Marc-Antoine 137
Leatherbarrow, David 163
Le Camus de Mézières, Nicolas 120
Le Corbusier 17, 19, 20, 86
Lee, Vernon 101
Leroi-Gourhan, André 129
Levitin, Daniel 83
Lewis, Jerome 156, 163
Lipps, Theodor 16, 101
Loos, Adolf 85
Lorenz, Konrad 30–1, 33, 37
Lubbock, John 14
Lumsden, Charles 33
Lynch, Kevin 36, 38, 78, 117

Mahler, Alma 17
Maldonado, Tomás 28
Malloch, Stephen 150
Malpas, Jeff 117, 118
Marcuse, Herbert 18
Marx, Karl 16, 18, 19
May, Ernst 19
McEwen, Indra Kagins 159
McGilchrist, Iain 170
meme 33

memory 80–1
Merleau-Ponty, Maurice 45, 52, 90, 112, 117
Merrifield, Colleen 125
Metcalf, Bruce 132
Metzinger, Thomas 135
Meyer, Hannes 19
Michelangelo 108
Mies van der Rohe, Ludwig 17, 25
mirror neurons (mirror mechanisms) 54, 55, 67–70, 107, 127–8
Mithen, Steven 142
Molino, Jean 156
Montagu, Ashley 27
Montero, Barbara 72
Moore, Charles 117
Morris, Desmond 30–2, 37, 147
Mumford, Eric 19
Mumford, Lewis 24
music, origin of 142–3, 157–8
Muthesius, Herrmann 16–17, 86

Narvaez, Darcia 168–9
nature/nurture debate 27–35
Naumann, Friedrich 16
Neanderthals 14, 136, 142
neoliberty 20–1
neural plasticity 48, 59–60
Neutra, Richard 5, 35–6, 41, 82, 84
Newman, Oscar 37, 38
niche construction 4, 47–9, 51, 52, 119, 148
Noë, Alva 89
Norberg-Schulz, Christian 28, 117
novelty 92–6

O'Keefe, John 79
olfactory system 81–2
Oud, J. J. P. 86
Oyama, Susan 50–1

Palladio, Andrea 23
Pallasmaa, Juhani 65, 73, 75, 128, 131
Panathenaea 159
Panksepp, Jaak 93, 157
parahippocampal place area (PPA) 78–9
Parsons, Talcott 33
Pasqualini, Isabella 115

Paul, Sherman 9, 10
Pausanias 158
Paxton, Joseph 14
perception 45, 52, 55, 132. *See also* aesthetic perception
    and emotion 90–2
    new models of 62–84, 89–91
    olfactory system 81–2
    sensorimotor underpinnings 3, 10, 52, 89, 107
    sound 82–4
Pérez-Gómez, Alberto 123, 162, 168
peripersonal space 113–16
Perrault, Claude 1, 92
Pevsner, Nikolaus 20–21
Phidias 121
place 117–33
place cells 79
Plato 86
play 3, 158, 162–3
pleasure circuit 73–4
Plotinus 86
Pollock, Jackson 108
Porteous, J. Douglas 82
Portoghesi, Paolo 20
poststructuralism 1
"presence" 97, 121
Pribram, Karl 33
Prichard, James 14
primitive hut 135–6
proprioception 62–4, 72–3
Proshansky, Harold 38
Proust, Marcel 82
Prum, Robert 165–6

Quantrill, Malcom 160

Ramsay, Allan 87
Rasmussen, Steen Eiler 44
Rauschenberg, Robert 25
Relph, Edward 117–19
retrosplenial cortex (RSC) 78–9
Richerson, Peter 34
Riemerschmid, Richard 16
ritualization 3, 155–64
Rizzolatti, Giacomo 77, 107
Robinson, Sarah 66, 73
Rodwin, Lloyd 36, 38
Rogers, Ernesto 19, 25
Romanian orphans 152–3
Romulus 159
Rooney, Kevin 75
Rosch, Eleanor 52
Rossi, Aldo 19–23
Rousseau, Jean-Jacques 29
Rowe, Colin 130
Ruyle, Eugene 33
Rykwert, Joseph 137, 158, 162, 163
Ryle, Gilbert 28

Scaff, Lawrence 17
Scarpa, Carlo 128
Scarry, Elaine 86, 168
Schäfer, Carl 17
Schafer, R. Murray 83–4
Schiller, Friedrich 162
Schinkel, Karl Friedrich 1
Schmarsow, August 111–12
Schmidt, Hans 19
Schmidt, Karl 16, 17
Schönigen javelins 143
Schore, Allan 151
Schumacher, Fritz 16
Schwarz, Rudolf 117, 169
Schwarzer, Mitchell 111
Scott Brown, Denise 24, 26, 37
Scott, Geoffrey 101
Scruton, Roger 86, 130–1, 168
Seamon, David 117
semiotics 1
Semper, Gottfried 14, 108, 111, 121, 163
Sennett, Richard 130
sensory deprivation 60–1
sensory enrichment 62
Sheets-Johnstone, Maxine 63, 71
"significant form" 102, 105–6
Silverstein, Murray 39
Skinner B. F. 27
Smail, Daniel Lord 43
sociability 3, 55
social deprivation 61, 152–3
sociobiology debate 31–5, 50
Sommer, Robert 37–8, 113, 117
song, origin of 142–3
space. *See* architecture
Spencer, Herbert 158
Sperber, Esther 97

Sperry, Roger 64
Stalin, Josef 19
Stam, Mart 19
Stamps, Arthur 94
Sterelny, Kim 148
Sullivan 7, 9–13, 15, 17, 100
Sütterlin, Christa 105

tactility (hapticity) 65–7, 127–8
Tafuri, Manfredo 20
Tan-Tan figurine 144
Terra Amata 135–6, 141
Tessenow, Heinrich 17
theory. *See* architecture
Thibaud, Jean-Paul 123
Thiis-Evensen, Thomas 121
Thompson, Evan 52–4, 71, 89, 91
Tilley, Christopher 70, 118
Tomasello, Michael 147–8
Trevarthen, Colwyn 150–1, 157
Tuan, Yi-Fu 82, 117
Turner, J. M. W. 167
Tylor, Edward 14

Uexküll, Jakob von 44
Ulrich, Roger 38–9, 41, 124
Umwelt (surrounding world) 44, 46, 67

van Eyck, Aldo 25, 51, 123
Varela, Francisco 52–3
Vartanian, Oshin 94, 114–15
Vasari, Giorgio 92
Venturi, Robert 23–6, 37
Vesely, Dalibor 5, 155, 170, 172

vestibular system 63–4
Vierzehnheiligen 170
Virchow, Rudolf 14
Vischer, Robert 68, 69, 70, 99–100, 101, 106
visual system 74–9
Vitruvius 7, 84, 85, 92, 136, 159–60

Wagner, Otto 11, 16, 85
Weber, Alfred 17
Weber, Carl 17
Weber, Marianne 17
Weber, Max 15–18, 23, 24, 26, 30
Webber, Melvin 37, 38
Wheeler, Peter 139
Whewell, William 14
Whitelaw, Allison 41
Whitman, Walt 9
Wiessner, Polly 144
Wilson, Edward 31–3
Wittgenstein, Ludwig 28, 161
Wohnkultur (culture of living) 16, 17
Wölfflin, Heinrich 25, 70–1, 100, 101
Wrangham, Richard 139
Wray, Alison 141
Wright, Frank Lloyd 20, 60, 121, 125
Wundt, Wilhelm 71, 111

Xenakis, Ioannis 91

Zeisel, John 38, 41
Zeki, Semir 105–6
Zevi, Bruno 20, 117
Zumthor, Peter 46–7, 84, 122, 131

www.ingramcontent.com/pod-product-compliance
Lightning Source LLC
Chambersburg PA
CBHW072146290426
44111CB00012B/1988